P9-EEO-352

BREAKFAST
WITH
SENECA

BREAKFAST
WITH
SENECA

A Stoic Guide
to the Art of Living

DAVID FIDELER

W. W. NORTON & COMPANY
Independent Publishers Since 1923

This book is intended for educational and informational purposes only. It is not a substitute for professional psychological, psychiatric, or medical advice, diagnosis, or treatment. Readers requiring such advice or treatment should consult a qualified mental health or medical professional.

Frontispiece: Bronze sculpture of Seneca in Córdoba, Spain.
Photography by Ken Welsh / Alamy. Used with permission.

For information about permission to reproduce selections from this book, write to Permissions, W. W. Norton & Company, Inc., 500 Fifth Avenue, New York, NY 10110

For information about special discounts for bulk purchases, please contact W. W. Norton Special Sales at specialsales@wwnorton.com or 800-233-4830

Manufacturing by Lakeside Book Company

Library of Congress Cataloging-in-Publication Data

Names: Fideler, David R., 1961– author.
Title: Breakfast with Seneca : a Stoic guide to the art of living / David Fideler.
Description: First edition. | New York, NY : W. W. Norton & Company, [2022] | Includes bibliographical references and index.
Identifiers: LCCN 2021035112 | ISBN 9780393531664 | ISBN 9780393531671 (epub)
Subjects: LCSH: Seneca, Lucius Annaeus, approximately 4 B.C.–65 A.D. | Stoics. | Ethics. | Philosophy, Ancient.
Classification: LCC B618 .F53 2022 | DDC 188—dc23
LC record available at https://lccn.loc.gov/2021035112

W. W. Norton & Company, Inc., 500 Fifth Avenue, New York, N.Y. 10110
www.wwnorton.com

W. W. Norton & Company Ltd., 15 Carlisle Street, London W1D 3BS

1 2 3 4 5 6 7 8 9 0

For my son, Benjamin—
Some wisdom to grow into.

I am working for later generations, writing down some ideas that may benefit them.

—Seneca, *Letters* 8.2

CONTENTS

PREFACE

MY RELATIONSHIP TO SENECA AND HIS WRITINGS changed once the crisis hit.

I was sitting in my office when an email arrived from a dear friend. I opened it with curiosity, expecting to find something pleasant. But the text screamed out at me. She had written, only moments before, "I just took half a bottle of tranquilizers. I'm sorry for the pain I caused you in your life."

That was the entire message.

I went cold in disbelief and read it twice just to make sure.

Then, while feeling unspeakable grief, I immediately got into my car, drove over to her place, and took her to the emergency room. She was in the hospital for a couple of days, and then transferred to a psychiatric hospital. Once in the psychiatric hospital, she begged me to help her get out. This was the beginning of her ordeal, and I was essentially the only person around to help her.

Of course, it was an ordeal for me, too. We had been in love. And it literally felt like the bottom had fallen out of my world. Her life could have come to an end. Fortunately, it didn't. But for me, the raw emotions and despair I was feeling were overwhelming. It felt like my life was ending, too: not physically, but emotionally.

Fortunately, I had a good friend who visited me once a week. I saw a therapist for a while. But most helpfully, I started reading the writings and letters of Lucius Annaeus Seneca (c. 4 BC–AD 65) each day, as a way to recover my mental and emotional equilibrium. While Seneca had been an interest of mine before this happened, after the crisis his words became a kind of medicine.

Perhaps not by coincidence, some of Seneca's most famous writings are long messages of consolation, written to specific friends, about how they could overcome their experiences of grief. In any case, it worked. Over time, Seneca's wise and steady voice helped me to regain the feeling of being a normal human being. It also put me in touch with a profound thinker who possessed a much deeper and more satisfying vision of human life than we are encouraged to hold by society today. I had discovered a wise mentor and companion who offered a steady stream of reliable and practical advice about the human condition, human psychology, and how to live a happy, flourishing life.

What I also discovered in Seneca's writings is that nothing significant has changed in human nature over the last two thousand years, which made everything he had to say contemporary. Vanity, greed, ambition, pursuit of luxury, and runaway consumerism—aspects of Rome's elite, decadent society that Seneca described in detail—are all still very much with us.

But countering these negative aspects of human behavior, Seneca teaches his readers how to overcome worry and anxiety; how to live a good life under any conditions; how to live with purpose and cultivate excellence; how to contribute to society; and how to overcome grief and all kinds of obstacles that might (and certainly will) cross our paths.

After that first reading of Seneca, I kept returning to his

pages. There's always something to be reminded of, or something to understand more deeply. Then there's another dimension to Seneca's work: he has one of the best writing styles of all times, and encapsulates his thoughts in pithy, epigrammatic lines like: "Our lack of confidence does not result from difficulty; the difficulty comes from lack of confidence."[1] Ralph Waldo Emerson loved to read Seneca too, and even imitated his style.

I FIRST STARTED READING Seneca when I woke up, with a morning coffee.

Then, over a decade ago, I moved overseas to the beautiful city of Sarajevo in southern Europe, where I live with my wife and son. Of course, I brought Seneca along for the adventure, and once settled here, I developed a new habit. After working in the morning, I'd stroll down the hill and read Seneca during lunch, next to some ancient Roman inscriptions housed in a local museum.

Now, when possible, on my perfect kind of morning, I'll go out and have breakfast with Seneca—hence the title of this book. After dropping my son at school and working out in the gym, I pick up a filter coffee with milk and settle down at a table at Hotel Central, a magnificent building from Austro-Hungarian times. There I pull out an e-reader with Seneca's complete letters and his other writings, and order an omelet. That's my favorite morning ritual. No one has any idea what I'm reading, let alone that I'm most often reading the same author, but I can usually get through one or two letters before heading home.

SENECA STRESSED HOW PHILOSOPHY and friendship should go together. As he wrote, "The first promise of real philosophy is a feeling of fellowship, sympathy, and community with others."[2] Because Seneca's principal works are letters, and essays written for specific Roman friends in an intimate and conversational style, a spirit of friendship permeates his writings.

Seneca believed that real philosophy is a joint undertaking—it's not something we do alone, but a journey we undertake with others. That's why he wrote the letters in the first place. But this idea goes back at least to Socrates, for whom philosophy and dialogue were a shared journey, a collaboration between friends.

Of course, I'm not talking about what philosophy has become in the modern academic world, which is something quite different. But philosophy in ancient times was closely allied with friendship. (See chapter 1, "The Lost Art of Friendship.") If it were possible to restore that connection today, it would be a happy development.

It's easy for modern readers to feel friendship with Seneca also, due to the details of his personal life that he shares in some of his letters. While the letters themselves, written during the last two or three years of his life, are devoted to practical philosophy and what it means to live a good life, Seneca confided many personal details to his friend Lucilius: what it's like to be old, details about his travels and other annoyances, how he almost died from an asthma attack, and the crazy behavior of people in Roman society. (Seneca, who had lived among the wealthiest and most powerful people in Rome, was a chief adviser to the emperor Nero, so he saw every kind of bad behavior, including political assassinations.)

DESPITE THE VERY HIGH level of interest in Stoicism today, no one has written a book explaining Seneca's teachings for the general reader, even though he's been called "the most compelling and elegant of the Stoic writers."[3] I hope this book will fill that void, and provide a bird's-eye view of his thinking. (Seneca is very consistent in his thinking, but his ideas about specific topics are scattered across hundreds of pages.)

This book might satisfy the entire curiosity of some readers about Seneca's philosophy. But for those who wish to continue on to Seneca's actual writings, or to host their own breakfasts with Seneca, may this guide serve as a helpful companion on that quest.

—*David Fideler*

BREAKFAST
WITH
SENECA

A Life Truly Worth Living

SENECA (C. 4 BC–AD 65) WAS ONE OF THE GREATEST and most learned writers of his time. As an unhappy adviser to the ill-fated regime of the Emperor Nero in Rome, he also became one of the richest men in the world. But the reason most people are interested in Seneca today has to do with something else: it's because he wrote about Stoic philosophy, which has undergone a tremendous, popular revival in recent years.

While the Stoic school started in Athens roughly three hundred years before Seneca was born, the writings of the Greek Stoics are mostly lost. They only survive in brief quotations or fragments. This makes Seneca the first major Stoic writer whose philosophical works have come down to us in a nearly complete form. He had one of the most well-informed and curious minds of his age, and displayed a daring intellectual freedom and open-mindedness in his writings. It is this quality that makes him seem very modern.

In this book, which features fresh translations from his work, I explain Seneca's key ideas and wise teachings in the clearest way possible. This is also an introduction to Stoic philosophy in general, because it's impossible to fully understand Seneca's thinking without understanding the Stoic ideas on which it was based. To further explain and amplify the ideas that Seneca held, I also quote from two later Roman Stoics, Epictetus (c. AD 50–135) and Marcus Aurelius (AD 121–180).

PHILOSOPHY AS "THE ART OF LIVING": STOICISM AND ITS LASTING APPEAL

The mind would rather amuse itself than heal itself,
making philosophy into a diversion when it is really a cure.
—Seneca, *Letters* 117.33

Before we start exploring Stoicism, we must clear up one popular misconception. Stoicism has nothing to do with "keeping a stiff upper lip" or "bottling up your emotions," which everyone knows to be unhealthy. While Seneca was a Stoic philosopher, it's essential to recognize that over the centuries the meaning of *stoic* has changed radically: the word *stoic* today, written with a small *s*, has no relationship with the capital-*S Stoicism* of the ancient world. While the modern word *stoic* means "to repress your emotions," the ancient Stoics never advocated anything along those lines. Like everyone else, the Stoic philosophers had no issue with normal, healthy feelings like love and affection. As the philosopher Epictetus wrote, the Stoic should not be "unfeeling like a statue." Rather, the Stoics developed a "therapy of the passions" to help prevent extreme, violent, and negative emotions that can overwhelm the personality, like anger, fear, and anxiety. Rather than repress these negative emotions, their goal was to transform them through understanding.

Some important Stoic ideas go back to the Greek philosopher Socrates (c. 470–399 BC), who famously said, "The unexamined life is not worth living." In other words, "Know yourself": self-knowledge is essential for leading a happy life. Socrates also suggested that in the same way gymnastics is designed to keep our bodies healthy, there must also be some kind of art that would care for the health of our souls. While Socrates never gave this "art" a name, the clear implication was that it is the role of *philosophy* and the philosopher to "care for the soul."[1]

These two ideas—that knowledge is critical for happiness and living a good life, and that philosophy is a kind of therapy for the soul—were essential foundations on which Stoicism was based. As a school, Stoicism originated in Athens around 300 BC, where the philosopher Zeno of Citium (c. 334–c. 262 BC) lectured at the Stoa Poikilē or "Painted Porch"—hence the name of the school.[2]

Like other philosophers of the time, the Stoics were intensely concerned with the question *What is needed to live the best possible life?* If humans could answer that question, they believed, we could then flourish and live happy, tranquil lives—even if the world itself seems to be crazy and out of control. This made Stoicism a supremely practical philosophy, and also explains its revival today, because our own time—socially, politically, economically, and environmentally—also strikes people as feeling crazy and out of control.

Even if the world seems out of control, the Stoics taught that we could lead meaningful, productive, and happy lives. Moreover, even in adverse situations, our lives can still be tranquil and characterized by psychological equanimity. It is this strong emphasis on the project of living a good, meaningful, and tranquil life that made Roman Stoicism so popular as a philosophical school during the times of Seneca, Epictetus, and Marcus Aurelius, and it's also what makes Stoicism popular today, in times that are no less stressful.

This emphasis on living a good life also separates Stoicism from modern academic philosophy, which has given up on such practical human concerns in favor of abstract theoretical issues, most of which are meaningless to others outside of the philosopher's ivory tower. But as the ancient philosopher Epicurus (340–270 BC) stressed,

> Empty is that philosopher's argument by which no human suffering is therapeutically treated. For just as there is no use in a medical art that does not cast out the sicknesses of bodies, so too there is no use in philosophy, unless it casts out the suffering of the soul.[3]

Similarly, the Stoics saw philosophy as a way of curing the "diseases of the soul." They saw it as resembling "a medical art," and even called the philosopher "a doctor of the soul." The Stoics also called philosophy "the art of living," and Seneca described his own teachings as being like "medical remedies." He found these "remedies" to be helpful in treating his own conditions and wanted to share them with others, including future generations.[4]

EIGHT CORE TEACHINGS
OF ROMAN STOICISM

As you might expect, Stoic philosophers held different ideas about many topics, but there are several key points that all Roman Stoic philosophers agreed on. That's what made them Stoics and not members of another philosophical school. These foundational ideas of Stoicism are reflected in the works of Seneca, too, and most of them go back to the earliest Greek Stoics.

While we'll explore these ideas more deeply in the chapters that follow, it's worth mentioning these eight main ideas of Stoic thought here, as a quick taste of what is to come. (That said, if you'd rather consider these points later, please feel free to skip ahead to the next section of this introduction.)

1

"Live in agreement with nature" to find happiness.

Like many thinkers that came before and after, the Stoics believed that rationality exists in nature. We can see evidence of this in nature's patterns, processes, and the laws of nature, which allow nature's forms to work in an excellent way. Because human beings are a part of nature, we are capable of being rational and excellent too. According to Zeno of Citium, the founder of Stoicism, if we "live in agreement with nature," our lives will then "flow smoothly." (Of course, it's hard to imagine living a happy life if you are constantly struggling against nature.) While living in agreement with nature had multiple meanings for the Stoics, one of the central, most important meanings was that we should strive, as human beings, to develop our own human rationality and excellence.

2

Virtue, or excellence of one's inner
character, is the only true good.

While there are several dimensions to this, I'll just mention one now: if you lack this kind of inner goodness, you won't be able to use anything else in a good way, to benefit either yourself or others.

For example, the Stoics did not see money as a good in itself, since it can sometimes be used well and can sometimes be used poorly. If you possess wisdom and moderation, which are virtues, it's likely that you could use money in a good way. But if someone lacking wisdom or moderation ends up blowing thousands of dollars over a weekend on drugs and other vices, few people would consider that to be good or healthy—or a good use of money either. As Seneca wrote, "Virtue itself," or excellence of character, "is the only true good, since there is nothing good without it."[5]

What makes a virtue like justice or fairness truly good is that it is *always* or consistently good. By contrast, other things can be used well or badly. They are not intrinsically or consistently good.

3

Some things are "up to us," or entirely under our control, while other things are not.

For the Stoics, the only things *fully* under our control are our inner powers of judgment, opinion, and decision making, our will, and how we interpret the things we experience.

To reduce emotional suffering, a person needs to focus on what is under his or her control, while still trying to create a better life and a better world for others. (We will explore this in chapter 6, "How to Tame Adversity" and chapter 8, "The Battle Against Fortune: How to Survive Poverty and Extreme Wealth.")

4

*While we can't control what happens to us in
the external world, we can control our inner
judgments and how we respond to life's events.*

This is highly significant to the Stoics, because extreme, negative emotions originate from faulty judgments or opinions. But if we understand and correct the faulty interpretations by viewing things differently, we can also get rid of the negative emotions. (See chapter 3, "How to Overcome Worry and Anxiety" and chapter 4, "The Problem with Anger.")

5

*When something negative happens, or when we are
struck by adversity, we shouldn't be surprised by it, but
see it as an opportunity to create a better situation.*

For the Stoics, every challenge or adversity we encounter is an opportunity to both test and develop our inner character. Also, to believe that misfortunes will never befall us would be out of touch with reality. Instead, we should actively *expect* occasional bumps in the road, and sometimes major ones. (See chapter 6, "How to Tame Adversity.")

6

*Virtue, or possessing an excellent character, is its own
reward. But it also results in eudaimonia or "happiness."
This is a state of mental tranquility and inner joy.*

Eudaimonia has been translated variously as "happiness," "human flourishing," "well-being," and "having the best mind-set possible." But for the Stoics, "having a life that is truly worth living" is probably the most accurate translation. (See chapter 14, "Freedom, Tranquility, and Lasting Joy.")

In one of their famous "paradoxes" or paradoxical sayings, the Stoics said that a perfectly wise person, a Stoic sage, would possess *eudaimonia* even while being tortured on the rack! While we couldn't describe a person who was being tortured as being "happy" in the modern sense of the word, we *could* imagine that he possessed *a life truly worth living*, especially if he was being tortured for standing up to an evil tyrant.[6] Similarly, many heroic people have given up their lives fighting for the greater good, to benefit society. In other words, living the best possible life, or a life truly worth living, might involve some pain.

7

Real philosophy involves "making progress."

Philosophy involves critical thinking, intellectual analysis, and trying to understand the world scientifically. But ultimately, for the Stoics, the most important dimension of philosophy is *ethics*, which has a very practical dimension. The Roman Stoics saw real philosophy as a kind of path in which one makes progress toward virtue or developing a better character. (See chapter 1, "The Lost Art of Friendship.")

8

It's essential that we, as individuals, should contribute to society.

The Stoics were the most prosocial philosophers in the ancient world. They taught that humanity is like a single organism, and that we, as parts of that organism, should contribute to the greater good of society as a whole. (See chapter 10, "How to Be Authentic and Contribute to Society.") Significantly, the Stoics were't just interested in improving their own lives. They were interested in improving the lives of all humanity.[7]

SENECA'S LIFE AND THE
TRANSFORMATION OF ADVERSITY

This is a book about Seneca's ideas and not his life. Naturally, though, there's some relation between the two, so a few details are in order. (For those who would like to learn more about Seneca's life, I recommend the excellent biography by Emily Wilson.[8])

Seneca was born around 4 BC to a well-to-do equestrian family, or family of Roman knights, in what is now the city of Córdoba, Spain. His father, Seneca the Elder (54 BC–AD 39), was a teacher of rhetoric and oratory. Like today, being an excellent communicator was a vital skill for creating a successful career in the Roman Empire, and Seneca's family excelled at this.

Little is known about Seneca's life as a child, but his father took him to Rome when he was five years old or a bit older. As an adolescent, he studied with various teachers in Rome, including several philosophers.

Unfortunately, Seneca suffered from some kind of chronic lung disease since childhood, likely a combination of asthma and tuberculosis. When he was around twenty-five, his aunt took him to Alexandria in Egypt in an attempt to quell the disease, which might have been made worse by living in Rome. Surprisingly, he ended up staying in Egypt for ten years, and only returned to Rome around the age of thirty-five. Fortunately for Seneca, his aunt had political connections, and due to her influence he was able to join the Roman Senate, when Rome was under the rule of Caligula.

In the previous century, Rome had been a republic. But with the dissolution of the republic, the newly created Roman emperors possessed, for all intents and purposes, absolute powers, which led, of course, to terrible abuses. The reigns of Caligula (AD 12–41), Claudius (10 BC–AD 54), and Nero (AD 37–68), under which Seneca lived, were corrupt beyond imagination, and filled with examples of murders, poisonings and assassinations, sexual infidelity (including reports of incest), exiling innocent people from Rome, brutal torture, and other terrible acts, many of them based simply on whim. It was like a television soap opera gone bad in the worst possible way, but with deadly, real-life consequences.

As a senator under Caligula, Seneca began to accumulate vast personal wealth, which he would continue to do throughout his life. But these financial rewards were mixed blessings indeed, because as Seneca rose to the pinnacle of social status and power in Rome, his life became increasingly dangerous.

At the height of his career, under the Emperor Nero, it seems that Seneca actually ran the Roman Empire—with the help of Burrus, the leader of the Praetorian Guard. Nero was a mere teenager, only sixteen years old, when he became emperor, and lacked the experience to govern the world's greatest empire on his own. During the first five years of his reign, Seneca guided him, and things went well for both men and for the Roman Empire. Seneca was also elected consul, which was the highest political office anyone could hold in Rome. However, after that peaceful five-year period, Nero assumed full control and started to act in murderous ways.

Unfortunately, when Seneca wrote his *Letters*, as an old man, he knew that his life was under threat from Nero, who had a bad habit of killing people he no longer liked. Knowing that his life was in danger, Seneca twice tried to separate himself from Nero, without success.

When Seneca was around forty-three, his troubles first started with Caligula, who wanted him put to death out of jealousy, just because he felt overshadowed by a brilliant speech Seneca had given to the Senate. Fortunately, one of Caligula's mistresses talked him out of killing Seneca because Seneca was ill, and she thought he would die soon in any case.

Later, when Seneca was forty-five, the Emperor Claudius had him exiled to the island of Corsica for eight years and took half his estate, on trumped-up charges, as an alternative to having him killed. This exile, entailing a total separation from his wife, took place only a few weeks after the death of Seneca's only son, still just an infant.

After spending eight years on Corsica, where he got a fair amount of writing done (because there was nothing else he could do there), Seneca was finally called back to Rome, but only under the condition that he would become a tutor to the young Nero, who at the time was eleven years old.

Despite Seneca's efforts to help Nero develop a good character, the project was a total failure. Nero had no interest in philosophy or ethics. He was only interested in self-gratification and power at the expense of others, which turned him into a monstrous tyrant. In the end, Nero had many who surrounded him killed, including his own mother, brother, and wife (whom he found to be boring, compared to his mistress). Nero finally had Seneca killed too, when Seneca was sixty-nine, after a failed conspiracy to remove

Nero from power. In this new killing spree, many people lost their lives, including Seneca's two brothers and his nephew.

But despite these severe hurdles, which would psychologically destroy many people today, Seneca's Stoic philosophy helped him to endure the hardships and to transform the adversities into something positive. Even when Nero forced Seneca to commit suicide as an old man—which was far preferable to the alternate forms of execution available—Seneca used the occasion of his own death to give a final talk about philosophy to several friends who were present, just as Socrates did when he was forced to drink hemlock poison.

Like a good Stoic, Seneca had prepared himself for death over the course of many years, as part of his philosophical training, and didn't show a single trace of worry or concern when surrendering his life.

He is reported to have said, quite matter of factly, "Who didn't know about Nero's brutality? After killing his mother and brother, there was nothing left but to add the murder of his guardian and teacher."[9] And while Seneca's last words about philosophy haven't come down to us, one could imagine him echoing the words of Socrates about his death: "While you can kill me, you can't harm me."[10] Or, as we might also put it, "While you might kill me physically, you can't destroy my inner character."

SENECA'S WORLD IS OUR WORLD

If you read Seneca's writings, one of the most striking things you'll notice is how he seems to be precisely describing our present-day world, even though he was writing two thousand years ago.

The wealthy citizens of Rome had developed consumerism into a fine art, and reveled in physical luxury and hedonism. As in our own time, when we can go into a supermarket in the middle of winter and buy oranges and avocados grown halfway around the world, the Romans had developed international trade to such an extent that rare goods, foods, and luxury items flooded into Rome from distant lands.

The upper-class Romans became obsessed with displaying their wealth as a sign of social status. What we now call "keeping up with the Joneses" even existed in ancient Rome. As Seneca describes it,

How many things we acquire only because others bought them and because they are in a good many homes. Many of our problems are explained by the fact that we copy the example of others: rather than following reason, we are led astray by convention. If only a few people did something, we wouldn't imitate them. But when the majority starts to act a certain way, we follow along, too, as if something should be more honorable just because it's more frequent.[11]

The wealthy built seaside villas, crafted out of exotic, imported marble, which featured spectacular views of the ocean, swimming pools and elegant baths, and every luxury imaginable. Some cooled their drinks and swimming pools during the hot summer months with snow and ice, transported over vast distances. Others hosted extravagant feasts, dinners, and parties, often costing astronomical sums of money, with the rarest delicacies imported from around the world, which they then vomited out to make room for more. Whereas the Romans had lived modestly in earlier times, this was no longer the case.

Finally, the high-spending Roman culture of Seneca's time displayed the same kinds of excesses associated with today's celebrities, which we read about now in Hollywood tabloids and on celebrity gossip websites. Seneca weighs in:

> Self-indulgent people want to be the focus of attention throughout their entire lives. Should the gossip go silent, they feel badly, and will do something new to arouse notoriety. Many of them drop large sums of money, and many keep mistresses. To make a name for yourself in this crowd, you need to combine extravagance with notoriety. In such a busy town, ordinary vices don't get reported.[12]

The simple reason these things sound commonplace today is because human nature hasn't changed. While our culture today is far more advanced technologically, in a psychological sense we are exactly the same as the people of Seneca's time. We are complex creatures who suffer from greed, ambition, worry, fear, grief, anger, financial anxiety, sexual desire, and addictions— along with a desire to be good people and to make the world a better place.

While Stoicism advocated simple living, it did not prohibit the accumulation of wealth, as long as wealth could be used wisely. But as one of the wealthiest men in the Roman Empire, whose professional colleagues included the top members of the social elite, Seneca had firsthand experience of the consequences of the pursuit of excess luxury. Most likely it was this firsthand experience that made Seneca recognize the emptiness and shallowness of high living, and led him to write against it:

> We admire walls veneered with a thin layer of marble, even though we know what defects the marble is hiding.

We deceive our own eyes, and when we have bathed our ceilings with gold, what are we delighting in, except a lie? For we know that beneath this gilding lurks some ugly wood. Nor is such skin-deep decoration spread only over walls and ceilings. All those famous men you see strutting about grandly possess gold-leaf happiness. Look inside, and you'll see how much corruption lies beneath that flimsy veneer of status.[13]

What makes Seneca unique in the Stoic tradition was his deep psychological insight into the human condition, including human ambition and fears. He was the first person in the Western world who deeply explored the psychology of consumerism. He also made significant contributions to the understanding of the emotions and anger, which are still valid today. In short, Seneca wasn't an academic theorist, but someone who had "seen it all" in real life: both the best and worst sides of human nature.[14] He had firsthand experience of what he wrote about, and a unique ability to understand the inner, psychological motivations of others. This is what makes Seneca such a valuable guide to modern readers, two thousand years later.

In the end, Seneca's time is our time. He's our contemporary, and we deeply share the same concerns.

CHAPTER 1

The Lost Art of Friendship

> Nothing will ever please me, no matter how excellent
> or beneficial, if I must keep the knowledge of it to
> myself. . . . No good thing is pleasant to possess without
> friends to share it.
>
> —Seneca, *Letters* 6.4

WHEN SENECA WAS IN HIS SIXTIES, HIS GOOD FRIEND Lucilius was wrestling with a significant problem.

Lucilius was a bit younger than Seneca and held a position in Nero's administration, governing the region of Sicily. Like Seneca, Lucilius was ambitious, talented, hardworking, and successful. He had established a high-ranking career, and even fame, in the social world of his time. But at some point in the process of achieving that high level of success, Lucilius had neglected his inner well-being. In modern terms, he was experiencing a crisis of meaning.

Seeking advice from a trusted friend, Lucilius turned to Seneca for help. Lucilius wanted to retire and live a more thoughtful and fulfilling life, but he also had become used to his wealthy lifestyle and the public acclaim he often received. And like many people today, Lucilius wondered if he had enough financial resources to retire and maintain his lifestyle, or if he should keep on working a few more years to build up his savings. While Lucilius yearned to be free, he also feared the consequences of leaving his well-paid position.

While Seneca scholars never mention it, this is the background story behind Seneca's letters to Lucilius.

Lucilius's questions about how to adjust his path in life gave Seneca an excuse to create his wonderful *Letters*, written not just for Lucilius but for a wider circle of readers. At the same time, the *Letters* were a cleverly designed introductory course to Seneca's own brand of Stoic philosophy. But behind this entire project was a belief in the deep and transforming power of friendship. Throughout his *Letters*, Seneca discusses many aspects of friendship, but this passage highlights why friendship is so essential:

> Friendship creates between us a partnership in all things. Nothing is good or bad for us alone: we live in common. Nor can anyone live happily who only cares for his own advantage. You must live for another if you would live for yourself. This fellowship, maintained with special care and respect, unites humanity as a whole, and holds that we all have certain rights in common. But it's also beneficial for nurturing the more intimate kind of friendship, of which I've been speaking. For someone who has much in common with another human being will have everything in common with a friend.[1]

While Seneca expressed his philosophy of living to Lucilius in letters and correspondence, he wrote his earlier philosophical works for other friends, relatives, and people he knew personally. His goal was to help them achieve mental tranquility, overcome grief, or address different challenges. As we can see, for Seneca philosophy, as the art of living, was not based on creating an abstract system for other intellectuals. Instead, it involved person-to-person relationships since, in Seneca's view, philosophy should help living people in the real world.

Seneca repeatedly criticized the academic philosophers of his time, who reduced philosophy to uncompelling logical arguments. Their approach seemed unconvincing, and it was irrelevant to addressing human needs. Seneca strongly distinguished between "real philosophy" and its alternative, which he saw as wordplay, a mere intellectual game. Many philosophers of his time, he said, focused on analyzing syllables and splitting hairs rather than exploring living ideas, which could enhance human life. He insisted that real learning is for life, not for the classroom.[2] Seneca's philosophical ideas were both systematic and consistent, but, as a writer, he understood the importance of presenting those ideas in an attractive and compelling way. By conveying philosophy with literary skill and dramatic impact, he brought philosophy to life and made it memorable.

While Lucilius saw Seneca as a close friend, he also looked upon Seneca as his philosophical mentor and adviser, a role Seneca was happy to play. Sometimes a friend can be a superb mentor. Often, someone who knows you well can offer candid feedback that would feel out of place—or even hostile—coming from a stranger. Consequently, there are many places in the *Letters* where Seneca "pushed back" quite hard against the kinds of false opinions (seen from Seneca's Stoic perspective) that were causing Lucilius mental anxiety.

Seneca knew Lucilius well and, when necessary, helped him take a serious look at the underlying beliefs that were causing his problems. Seneca would then encourage Lucilius to look at things from another perspective, helping him to reframe the situation. Some of Seneca's letters closely resemble modern-day psychotherapy sessions, in which a therapist challenges his client to question his or her patterns of thinking. In all of Seneca's philosophical writings, he plays a mentor's role, offering sensible advice and rational arguments to address real-life difficulties. He does this by helping his readers to reconsider their underlying beliefs. For Seneca and the Stoics, unless you can remove or deconstruct the false beliefs that cause mental suffering, it's impossible for anyone lead a happier life.[3]

INSTRUMENTS OF FRIENDSHIP

> Whenever your letters arrive, it seems I am with you. I feel that I'm about to speak my answer instead of writing back.
>
> —Seneca, *Letters* 67.2

Being together with a friend is the best way to enjoy each other's company and have meaningful conversations. But that's not always possible. In ancient times, a letter was an instrument to build, maintain, and strengthen friendships, bridging the space of separation. As Seneca wrote to Lucilius, "I never receive a letter from you without being instantly in your company."[4] Letters continued to perform this function until they were largely replaced by email, which wasn't that long ago.

Unfortunately, I think we lost something vital with the invention of email. While emails are quick and efficient, they tend to feel disembodied and insubstantial. By comparison, a well-written physical letter can offer a significantly different experience, one that more profoundly communicates an individual's personality and inner thoughts. While we forget emails quickly, an engaging letter can feel nourishing and is something you might save in a special place.

The fact that letter writing has gone out of style is, I believe, at least one small contributor to the "epidemic of loneliness," about which we now read so much. Ironically, while social media platforms like Facebook connect us with hundreds of others, many people feel more lonely than ever. I think I understand why: the level of communication that takes place on social media is so diminished, compared to the kinds of *real* conversations we need to be happy and to flourish as human beings. While letters can embody ongoing conversations, social media is primarily made up of *comments*—and those are two very different things.

Of course, it is possible to write a real letter to someone by email. And, thankfully, that sometimes happens. But since most emails are just quick notes, the medium itself encourages us to communicate less thoughtfully than before, back in the day when people wrote physical letters. Put another way, with email we communicate much faster and more frequently, but also less deeply.

In his letters to Lucilius, Seneca offers us a model of what a deep kind of friendship might resemble. But in our fast-paced, utilitarian culture, with its focus on achieving quick results and immediate gratification, we often seem to forget what deep and satisfying friendships require.

THREE LEVELS OF FRIENDSHIP

Aristotle (384–322 BC) emphasized the importance of friendship over two thousand years ago, when he wrote that there were three different kinds of friendship—and how living a happy life was not possible without meaningful friendships. While you are unlikely to study friendship in a college philosophy course today, it was so crucial to Aristotle that he devoted one-fifth of his main work on ethics, the *Nicomachean Ethics*, to exploring the nature and significance of friendship.

The most basic level of friendship, Aristotle explains, relies on mutual advantage. We can see these kinds of *advantage-friendships* as resembling connections you might make at a networking event for work. These are the most shallow and short-lived types of friendship. Because they are often self-centered, when the advantage someone offers disappears, the friendship dissolves also. Personally, I wouldn't call these people *friends* but *acquaintances*. In the words of Seneca, "Real friendship is stripped of its dignity when someone makes a friend just to increase his personal gain."[5]

The next form of friendship relies on mutual pleasure. These *pleasure-friendships* consist of people who enjoy one another's company. This could include a drinking buddy, someone you like going to movies with, or anyone you enjoy spending time with.

The deepest level of friendship for Aristotle, however, is based on mutual admiration, in which each person sees something he or she admires in the other person's character. These *character-friendships* are based on something good or virtuous you notice in another person. Character-friendships require trust and an investment of time, and are the types of bonds that can easily last a lifetime. Aristotle called this kind of friendship "perfect," and it involves sharing your inner life with another person. Like all friendships, it involves genuinely wishing well for the other person. And because it requires time, the number of real friends you can have is limited.

For both Aristotle and Seneca, no human life can be fully satisfying in isolation, without real friendships based on the love and knowledge of others.[6] Equally important, by spending time with others and engaging in dialogue, we can also develop our inner qualities. Friends are like mirrors to one another, because when you see good qualities in another person that aren't developed in yourself, it inspires you to improve your character, to become a better person.[7]

This is the lost art of friendship that Seneca and Lucilius practiced, which was not just philosophical but filled with genuine affection. Based on engaging dialogue and the desire for another person's well-being, this is a kind of friendship I'm convinced many people are hungry for today, but one for which we don't have many good role models. Certainly, those rare, deeper-quality friendships, which feel inwardly meaningful, make us feel more human and more fully alive. These kinds of friendships not only improve the quality of our lives—they make us into better people.

MAKING PROGRESS TOGETHER

Seneca was in high spirits when he wrote one of his first letters to Lucilius. As he wrote with excitement in the very first line, "I can now see, Lucilius, that I'm not just being improved but transformed!"[8]

Seneca wasn't just trying to help Lucilius, as a mentor, to improve his character. As this line shows, he was hoping the same *for himself*. Although Seneca had been studying Stoicism since he was a teenager, he still felt he had an immense amount of personal progress to make.

After telling Lucilius he was experiencing a transformation, Seneca explains this insight in greater depth. He knows that he has "many traits that should be identified, and decreased or strengthened."[9] He believes this realization is significant. It's proof of a mind that has transformed itself for the better, because he's now able to see his own faults.

What Seneca was feeling is the exact kind of transformation he wanted to see in Lucilius, too. Perhaps with his excitement Seneca was trying to emphasize and model these insights for Lucilius. For Seneca, if two friends could help each other improve their characters and make progress together, that would be an ideal type of friendship.

Friendships and meaningful relationships are crucial in Seneca's philosophy for another reason (see chapter 9, "Vicious Crowds and the Ties That Bind"). That's because the people we surround ourselves with make a huge impact on our own character. For Seneca, we should choose our friends carefully, because it's easy to pick up, or unconsciously absorb, bad character traits from other people. Alternately, being around people with good character traits helps us to develop good character, too. Those friendships help us to make progress.

MAPPING OUT A PATH:
STOICISM AS PROGRESS

As Seneca realized, only when you become aware of your faults, or what you might lack, is it possible to make real progress.

This idea was first associated with Socrates. He learned it from a wise priestess by the name of Diotima. As Diotima told Socrates, the gods possess perfect wisdom, so they don't seek it. Most people don't even know that they lack wisdom, so they don't seek it either. In the end, it's only possible to seek wisdom if you realize something is lacking.[10]

Put another way, if you're not aware of your faults, if you don't engage in self-inquiry, or if you don't seriously examine your values, you really are unconscious of these things, and little to no progress is possible.

For the Roman Stoics like Seneca, everything was focused on making progress toward wisdom and developing a better character, with the ultimate goal of becoming a Stoic sage or wise person.

While that makes perfect sense, one of the strangest and most damaging ideas of the earliest Greek Stoics (in my view) was that virtue itself, or having a good character, was an all-or-nothing matter. This meant that only the Stoic sage was virtuous, while everyone else was described as being foolish, vice-ridden, and even insane. This idea had come from the Cynics, which helps to explain its unusual and questionable nature.

Zeno of Citium, the founder of Stoicism, was strongly influenced by the life and thought of Socrates. But Zeno was also influenced by another Greek philosophical school, the Cynics. Seeking a radical state of freedom, the Cynics lived on the streets of Athens as beggars and were infamous for their extreme sayings and personal behavior that openly defied social conventions. (Plato supposedly described Cynic philosopher Diogenes as "a Socrates gone mad."[11]) Nearly all of Zeno's more radical ideas went back to the Cynics. Similarly, the idea that virtue is an all-or-nothing matter (and the idea of the sage) came from the Cynics.[12]

Certainly, there is nothing wrong with the basic idea of the Stoic sage. It's actually a very helpful concept. The problem is with the idea that virtue is an all-or-nothing matter: someone can *either* be a perfectly virtuous sage *or* be completely lacking in virtue. Consequently, in my view, Zeno's notion of an extreme dichotomy between a sage and the rest of humanity was not a helpful idea. While certainly attention-getting, it was harmful to the Stoic school, and it brought quite a bit of ridicule on the Stoics from other ancient philosophers.[13]

Put another way, most modern philosophers would identify the idea that virtue must be "all or nothing" as a *false dichotomy*, which is a logical fallacy. Similarly, a modern philosopher would not expect anyone to be perfectly virtuous; they would look for an overall excellence of character instead.

In this regard, the later Roman Stoics, like Seneca, strike me as far more realistic than the original Greeks. While the Greek Stoics had described the sage as an aloof and emotionally detached type of being, Seneca made the sage seem more human. He also stressed how the Stoic sage is, like everyone else, subject to normal human feelings. Most importantly, the Roman Stoics placed their emphasis on people who were trying to make progress toward virtue or toward improving their characters. This meant there are three groups of people in relation to Stoic philosophy: *sages*; *"progressors,"* or people making progress toward becoming sages; and a third group of people who don't make progress. While we could call this third group *non-progressors*, the Roman Stoics didn't give this group a name or even define them.[14] Despite that, as we can clearly see from the writings of Seneca, this group is made up of people who are unconsciously tied to, or enslaved by, false and unexamined beliefs. For our purposes, we'll call this group *the unenquiring* (see figure 1), echoing Socrates, "The unexamined life is not worth living."

I'll now try to map out this model more fully, to help explain why the Roman Stoics saw Stoicism as a kind of path and how

Fig 1: Three broad types of people on the philosophical
path, according to the Roman Stoics.

they thought it was possible to make a bit of progress each day
through self-reflection, practice, and training. While it's unlikely
for anyone to reach the level of a Stoic sage, it's still possible,
they maintained, to make progress in that direction.

At the apex of figure 1, we find the figure of the Stoic sage,
a perfectly wise person. A Stoic sage in normal circumstances
is happy, joyous, and tranquil, and displays psychological equanimity. In addition, a sage doesn't experience any passions (*pathē*
in Greek) or violent emotions, like extreme anger, because those
kinds of intense emotions arise from faulty inner judgments. What
keeps the Stoic sage free from negative emotions is that he or she
only makes sound judgments, so violent emotions never even have
a chance to arise. (That said, a Stoic sage *will* experience normal
human feelings, a topic discussed in chapters 4 and 12.)

As we can see, the Stoic sage is an extremely rare kind of
philosophical creature. Seneca said it's so rare that a sage only

appears like the Egyptian phoenix, once every five hundred years. (That's why I've included a little phoenix on top of the diagram, as a reminder of its rarity.) And while almost every Stoic philosopher spoke about the sage or wise person, not a single one of them claimed to be a Stoic sage. Within the Stoic school, stretching over centuries, the person most commonly identified as being a true sage was Socrates.[15]

So if the sage is not impossible, but incredibly rare, what practical value does the idea have? In the end, the sage is a kind of role model: a compass or north star, to give students something to aim for, and to keep them moving in the right direction. In the words of Emily Wilson, Seneca's biographer, "The figure of the perfect Stoic sage is of interest to Seneca not as an abstraction but as a tool to enable his readers to behave better toward one another."[16]

Seneca himself didn't claim to be a sage. As he admitted, "I am far from being a tolerable human, much less a perfect one."[17] But Seneca referred to the sage or the wise person often, because it was a useful tool. In fact, Seneca defines the nature of the sage so well in his writings that a student of Stoicism could find himself in almost any situation and ask, "How would a Stoic sage respond to this situation?" Even though it might not be perfect, it's a tool that works.

At the opposite and least philosophically inclined level of my pyramid, *the unenquiring* corresponds to the group of people that Socrates described as unaware: because they don't realize they lack wisdom, they will never desire to seek it out. (Even worse, some in this group might believe they are *already* wise, which is just as limiting.)

In modern terms, we'd say the lives of the unenquiring are deeply shaped by beliefs absorbed through socialization and social conditioning, which they haven't yet begun to actively question. Because of this, they tend to take things at face value, maybe things like the implied messages of advertisers, "Buying this product will increase your status and self-worth." From the ancient Stoic perspective, deeply entrenched false beliefs like this inspire people to seek out luxurious pleasure, wealth, possessions, fame, and social approval. But in the Stoic view, all of these things are "false goods," instead of the *real good* of having an excellent inner character, which would also allow us to use external things in a wise and beneficial way. In addition, the false opinions held by the unenquiring frequently cause them to experience extreme negative emotions like worry, fear, anxiety, and anger.

Given the fact that you're now reading this book, it's almost certain that you're a curious person, interested in learning new things, and that you're *not* totally unaware (or totally wise, either) but fall into the middle group of people, we call *progressors*. A progressor is someone who realizes that he or she is *not* already wise, and is thereby capable of improving and becoming a better person. This is the audience that Seneca wrote for, and he placed himself and Lucilius into this category too.

Progressor is a translation of the ancient Greek term for a student of Stoicism, a *prokoptōn*, or "one who makes progress." Since none of the Stoic philosophers claimed to be perfect sages but tried to make progress each and every day through the use of self-reflection and various exercises, all of the Stoic philosophers were progressors.

In the end, to make progress as a human being, you must first realize that you are imperfect (or have reason to improve) and, second, have a desire to improve. It's no coincidence that one of Seneca's most frequently used words in his letters is "progress," or making progress toward wisdom. And as he concluded, "most of progress consists in the desire to make progress."[18] For without that desire, progress itself is impossible.

Strangely, one question the Stoics, as a school, never explored in depth is, *What causes someone to become a progressor in the first place?* While the precise answer to this would vary from person to person, obviously some kind of "wake-up call," as we say today, is generally needed. It could be a personal crisis, a personal loss, repeated failures, or just a slowly growing realization that life is too precious to waste on the false goods that the world is constantly trying to sell to us. Alternately, the wake-up call could be a persistent feeling of unhappiness or depression—because a person's real, inner needs are not being met by his or her current beliefs or lifestyle.

MAKING PROGRESS EVERY DAY

> Don't demand that I should be equal to the best, but
> better than the worst. It's enough for me if, every day, I
> reduce the number of my vices and correct my mistakes.
> —Seneca, *On the Happy Life* 17.3

Roman Stoicism is a kind of path that focuses on making small, incremental amounts of progress each day, one step at a time. No one is perfect, and that's why Stoicism, at least in part, is a *practice*: and it's not just a practice that you undertake, but something that you practice *at*—in the same way a musician or an athlete practices—to get better at what you do.

Every day new situations arise that test our characters in small or significant ways, giving us ongoing opportunities to be mindful, virtuous, and to make the best (or wisest) judgments possible.

The *Meditations* of Marcus Aurelius highlights the fact that

Stoicism is a daily, incremental practice. Over the course of many days, Marcus reflected in his private journal on how to live a better life. By writing these notes to himself, he rehearsed his Stoic beliefs and reflected on how he could apply them in his life.[19] That's also one of the reasons Seneca wrote his philosophy in letters. Each day brings a new opportunity for self-reflection and progress, and a series of letters is itself "a work in progress"—just as developing one's character is a work in progress, too.

Other Stoic exercises show progress to be incremental, like the daily review of one's activities before bedtime, which was practiced by Seneca and other philosophers. In this exercise, Stoics would examine the mistakes they made during the day and consider how to act better in the future. As Seneca explains, after his wife has fallen asleep, "I carefully examine my entire day and review my deeds and words. I don't hide anything from myself, and overlook nothing. For why should I fear anything from my errors, when I'm able to say: 'Make sure you don't do that any longer, and now I forgive you.'?"[20]

In the various forms of this simple practice, one asked several questions:

- Where did I go wrong?

- What did I do right?

- What did I leave undone?

- What could I do better in the future?

This was not the only kind of "philosophical exercise" practiced by the Stoics. Others are mentioned throughout this book and a short listing is given in the appendix, "Stoic Philosophical Exercises." But as we can see, especially from this exercise, a Roman Stoic was encouraged to review his or her behavior each day, in order to make steady, incremental progress.

EXPERIENCING A SAGE-LIKE MOMENT

While none of the Stoic philosophers claimed to be a perfect sage, when I deeply study the most compelling writings of the Roman Stoics—Seneca, Epictetus, and Marcus Aurelius—I can't believe that they didn't experience sage-like *moments*. In those moments, they would have felt total peace of mind, felt in harmony with the universe, felt capable of making the best judgments, and felt a deep sense of joy. In fact, now and then, I've tasted these sage-like moments, too, even if they didn't last.

According to traditional Stoic arguments, being a sage is an all-or-nothing matter. But to me, something is missing in those arguments. What is the point of aspiring to be a sage if it's not even possible to taste what that state might be like occasionally? While our day-to-day lives may feel far from perfect, there are those rare moments, sometimes experienced in nature, when we can glimpse the sublime beauty and perfection of the world, despite what suffering or mayhem might be taking place elsewhere.

Aside from experiencing those moments, which I believe can be experienced by anyone, it doesn't matter if we become a perfect sage. What mattered for Seneca and the Roman Stoics is that we make some kind of steady progress, enhancing our excellence of character, so that we can live good and meaningful lives, no matter what outer circumstances we might face.

For Seneca, making progress in life is not an isolated experience: it involves friendship, spending time with kindred spirits, and receiving a helping hand from others. The Stoics believed strongly in the value of human community. The highest kind of friendship, in theory, would exist between perfectly wise people. But since perfectly wise people don't even exist (or are extremely rare), the next best kind of friendship exists between people devoted to helping each other make inner progress, to become better human beings. While all friendships have value, the most remarkable are those that help us—and others—to understand the world and ourselves more deeply.

CHAPTER 2

Value Your Time: Don't Postpone Living

Combining all times into one makes life long.
——Seneca, *On the Shortness of Life* 15.5

IT'S A BEAUTIFUL, SUNNY FALL MORNING, WITH A slight chill in the air, and I've picked up a warm filter coffee to go. Now seated in my favorite restaurant, I'm ready to order a delicious breakfast. But I'm feeling especially happy this morning, as if a joyful reunion is about to take place. It's because I'm going to spend some time with my old friend Seneca, but on a special occasion. For on this brisk but sunny morning, just as the world is coming alive and people are rushing off to work, I'm starting another reading of Seneca's *Letters*, starting with the very first one.

This first letter, which is less than two pages long, is a warning about how people undervalue their time, written in a dazzling literary style. While Seneca didn't give his letters titles, this one has been titled "On Saving Time," or "Taking Charge of Your Time," by different translators.

OUR MOST VALUABLE POSSESSION

Seneca believed that time is our most valuable possession. Because our lives are finite, each person has only a limited amount of time remaining. Many people, however, and for whatever reason, don't value their time and waste their lives on meaningless pursuits. Then, as they reach the end of their lives, they finally realize the mistake they've made and experience a deep sense of regret.

In this first letter, Seneca is responding to Lucilius, who had written to Seneca about his desire to lead a better life, and how best to maintain his inner focus. These are the first few lines of Seneca's response, starting at the very beginning:

LETTER I
From Seneca to Lucilius, greetings
Continue, dear Lucilius, to free yourself: gather and protect your time, which until now was being taken from you, stolen from you, or simply vanished. Convince yourself of these words: some moments are robbed from us, some are stolen, and some just slip away.[1]

For Seneca, we lose much time, and much of life, through carelessness. When we are not paying attention, life just slips away. He then asks Lucilius, "Can you show me a single person who considers the worth of his time, who values the worth of each day, who realizes that he is dying every day?" And to make the matter even more pressing, Seneca adds, "We are mistaken to think that death lies in the future: much of death has already passed us by, unnoticed. Any years behind us are already in the hands of death."[2]

When he wrote this, I don't think Seneca was being unpleasant or moralizing, looking down his nose at the behavior of others and telling them how to live. Most likely, he was basing these insights on his own experience. When writing this letter, Seneca was around sixty-six years old, and if the reports from the ancient world are true, Nero was trying to poison him. In fact, around the same period Seneca wrote this letter, in another writing he looked back over his life with regret, and reflected on all the time he had wasted. As he frankly admitted, "Old age accuses me of having consumed my years in useless pursuits," a situation Seneca was trying to remedy then, before it was too late: "Let us press on all the more and allow my work to repair the faults of a wasted lifetime."[3] If we read a bit between the lines, it's tempting to imagine Seneca was thinking about the work he did for Nero when musing about his squandered years. For while Seneca's work for Nero was highly lucrative in a financial sense, in the end Nero grew tired of Seneca and wanted him dead. Given that outcome, Seneca must have seen his work for Nero as being a waste of time, when he could have been doing something better. In fact, not long before he started writing the *Letters*, Seneca tried to disentangle himself from Nero as much as possible. Wanting to retire, Seneca made two attempts to return some of the wealth and properties he had received from Nero. But both times, Nero refused to take anything back and refused to let Seneca retire officially.

LOSING TIME

Seneca encourages Lucilius not to fall into a similar trap of wasting his time, and to value every hour, for time alone belongs to us. Strangely, he points out, while people often prize external things, which have little real value, they frequently don't value the most precious thing that is truly their own: the limited time that makes up our lives.

While Seneca's first letter on the value of time is short, the importance of time—and the importance of not wasting our lives on meaningless pursuits—is a central theme running through all of his writings. It's also a unique contribution he made to Stoic philosophy, because other Stoics didn't discuss this topic. Significantly, when Seneca was much younger and at the height of his professional career, he wrote a little book, *On the Shortness of Life*, also about making the best use of time. It might even have been written when he was at his busiest, helping to run the Roman Empire, when Nero was still a teenager.

"Life, if you know how to use it, is long," Seneca writes. "It's not that we have a short time to live, but that we waste much of it. Life is long enough, and it's been given to us in sufficient measure to accomplishing even the greatest things, if our life is well invested. But when life melts away through carelessness and the pursuit of luxury, and when death finally presses down on us, we realize that life passed us by before we even knew it was passing."[4]

According to Seneca, people fritter their lives away in countless ways: some through limitless greed, others through the pursuit of "useless undertakings." Some through drunkenness, others through idleness. Some through political ambition, others through pursuing international trade. "Some are worn out by the self-inflicted slavery of serving the great." Others waste their time "pursuing the wealth of others or complaining about their own." Some lose their time by having no consistent goal, and throw themselves from one project to another, with no rhyme or reason. "Some have no goal by which to guide their course, and death takes them by surprise as they lie wilting and yawning."[5] While people tend to be very careful in guarding their physical property and financial savings, he says that when it comes to protecting their most valuable asset, many let it slip away.

THE CULT OF BUSYNESS, ANCIENT AND MODERN

Seneca is quite dubious about people who engage in constant "busyness," running around as if they have many important tasks to do, while accomplishing little of significance in the process. Sometimes, the way people communicate their busyness seems little more than a form of show. In his words, "Loving to rush around is not proof someone is hardworking—it's only the restlessness of an agitated mind."[6] Unlike work accomplished with real mental focus, *acting* like you're busy is a waste of time.

As Seneca noted, some people "believe that busyness is proof of their success," while a person with more character won't "be busy for the sake of being busy."[7] Seneca, of course, was no slouch. He saw hard work as being essential. But he certainly would have questioned the wisdom of "multitasking." He also would have questioned the value of participating in long, tiresome workplace meetings, in which nothing meaningful is accomplished. As we can see from Seneca's writings, these kinds of things existed in his time, too; and as in our own time, they caused people to lose sense of the things that really matter in life.

In one graphic passage, which is also satirical, Seneca wrote, "We must cut down on the rushing around that many people engage in, wandering through theaters, houses, and marketplaces." These people "intrude in other people's affairs and always appear to be busy. But if you ask one of them leaving his house, 'Where are you going? What are you planning to do?' he will reply: By Hercules! I do not know! But I'll see some people and I'll do *something*." For Seneca, having some kind of definite aim in life was important, so he notes, "They wander around without purpose, seeking business, and don't pursue what they intended to do but only what they stumble upon." He finally ends with this humorous jab: "Their wandering is aimless and without point, like ants crawling over bushes, up to the highest tip of a branch and then all the way back down."[8]

If Seneca wrote *On the Shortness of Life* toward the peak of his career, he would have been at the peak of his busyness too. Most likely he was thinking about a better way to live. He might have been wondering about how the lives of those around him, and perhaps his own life, had gotten so out of harmony with what he believed to be a fulfilling lifestyle.

The problem with busyness for Seneca is that it leads to mental preoccupation with trivial concerns. And when we become one of "the preoccupied," as he calls them, we're not able to focus our minds on anything more important than the tasks and checklists we're trying to keep up with. I'm quite sure that we've all been in a place like that at one time or another—I certainly have—and most of us need to work for financial survival, too, as did Seneca. The big question, then, is: How can we value our time and live fully in the present moment without becoming overwhelmed with trivial tasks and distractions? How can we avoid losing our inner selves in a flurry of busyness?

One crucial idea for Seneca is that we shouldn't postpone living now in the hope that we will one day be able to retire and live the life we always dreamed of. Far too many people try that approach and fail. Sometimes people die before they can retire. In other cases, because they have spent their entire lives working at a career, some people have never developed any outside interests they could pursue during retirement. Due to a lack of interests outside of work, some find retirement to be boring, or even die soon after leaving a lifelong position. In Seneca's time, things were no different. As he notes,

> You'll hear many say: "After my fiftieth year, I'll retire into leisure. And after my sixtieth year, I'll give up all public duties." But what guarantee do you have, I ask, that your life will last longer? Who will allow your plans to proceed just as you desire? Aren't you ashamed just to save for yourself the little that remains of life and to develop your mind using only the time that can't be spent on business? How late it is to begin living just when life must end![9]

While Seneca valued hard work, leisure is essential, too: he certainly would have agreed with the idea that we should work to live, not live to work. Also, if possible, we should seek out meaningful work, which can contribute to society.

For Seneca, we should attend to our essential tasks when working, but avoid trivial things. This will eliminate much of the inconsequential "busyness" he described; and when our necessary tasks are complete, we should rest and apply our minds to better things.

Of course, how someone will find the right balance between work and leisure will vary for each person. The real problem for Seneca is that people become addicted to wealth—or what they *believe* to be wealth—and this leads to a mindset in which more is always needed. This belief then leads to the hustle and bustle of the preoccupied life. But for Seneca, the person who has enough, even if it is little, is already rich, while those who always seek more are poor. When you have "enough," you also have time. But people engaged in a constant hustle to acquire more money and status postpone living now and lack the time needed to develop their inner lives.

OVERCOMING SLAVERY:
A STOIC PATH TO FREEDOM

Most readers of Seneca will miss an important fact, and I discovered it only recently: Seneca reveals the key to understanding the entire project behind his *Letters* in the very first line of his very first letter. It's like a secret message, hidden in plain sight.

While this message would have been evident to readers of the original Latin, it's not apparent to readers of English translations.

The very first line of Seneca's letter reads like this in English: "Continue, dear Lucilius, to free yourself: gather and protect your time, which until now was being taken from you, stolen from you, or simply vanished." But the first part of this line in the Latin more accurately states: "Continue, dear Lucilius, to free yourself for yourself."

The key phrase here is "free yourself for yourself," which in the original Latin refers to freeing someone from slavery. In other words, Seneca's first line of the *Letters* carries this meaning: "Continue, dear Lucilius—*keep freeing yourself from slavery!*"

If there was ever any good aspect of slavery in the ancient world, it could only have been that it was possible for a slave to become *free*. This process was known as *manumission*. During Seneca's time, some freedmen or former slaves became extremely successful, wealthy, and high-ranking members of Roman society.

Significantly, three hundred years before Seneca, the earlier Greek Stoics developed the idea that in addition to being enslaved physically, it's also possible to be enslaved psychologically. In a world where physical slavery was widespread, to speak about inner slavery was an extremely powerful idea, and one that carried an emotional charge. But the idea worked well because

Stoic philosophy promised total human freedom on an internal level. Zeno stressed this idea in one of his famous "Stoic paradoxes," the puzzling sayings the school was famous for. Full of dramatic impact, his cryptic maxim stated, "Only wise people are free, and everyone else is a slave."[10]

While this saying was meant to draw attention to Stoic teachings by creating a mental shock in the mind of a reader, similar to an Internet meme today, it implied two separate ideas. The first is that it's possible to be totally free, externally, but to still be a slave internally. The second is that *Stoicism as a philosophy was designed to free its practitioners from the slavery of false judgments and opinions that lead to negative emotions like fear, anxiety, greed, anger, and resentment.*[11] And that is the exact project of Seneca's *Letters*, too, as he reveals in the first line of the very first letter: it's all about finding true freedom in life.

To give an example, if someone is always angry, snapping out at those around him day after day, that person is psychologically enslaved by negative emotions. But freedom is possible, too. And while the Stoics spoke about "psychological slavery," we speak today of *addiction*, which is a related concept.

Elsewhere, Seneca explains, "That's how it is, dear Lucilius"—while "slavery holds on to a few, many more hold on to slavery." But if his desire for freedom is genuine, and if he wishes to lay his slavery aside, Seneca promises Lucilius that he'll discover the freedom he seeks by progressing down the path of Stoic training.[12]

For people in ancient Greece and Rome, freedom did not mean so much the freedom "to do whatever you like" (or license); it meant the freedom of self-mastery or "freedom from." It meant self-possession, belonging to yourself, and not being a slave to anything.

This idea that Stoic philosophy was a path leading out of

slavery to freedom was even more strongly emphasized by the next great Roman Stoic after Seneca, Epictetus, who was himself, literally, a freed slave. (His name, *Epictetus*, means "owned" in Greek.)

In his classroom lectures, Epictetus humorously scolded his students, calling them "slaves," when they were, in fact, the sons of wealthy Roman aristocrats. Like Zeno, Epictetus believed that "only the educated can be free."[13] He also said that a person training to become a Stoic resembles a slave working to become free.[14] That graphic description of Stoic philosophy, and its power to free the mind from suffering, is a huge claim to make, and it's one the Stoics genuinely believed.

Learning how to value and experience the fullness of time, for Seneca, is also a way to overcome another kind of slavery. It's probably no coincidence that people today, who despise their nine-to-five jobs, often refer to themselves as "wage slaves." But for modern people who feel imprisoned by time, Seneca offers the ultimate escape route.

LIVING IN THE FULLNESS OF TIME

For Seneca, "It takes an entire lifetime to learn how to live," but the preoccupied mind of a constant workaholic takes in nothing deeply. By constantly focusing on how to reach higher levels of status or wealth *in the future*, preoccupied minds can't fully enjoy the present moment. The greatest obstacle to living fully, Seneca writes, "is expectation, which depends on tomorrow and wastes today."[15]

Life is divided into past, present, and future. But since preoccupied people have always been busy, they have little in the way of happy memories from the past. By comparison, people with tranquil minds have many happy memories. Because they weren't always working, they had more free time to enjoy life deeply, and no one can take those memories away.

After discussing these points, Seneca makes a startling claim:

> Of all people, only those who find time for philosophy are really at leisure—they alone really live. For not only do they guard over their own lifetimes, they add every age to their own. All the years that passed before them are added to their own.[16]

Seneca then explains that the great founders of the philosophical schools in the past gave human beings a way of life to follow and have passed onto us many valuable treasures. But all of these gifts, and even the greatest thinkers of past times, are things (and people) we still have access to, due to the power of the human mind. Thanks to this power, we don't need to remain trapped in our own era. We can share in the work of past ages, and even debate with past philosophers like Socrates and Seneca, learning from them each day. In this way, we can "turn from this brief and fleeting span of time" and immerse ourselves in a more profound experience of time, "which is boundless, everlasting, and which we share with better minds."[17]

Seneca believed that by having access to the philosophical minds of the past, a person will experience a deep sense of happiness until his dying day. In Seneca's words, "He will have friends with whom he may consider the greatest and smallest matters, whom he may consult with daily about himself, and who will tell the truth without insult, offer praise without flattery, and who will provide a model on which to pattern his own character."[18] As he notes in another writing, "I spend my time with the very best company. No matter where, in which time they lived, I send my thoughts to be with them."[19]

In this way, Seneca gives his readers a way to value the full range of time, to join a broader human community, and to escape the slavery of being forced to live only in the present age. He writes, the life of a wise person is

> not constrained by the same limits that constrain others. He alone is freed from the conditions of the human race, and all ages serve him. . . . Some time passes? He holds it in memory. Time is present? He makes use of it. Time is to come? He anticipates it. Combining all times into one makes his life long.
>
> But life is very brief and anxious for those who forget the past, neglect the present, and fear the future. When they reach life's end, the poor wretches realize, too late, that they've been busy for a long time doing nothing.[20]

In this remarkable insight, Seneca suggests that the happiest people are not just trapped in the present age. Instead, they can experience the ultimate value of time by weaving past, present, and future together. Here he no longer refers to time as being some kind of limited resource that we might someday run out of if we don't use it wisely. We now transition from scarcity to being part of a timeless human community, which is inexhaustible.

Seneca challenges us to discover what is timeless and valuable about human nature, and to become better, deeper, and wiser people in the process.

We can now see that the alternative to "preoccupation" and racing around in a flurry of busyness is learning how to live more deeply. And for us today, this doesn't require becoming a philosopher. Instead, developing an interest in art, music, architecture, science or astronomy, history or literature, or a spiritual tradition, to name a few, could help any modern person to live more deeply. Through these interests, we can take in the wisdom and accomplishments of the greatest thinkers from the past, with whom we can still form relationships. In this way, our lives are no longer limited to the present age, but enlarged and nourished by a timeless community of the human spirit.

CHAPTER 3

How to Overcome Worry and Anxiety

We suffer more often in imagination than in reality.

—Seneca, *Letters* 13.4

EVERYONE HAS EXPERIENCED WORRY OR ANXIETY.
Just before writing this chapter, I was alone at home with my small son, who is in grade school. My wife was traveling to a couple of conferences, so it was my duty to take care of him and to make sure that he got to school on time.

All in all, we had a perfect time together, some fun conversations and enjoyable dinners, and we deepened our father–son bond. But there were a few moments when we were leaving the house and going to school when I experienced a bit of panic or anxiety. It wasn't entirely irrational, but a moment of neurotic thinking that most people suffer from, from time to time.

My anxiety focused on the idea that some kind of mishap could take place, added to by the fact that I live in a place where I speak only a bit of the language, which could make it difficult for me to get help. While I speak enough of the local language to get by in simple settings, like restaurants, and many people here in Sarajevo speak English, there are some who don't speak any English. In more complex situations, I rely upon my wife to handle translations, and now she was away in a nearby country.

Basically, I started thinking, *What if?*

What if I locked us out of the house without a key, and no one could help me? (Something similar happened a few months earlier, so we had to change the lock on the front door.) *What if* I was in a car accident, and my wife wasn't around to translate? (It could easily happen, since the driving is so terrible here.) *What if* I suddenly became incapacitated and couldn't take care of my seven-year-old son while my wife was away? *What if . . . ? What if . . . ?*

None of these worries were entirely irrational, and that's how the process begins. People start to worry about the future and also about things that are beyond their control. They start to worry . . . *What if?* And if things get bad enough, they then start to worry about the fact that they are worrying.

As a keen protopsychologist and student of human nature, Seneca carefully studied how worry and anxiety arise, and how it's possible to reduce or eliminate anxiety by using the techniques of Stoic philosophy.

WHY PEOPLE WORRY

For Seneca, being able to plan for the future is one of the most amazing gifts that human beings possess. The ability to plan ahead, and to create many things of value, depends upon foresight, which is our inner way of imagining the future.

But while Seneca likens foresight to "a divine gift," there is nothing worse than *worrying* about the future (or what *could* happen), which, for most people, is the leading cause of psychological anxiety. And when people worry like this, it's because they have taken "foresight, the blessing of the human race," and turned it into a source of anxiety.[1]

Throughout his writings, Seneca explores precisely *how* worry and anxiety arise, and how to eliminate these kinds of worries, or at least how to address them and reduce them significantly. He even describes specific exercises his readers can use to overcome their worries, fears, and anxiety.

Seneca explains that two major fears everyone needs to work on overcoming are the fear of death and the fear of poverty (or the desire for wealth). Since those are important topics, we'll explore Seneca's advice about how to do that elsewhere in this book. In this chapter, we look at the more general question of how fear and anxiety arise in the first place, and how to defuse them.

The first teaching of Stoicism is pure common sense: some things are "up to us" or fully within our control, while other things are beyond our control. So far, no one could possibly argue with that. The way the Stoics extend this idea, though, takes more effort to explain.

The next step, according to the Stoics, is to understand that all of the external things beyond our control that happen to us are not truly "bad," because all such things are just indifferent facts of nature. But they become "bad" based on the mental judgments we make about them, which then create emotional reactions. In fact, nearly all negative emotions originate from judgments or opinions. Today, psychologists call this the *cognitive theory of emotion*, which the ancient Stoics originated.

This is one belief that every single Stoic philosopher shared, and Marcus Aurelius expressed it this way: "Get rid of the judgment, 'I've been harmed,' and the feeling of being harmed vanishes. Get rid of the 'I've been harmed,' and you're free of the harm itself."[2]

Another way of stating this central idea is that while we don't have control over the external things that happen to us, we *do* have control over how we respond to them. For example, you can probably remember some rainy day when you were walking down a busy road and a passing car roared through a deep puddle and splashed you. While the splash was unavoidable, how you responded to it mentally was your choice. On the one hand, you could have simply thought, "Oh, I just got splashed." On the other hand, you could have screamed out, "You ruined my entire day!" Of course, that outburst would have been followed by feelings of rage and fantasies about how you could seek revenge on the driver.

For the Stoics, the first thought, "I just got splashed," is an objective mental observation about something beyond our control. But the second thought, "You ruined my entire day," is a judgment or belief that creates anger and emotional suffering.

When we feel upset, we usually think that we are reacting to outer things in the world, but we are actually reacting to things in ourselves: our inner judgments, beliefs, or opinions. And we react emotionally because of the internal judgments we are constantly making. For Seneca and the other Stoics, rather than being irritated by things in the outer world that might be perfectly normal and expected—like getting splashed, or the bad behaviors of other people—it's better to look at the inner judgments that cause us to feel so upset. In that way, we can learn to live a more tranquil life.

Seneca saw that human beings have powerful imaginations that shape our feelings and the kinds of mental judgments we make. When the power of foresight, which is a kind of imagination, becomes misused, it creates worry, fear, or anxiety, which is different from having a legitimate, rational concern. Because of this, most anxiety is about things that *could* happen to us in the future, like the *what-if* story I started this chapter with. *What if she leaves me? What if I have an accident and can no longer work? What if I reach retirement age and don't have enough money to live?*

These might be entirely legitimate concerns, and they might demand serious, rational attention. But they become something else—sources of fear and inner turmoil—when we lose our mental composure. For Seneca, fear is a form of slavery, and "there is nothing worse than worry about future events," which "sets our minds trembling with unaccountable fear."[3] The only way to avoid this, he explains, is to not "reach forward" mentally but to live in the present moment, and to realize that the present moment is complete and perfect just as it is. As Seneca explains often, you can only be anxious about the future if you view the present moment as being unfulfilling.

Whenever Seneca discusses fear or anxiety, he's always quick to point out how to overcome these kinds of worries: instead of mentally "time traveling" to some imaginary point in the future when something bad *might* happen, and worrying about it now, *live in the present moment.* Marcus Aurelius, who read Seneca, agreed. He wrote that the only life we truly have is in the present moment.[4]

For Seneca, worrying about the future (or having regrets about the past) is an entirely psychological phenomenon in which people indulge their negative emotions. As he explains, because the past and the future are both absent, and we can feel neither of them, the only source of pain can be a person's emotions, opinions, or imagination.

I don't know if Mark Twain ever read Seneca, but he is said to have expressed a similar thought: "I am an old man and have known a great many troubles, but most of them never happened." In other words, they were imaginary.

Seneca explains how to return to the present moment. He also describes other remedies for worry and anxiety. But before we examine these in depth, let's take a closer look at how worry arises in the first place.

AN IMAGINARY HOUSE OF MIRRORS

In his writings, Seneca draws upon the imagination in powerful ways. He conjures up stunning descriptions of scenery to create a mood or to set the stage for something he's going to explain. While a rational thinker, he also uses the imagination to sometimes offer an image of transcendent beauty, like his thought, "I wish that mankind could glimpse philosophy in all its unity, so that it would appear unveiled like the glory of the starry heavens at night."[5] Then, like other Stoic philosophers, Seneca sometimes offers an imaginary exercise or visualization, which can be psychologically beneficial. One such practice, which was made famous by Marcus Aurelius, is called today "the view from above": it involves imagining yourself far above our planet and looking down on the Earth below, to see how small we are, and realizing how tiny our personal troubles are in relation to the greater universe.

As we've seen, Seneca also praises the imaginative power of foresight, which allows us to create the future. But despite this positive belief in the goodness of the imagination, Seneca recognizes that the imagination can take negative forms. It can help give rise to human obsessions, and it can also give birth to worries and fears that spiral out of control. "Even when nothing is wrong," he writes, "and nothing is certain to go wrong in the future, most people burn with anxiety."[6]

When the imagination becomes mixed with raw emotion,

this can create a feedback loop in which imagination amplifies emotions and emotions then amplify the imagination. (Modern psychologists sometimes call this experience of "becoming anxious about being anxious" *meta-worry* or *meta-anxiety*.) In a situation like this, with the imagination and emotions each amplifying one another, the entire system can spin out of control, resulting in extreme anxiety, panic attacks, or other psychological symptoms. In a situation like this, when the imagination reflects fear and fear reflects the imagination, we could refer to it as an imaginary house of mirrors, fueled by emotion. While everyone experiences worry or anxiety at some point, people who experience extreme anxiety live in a place like this frequently. As Seneca writes, "Each person is as miserable as he imagines himself to be."[7]

Seneca didn't use the image of a house of mirrors. He used the image of a maze instead. Seneca says that the happy life is fully available, right here and now, in the present moment. But by seeking it elsewhere or in other things, people lose the freedom of confidence they would already possess if they were fully present. He then likens this state to running through a maze, in which you lose the awareness of your true self: "This is what happens when you speed through a maze: the faster you race, the worse you become entangled."[8]

HOW TO OVERCOME WORRY

In Seneca's philosophy, there are several ways to overcome worry, and they're all rather simple. But since Stoicism involves practice, and is a practical philosophy like Buddhism, these solutions must be applied for them to work.

One of the first and most effective ways to reduce worry is simply to monitor your inner judgments and the emotions they give rise to *as the process happens*, and as you start to feel anxious about future events. The Stoic philosopher Epictetus called this practice *prosochē*, "mindfulness" or "attention." Once we understand how emotions arise and learn to monitor this process in real time, at the exact moment that anxiety is first felt, we can make a conscious choice to follow Seneca's advice: this involves calling our mind back from the future to live fully in the present, because the future doesn't even exist.

For a Stoic like Seneca, it's reasonable to be *concerned* about future events but it's a mistake to *worry* about something in advance that might not even happen. As he wrote to Lucilius, "My advice to you is this: Don't be miserable ahead of time. Those things you fear, as if they were near at hand, might never arrive. Certainly, they haven't arrived yet."[9] This is one piece of advice that Seneca stressed many times over, throughout his writings. Marcus Aurelius also supported this view when he wrote, "Don't allow the future to trouble you," because when it does arrive, you'll face it with the same sense of reason you apply to the present moment.[10]

Second, since anxiety, fear, and psychological suffering arise from bad judgments, faulty opinions, or a misuse of the imagination, Seneca asks us to undertake a key Stoic practice: to analyze wisely our patterns of thinking in order to understand the source of the suffering. For if anxiety arises from faulty beliefs, by rationally analyzing those beliefs and dismantling them, we can also cure the distress. As Seneca puts it, "We agree with opinion too quickly. We don't test those thoughts that lead us to fear, or question them with care. . . . So let's examine things carefully."[11] Modern cognitive psychologists call this kind of inquiry *Socratic questioning*, another tip of their hat to ancient philosophy.

Albert Ellis, one of the modern founders of cognitive behavioral therapy (CBT), had studied the Stoics. When Ellis first started work with new clients, he always gave them a copy of this famous Stoic saying: "It's not things that upset us, but our opinions about them."[12] That, in essence, is the central, foundational thought behind the entire field of cognitive therapy. Ellis used a simplified scheme, known as the "ABC Theory of Emotion," which was directly based on Stoic philosophy (see figure 2). First, with *A*, there is an *Activating* event. Then with *B*, there is a *Belief*, opinion, or judgment. And finally there appears *C*, *Consequences*, which is usually an emotional result of the earlier belief.

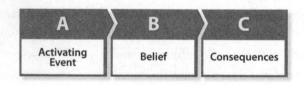

Fig 2: Albert Ellis's "ABC Theory of Emotion" was directly based on the Stoic idea that "it's not things that upset us, but our beliefs about them."

If you get splashed by a car on a rainy day and simply believe "I just got splashed," the main consequence is that you might feel a bit wet. But if you believe "My entire day has been ruined," which is the same as saying "I've been harmed," the consequence would most likely be extreme anger. From this, we can see that it's our unexamined, often irrational beliefs that cause emotional reactions. Fortunately, we can better understand those faulty beliefs, and even eliminate them, by analyzing them through the practice of Socratic questioning, either on our own or with the help of a therapist or mentor.

Nearly 20 percent of people in the United States suffer from anxiety disorders. But many individuals who study Stoicism and use Stoic mindfulness techniques have reported significant declines in the experience of negative emotions like anxiety and anger.

It's fascinating to see how cognitive therapy was influenced by Stoicism, especially since some of Seneca's letters to Lucilius read just like little psychotherapy sessions. Seneca knew Lucilius well enough to understand what many of his friend's underlying beliefs were, and it's educational to see Seneca questioning his friend's assumptions. It's also remarkable to watch Seneca explaining how other beliefs might lead to happier outcomes. This is exactly the same process a modern cognitive therapist would use today.

In this way, Stoicism was a precursor of modern-day cognitive behavioral therapy, and the founders of CBT, like Albert Ellis and Aaron T. Beck, directly drew upon Stoic teachings to create their modern therapeutic methods. In the first major textbook published on cognitive therapy, Beck flatly stated, "The philosophical origins of cognitive therapy can be traced back to the Stoic philosophers."[13] As Stoicism and CBT both show, by coming to understand and challenge the distorted thoughts, beliefs, and attitudes that cause suffering, psychological anxiety can be greatly reduced. Significantly, this cognitive "therapy of the passions," which originated with the Stoics, has been scientifically proven to resolve many kinds of psychological disorders. For example, CBT is the most studied form of psychotherapy, and is the "gold standard" in treating mental anxiety. In some studies, CBT has helped 75 to 80 percent of patients to recover from different types of anxiety, including panic attacks.

Another approach from Seneca, which is also used in CBT, involves dialing down the level of our emotions, especially emotions connected with the future. In Letter 5, Seneca writes, "Limiting desire helps to cure fears." He then quotes a line from the Stoic philosopher Hecato: "Cease to hope, and you will cease to fear."[14]

Seneca explains that hope and fear are conjoined because they are both emotions that become activated by our imagination about the future. He writes, "Both come from a mind that is in suspense, worried in anticipation of what is to come. The greatest cause of each is that we don't apply ourselves to the present but project our thoughts far into the future."[15]

While many concerns we have about the future might appear to be reasonable, Seneca taught that we should carefully analyze those concerns. In that way, we can respond to them in a thoughtful way, rather than in a way that generates emotional suffering. For example, Seneca noted that people have an irrational fear of death, even though death is a part of life. Since death is natural and something everyone should expect, to view it as being something terrible is a cognitive error. The later Stoic, Epictetus, agreed with him:

It is not things themselves that disturb people, but people's opinions about things. Death, for example, is nothing frightening, or Socrates would have thought so too. The fear arises from *the opinion* that death is frightening [emphasis added]. So whenever we feel frustrated, disturbed, or upset, we should never blame anyone else, only ourselves—that is to say, our own opinions.[16]

Ultimately, while the Stoics didn't believe in the existence of *real* misfortunes, they understood full well how things *feel* like misfortunes through the judgments we make or the opinions we hold. Also, as Seneca pointed out, it's just not possible to avoid emotional shock at some events. Those reactions are natural, instinctual, and not based on opinions. But even in such cases, it's possible to reduce the psychological impact, and to keep those emotional shocks from developing into something more serious.

For some conditions, like the fear of poverty, Seneca advocated specific exercises to lessen or eliminate the grip of the fear, and to prepare ourselves for the feeling of misfortune or emotional suffering. We'll take a look at some of these exercises in other parts of this book. In fact, Seneca frequently recommends that we consider in advance every possible adversity that could impact us. In this way, if such a mishap actually occurs, we'll be mentally prepared for it, and the blow of the misfortune will be decreased. But for Seneca, anticipating or even rehearsing the possibility of adversity in the future is not a form of worry or fear. It's a way to calmly and rationally consider things that *could* happen, draining future misfortunes of their emotional impact *should* they occur. (This also resembles a technique used by modern psychologists.)

While it takes awareness and practice, when a feeling of worry about the future first arises, we can question it, analyze it, and consciously decide to return to living in the present moment. But living in the present moment isn't just some kind of psychological solution for Seneca—it's one of the key things needed to lead a complete human life.

FINDING YOURSELF IN THE
PRESENT MOMENT

The present alone can make no one miserable.

—Seneca, *Letters* 5.9

Do you want to know why people are greedy for the future? It's because no one has yet found himself.

—Seneca, *Letters* 32.4

When you live in the present moment, you have finally found yourself, and you are living from the center of who you really are, your most essential self.

The idea of living from your own center, and being present at this very moment, without desiring future states or external things, is one of the keys to achieving Stoic happiness or joy. When we are fully present and living from our inner selves, we experience feelings of radiance, joy, and completeness. To use a metaphor, the soul starts to shine like the sun; and as long as we can maintain this sense of presence and self-sufficiency, the sun will keep shining. This doesn't mean there won't be external disturbances, but those disturbances will be like clouds floating below the serene, radiant face of the sun. Those clouds float by, but do nothing to alter or disturb the sun or its light.

This image of the sun and the clouds appears in two of Seneca's letters, and in both cases the sun and its light represent lasting goodness, virtue, and joy: any adversities or anxieties we experience, he writes, "have no more power than a cloud can have over the sun."[17] Similarly, when we experience true joy, "even if something obstructs it," it's just like a cloud, "which is carried below, and never overcomes the light of day."[18]

This symbolic image, which I find to be powerful, gives me a personal way to evaluate my mental or psychological state at any time. Do I possess the inner serenity of the sun, shining in the present moment, in which external disturbances are just like harmless clouds floating by my path? Am I experiencing the joyful state of being present and undistracted, with the right mental focus, and not worrying about some imaginary future event that might not even occur?

If my inner state is not focused, luminous, and joyful, I can remember and identify with Seneca's image of the sun. Then, returning to the radiance of the present moment becomes easy.

Ultimately, this kind of "unbroken and lasting joy," which Seneca speaks of and symbolizes by the sun, is a by-product of Stoic practice, and being fully present is one way to catch a compelling glimpse of it. But the way to make it into a continuous state—or as constant as possible, since no one is perfect—is through the development of virtue, one's inner character, and the practice of Stoic mindfulness. This allows the Stoic to experience tranquility of mind, despite whatever troubles life throws our way.

CHAPTER 4

The Problem with Anger

A TEMPORARY INSANITY

I hate to admit it, but, like Seneca, I'm not a perfect person. One of my character failings is that I've had a bad temper at times in the past. It's not as though I was always angry, by any means, but every now and then, something would set me off.

The good news is that I rarely get angry now, which I attribute to my study of Stoicism, and especially to Seneca, who wrote about anger in depth.

For the Stoics, anger (by which they meant rage) was the worst and most toxic of the extreme negative emotions, which they called "passions" (*pathē*).

In fact, in one of Seneca's more memorable descriptions, he called anger "a temporary form of insanity."[1]

Why is it that anger is so terrible and destructive, and how does it come into being? More importantly, how can we stop anger from taking root in the first place?

In answering these questions, Seneca is an almost perfect

guide. He took the issue of anger so seriously that he wrote a lengthy book, *On Anger*, divided into three parts. It's the most in-depth work of Stoic psychology that has come down to us from the ancient world, and the advice that Seneca offers about anger management is totally up to date. In fact, as the modern Stoic philosopher Massimo Pigliucci points out, if you read the American Psychological Association (APA) web page on how to manage anger, most of it matches the advice you find in Seneca's book on anger.[2] Some things, it seems, just never change.

When Seneca said that extreme "anger is a temporary form of insanity," he wasn't being metaphorical. In fact, he wants to impress upon the reader just *how* out of their minds humans act, like crazy people, when they're under the spell of anger.

At the beginning of *On Anger*, he writes, "You only need to see the symptoms of those seized by anger to know they are insane." He then launches into a vivid and compelling description to prove his point:

As the marks of a madman are clear—a bold and threatening expression, a scowling brow, a wild-looking face, quickened steps, restless hands, a changed complexion, quick and violent breathing—the appearance of an angry person is the same: his eyes blaze and flash, his whole face turns red with blood boiling up from deep within his heart, his lips quiver and teeth clench, his hairs bristle and stand on end, his breathing is harsh and noisy, his joints snap from writhing, he groans and bellows, his speech is broken and unclear, he claps his hands and stomps his feet, and his entire body becomes frenzied as he acts out his angry threats. It is such an ugly and horrible display that, when someone is distorted and swollen with anger, you can't say whether this vice is more revolting or more disfiguring.[3]

The outcome of great anger is madness, Seneca writes, and we should avoid it to maintain our sanity. Elsewhere, he points out that if a furious person's outward expression is so terrible, what must their mind look like on the inside?

Seneca reports that some people who experience extreme anger never regain their sanity. He refers to anger as "the greatest evil," and "one that surpasses all other vices."[4] While other vices like fear, greed, and envy merely "provoke" the mind, anger "topples" it.[5] While the other vices rebel against reason, anger undermines sanity itself. While other character defects "approach gently and increase unnoticed, our minds plunge headlong into anger."[6]

A HOSTILE FLAME:
THE DEVASTATING EFFECTS OF ANGER

Anger is bad enough for the poor person who falls under its spell but can be even worse for those on its receiving end. Seneca invites us to consider anger's destructive outcomes:

> If you wish to view its harmful effects, no plague has cost the human race more. You'll see massacres and poisonings, the vileness of rivals battling in court, the loss of cities, and the destruction of entire nations. You'll see leading citizens sold into slavery at public auctions. You'll see houses torched, the blaze overtaking city walls, causing vast regions of the country to burn with a hostile flame.[7]

Nor is that all. Anger causes some parents to threaten their children with death, or vice versa. It destroys households, plunges some into poverty, and encourages people to turn their friends into enemies. Anger is the worst vice, because it surpasses all others. What Seneca means by this is that in the same way that anger overturns the mind, it overpowers the other vices too. When someone is truly under the spell of extreme anger, anger reigns supreme.[8]

Anger arises from a mental judgment that "I've been harmed" or "I've been wronged," and once that opinion has been fully accepted, anger seeks out revenge or retribution, as a way to "pay back" the injustice. "That it should find a place in the peaceful heart of a human being," Seneca writes, "is at odds with our nature. For human life is founded on kindness and harmony, and is bound together into agreement and common aid not by terror, but by mutual love."[9]

For Seneca, anger is the absolute worst human emotion. But why?

"The problem with anger," Seneca writes, "is that it refuses to be controlled. It rages against truth itself, if truth seems to contradict its wrath. With shouting, frenzy, and the whole body shaking, it bears down on its targets, with abuses and curses thrown in."[10]

When someone gets angry, he asks, what's the point of flipping a table over or smashing a glass? Even stranger is how people sometimes express rage at inanimate objects. When a tool doesn't work properly, what's the point of throwing it to the ground and cursing at it, if it can't even sense one's anger?

Most people, because they've never really thought about it, assume that anger is a natural kind of emotion, and unavoidable in some way. Because of that, Seneca writes, some people believe that showing their anger in public is good because it shows how they are "open" and authentic, not trying to hide any part of their personality.

The Stoics, though, took an entirely different view of things. They believed that extreme anger could be avoided and never allowed to develop in the first place. Because intense anger is based on bad mental judgments, a wise person could avoid making those bad judgments through training and practice.

"FEELINGS" VS. "PASSIONS": THE STOIC THEORY OF EMOTIONS

How is it that anger, or any other extreme emotion, arises in the first place?

According to the Stoics, if we could learn the answer to that question, it would be possible to eliminate negative emotions before they even develop. Of course, no one said this would be easy. It might take long periods of education and training, and would require the development of considerable self-awareness. But even learning about the Stoic theory of emotions, in my experience, can significantly help reduce anger and other negative emotions and improve a person's overall mood.

In fact, shortly after first reading Seneca's book *On Anger* a few years ago, I found myself in a situation where I could have become very angry and felt the early signs of anger coming on. But before the anger had a chance to develop fully, I recalled what Seneca had written and was able to deconstruct the emotion before it ever took hold.

As we've seen, one common misconception about Stoics is that they don't experience feelings, or they suppress their emotions. That is untrue. Seneca consistently pointed out that even a Stoic sage will experience normal human feelings. Like other people, a sage doesn't resemble "some kind of rock." He or she will experience pain, grief, and other feelings.[11] Similarly, Epictetus said, a Stoic should not be "unfeeling like a statue."[12] Marcus Aurelius frequently wrote about love and even wept in public. The Stoics, as a school, were known for their love for humanity. As Seneca noted, writing about the Stoics, "No school is more kindly and gentle, none more full of love for mankind and more concerned for the common good."[13]

For the Stoics, the most primary human feeling is affection and love for others. Parents naturally feel love for their children, and human affection binds people and communities together. But to understand how anger comes into being, and how to defeat it, we must understand the three different kinds of emotions that the Stoics defined clearly, in addition to love:

1. **Feelings.** The first kind of emotions, known as "first feelings" or "protopassions" (*propatheiai* in Greek), are experienced by everyone, and include spontaneous, instinctual responses. These include things like blushing, sexual arousal, being startled if someone sneaks up behind you, having stage fright, changing your expression at a sad event, and so on. In this book, we'll refer to these as *feelings* or *natural human feelings*, which everyone experiences, including a Stoic sage. It is important to note that these feelings are involuntary and come and go on their own. Also, these feelings are morally indifferent. Since they are beyond our control, they have no positive or negative impact on our character.

2. **Negative emotions.** The next group of emotions, which these earlier feelings can help give rise to, are

known as "passions" (*pathē*). These are negative emotions like anger, fear, greed, envy, and so on. In this book, I refer to them as *negative emotions*, *extreme negative emotions*, or *unhealthy emotions*. These negative emotions arise from mental judgments, but judgments that are mistaken or false. Because they are based on false beliefs, these negative emotions are harmful to our character. In other words, they are vices.

3. **Good emotions.** The third and final group of emotions are "good passions" (*eupatheiai* in Greek). In this book, we will refer to them as *good emotions*, *healthy emotions*, or *positive emotions*. These include joy, cheerfulness, sociability, goodwill, and forms of friendship and love. Just like negative emotions, positive emotions are based on mental judgments. But good emotions are based on rational and accurate judgments, while negative emotions are based on false judgments. And as you might imagine, good emotions are not indifferent or bad, but *good* for our personality and character.

And that's that: For the Stoics, *feelings* are just feelings, neither good nor bad, and everyone experiences them. *Healthy emotions* are good, and based on sound, accurate judgments. For the Stoics, the real enemies are the *extreme negative emotions* or passions, which are based on false opinions and harmful to one's inner character. Seneca pretty much summed up the Stoic view about negative emotions when he wrote, "Anyone enslaved to a passion is living under a tyrant."[14]

If you live under a negative emotion's tyranny, you will never experience peace of mind because your mind is not under your own control. It's under the control of something else: a false judgment or opinion, which will cause you to act in harmful and self-destructive ways. When Seneca said that "anger is a temporary form of madness," it's something that applies to *all* of the passions or extreme negative emotions. In the words of Stoic scholar John Sellars, they are like "little mental illnesses" that take over our minds. It's just that anger is the most powerful.[15]

What does it mean that a passion is based on a judgment? Take the example of *greed*. For a Stoic, someone who suffers from greed agrees with the judgment that having a lot of money is not just a possible advantage but *essential* for human happiness. Ultimately, this is based on a widespread social belief, like many other false opinions, that are "deeply ingrained errors about the value of external objects."[16] Significantly, the Stoics were among the first thinkers to deeply explore the adverse effects that social conditioning can have on our inner development.

Let's also imagine, as a thought experiment, that my friend Mike was walking through the city one day and noticed a gorgeous woman on the other side of the street. Mike might think, "Oh, she's beautiful!" Perhaps he felt his heart was beginning to melt a bit, but he kept walking and quickly forgot about her. For the Stoics, this would just be a normal *feeling*, and nothing more. But if Mike saw the beautiful woman and became obsessed with her, thinking, "I could never be happy living without her!" that would be the beginning of a full-blown passion, or negative emotion, because it would no longer be based on just a feeling, but a false and potentially harmful judgment.

THIS BRINGS US TO the point where we can now understand how anger and other negative emotions come into being.

Seneca was not by any means the first Stoic to write about

this process, but he is our single most important source, because the earlier writings have been lost.[17]

Anger itself, as Seneca tells us, is always based on two mental judgments. The first judgment is "I've been harmed" or "someone has treated me unjustly." The second judgment is "If I've been harmed, I should seek payback through retribution or vengeance." Should these two judgments be combined, the outcome is likely to be a manifestation of extreme anger.

Seneca explains in some detail how extreme anger comes into existence, following a three-step process. This mirrors the ABC Theory of Emotion, discussed earlier, in chapter 3:

A. In the first step or "movement," there is an involuntary motion, or a natural, instinctual feeling. This natural feeling is a protopassion and a kind of warning that something worse might be coming. Seneca calls this raw feeling a "jolt," an "agitation," and "a first movement." This is not a passion but an impression or feeling that could turn into a passion. In the case of anger, the two involuntary impressions that first come to mind are "I *feel* harmed" and "I *feel* like I should take vengeance."

B. In the second step or movement, the mental judgment appears, "I *have* been harmed, and I *deserve to* seek vengeance."

C. In the third step or movement, someone has given approval to the judgment, and all hell breaks loose, because reason has been overturned and overpowered: anger flares forth and takes command, and vengeance is sought. At that point, it's just too late to pull back from anger, because the mind has already "gone over the cliff" and is out of control. The temporary insanity has begun.[18]

HOW TO CURE ANGER

If we look at the three-step process through which anger comes into being, it becomes clear that the only way to stop anger is during the first two stages. By the time the third stage is reached, it's too late. What makes anger management difficult is that these three movements can take place so quickly—sometimes in a flash. If you carefully study Seneca's explanation of the three steps and compare it with your own experiences of getting angry, I think you'll see that he's correct about the process. But in terms of real-life experience, the three steps happen so quickly it often feels like a blur.

Thus, the most important thing we can do is slow down the process when there is the first, initial sense that anger may be coming on. The first movements of anger, Seneca explains, cannot be controlled by reason because they are instinctual feelings. However, "practice and constant watchfulness will weaken them."[19]

Once the second step is reached, judgment or deliberation is in effect, which is rationality at work; as Seneca notes, only the power of rationality, or a good judgment, can erase a bad judgment.

Time and again, Seneca states that the most powerful tool for defeating anger is *delay*, to slow down the entire three-step process. That gives us time to intervene and rationally analyze any bad judgments:

> The greatest cure for anger is delay. Ask this from anger at the start, not so it will forgive, but so it will evaluate.

While its first assaults are heavy, it will retreat if forced to wait. But don't try to destroy it all at once. If picked away at bit by bit, it will be defeated.[20]

He also puts it like this:

Anger arises from a belief that you have been wronged, which one should not accept lightly, at face value. You should postpone judgment even if it seems clear and evident, because some false things appear to be true. We must always allow for some time to pass: a period of time reveals the truth.[21]

From the earliest days of the school, the Stoics emphasized how important it is to analyze the "impressions" presented to our minds. Like Seneca did in the quotation above, they warned us not to make snap judgments because impressions can be deceiving. In fact, Epictetus said that "testing impressions is the philosopher's single most important task, and no impression should be accepted unless it has been carefully tested."[22]

How a Stoic can stop anger from developing into a full-blown negative emotion is beautifully summed up in the remark attributed to the psychologist Viktor Frankl: "Between stimulus and response there is a space. In that space is our power to choose our response. In our response lies our growth and our freedom."

While Viktor Frankl never actually said that, and the quote appears to be based on a passage from psychologist Rollo May, the Stoics would have endorsed both statements, whoever said them. This is the original passage from Rollo May:

Human freedom involves our capacity to pause between stimulus and response and, in that pause, to choose the one response toward which we wish to throw our weight. The capacity to create ourselves, based upon this freedom, is inseparable from consciousness or self-awareness.[23]

That is why Seneca says that the greatest cure for anger is *delay*. Put into Stoic terms, a "stimulus" is an "impression." We need to pause, carefully test impressions, and decide or "choose" whether they should be accepted.

Importantly, for Seneca and the Stoics, an extreme, negative emotion cannot come into being without the mind first agreeing to an impression and then accepting a false mental judgment. By pausing, it's possible to question the impressions. It's also possible to challenge a mental judgment or belief before it's accepted. In terms of Stoic psychology, this is the best way to stop anger, because, as Seneca notes, anger "only acts with the mind's approval."[24] In the end, anger can arise only when we *decide* it is justified.

Fortunately, the first feelings of anger are clear warning signs of impending danger, in the same way that symptoms appear before a disease, and as signs of rain appear before a storm. As Seneca advises,

The best approach is to reject the first provocations of anger at the outset, to resist its smallest beginnings, and to make every effort not to fall into it. For if it starts to lead us off course, the path back to safety is steep, since reason evaporates once anger has been let in and we've decided to give it any authority. It will then do whatever it wants—not what we allow it to do. The enemy, I say, must be kept away from the entrance to the city gates from the very beginning: for once it has stormed inside, it ignores every plea for restraint from those taken captive.[25]

As he notes in a letter, "Every negative emotion is weak at first. But it rouses itself and increases its strength as it advances. It's more easily shut out in the beginning than driven out later."[26] If we stay strictly within the Stoic theory of the emotions, two fundamental anger management techniques stand out:

1. *Take a Step Back.* The best way to stop anger, in the very beginning, would be to notice the first feelings or impressions that "I have been wronged," and to pause, take a time out, give them time to subside, and not consent to them. The American Psychological Association (APA) also recommends this technique. Psychologists today call this *cognitive distancing*, which can take many different forms.

Long ago, I had a girlfriend who used this technique, and it's a good thing she did, because she was a well-trained athlete who held a fifth-degree black belt in karate. Though she was short in stature, she was extraordinarily muscular and fierce as a martial artist. Without exaggeration, she literally could have killed anyone with her bare hands.

One day we were together at my home, and I can't recall what I said, but she felt some anger coming on because of it. At that moment she explained to me, calmly and without emotion, "I'm sorry, David, but I need to leave for a couple of hours and cool down, because if I lost my temper, you would be in extreme physical danger, and I could possibly kill you." Like a true professional, she had trained for this moment and delivered her line without a single trace of anger, even though she felt something simmering.

Of course, I was thankful that she possessed this incredible self-awareness, and grateful she didn't kill me. When she returned, everything was fine. She was her usual calm self. This was the only time something like that happened between us, perhaps because it put me on warning!

2. *Restructure Your Beliefs.* If the growing sense of anger has moved past the stage of just being a "first feeling," it's time to question your judgments and beliefs before concluding that revenge is justified. This is another way to take a step back before a final judgment has formed. Again, the APA recommends this technique, and I've even stolen the phrase "Restructure Your Beliefs" from their website, just to show how Seneca's psychological insights are timeless.

As we've seen, the final step before real anger flares forth is making the judgment that "I've been wronged, so vengeance is justified." So you clearly want to apply some critical thinking before allowing this judgment to take hold, and to destroy the false belief if possible. Under the heading "Cognitive Restructuring," the APA tells us,

> Logic defeats anger, because anger, even when it's justified, can quickly become irrational. So use cold hard logic on yourself. Remind yourself that the world is "not out to get you," you're just experiencing some of the rough spots of daily life. Do this each time you feel anger getting the best of you, and it'll help you get a more balanced perspective. Angry people tend to demand things: fairness, appreciation, agreement, willingness to do things their way. Everyone wants these things, and we are all hurt and disappointed when we don't get them, but angry people demand them, and when their demands aren't met, their disappointment becomes anger.[27]

Good work, APA—spoken like a real Stoic! Except for the suggestion that anger can sometimes be "justified," which Seneca argued against vigorously. In fact, Seneca and the other Stoics argued that a wise person could never be harmed by anything trivial. In the words of Epictetus, "No one will harm you without your consent; you will only be harmed when you think you are harmed."[28] Or as Marcus Aurelius put it, "Discard the judgment and you'll be saved. Who, then, is stopping you from discarding it?"[29] Both of those quotations are helpful in terms of overcoming a belief that you have been harmed.

Another way to restructure the belief that you've been harmed is through the use of humor. Since many of the things that make people angry are entirely meaningless in the grand scheme of things, there's no harm in laughing off something trivial, or making it into a joke. One day when Socrates was walking down the street, someone hit him in the head. This remark was his only response: "It's too bad, these days, that you don't know when you need a helmet when going out for a walk."

IN ADDITION TO THOSE two central techniques, Seneca mentions many other approaches for avoiding anger. If you're interested in learning more about these, I highly recommend reading his book *On Anger*. I will mention a few here, which he writes about in depth:

- Realize that people often have no idea about what they're doing, and do things in error, so don't take their actions too seriously.

- Be magnanimous: with a lofty mind, be above feeling injured by trivial things. Look down on them as being unworthy of your attention.

- Look carefully at the extreme ugliness of anger, and also at its danger. This will provide a strong deterrence to becoming angry. (That's why Seneca provided the graphic descriptions of how anger is so ugly.)

- Associate with good-natured people who are unlikely to make you angry and unlikely to put up with your own anger. People with character defects are much more likely to upset you and negatively influence you.

- Don't allow yourself to become mentally or physically exhausted, which encourages irritation and anger.

- If feeling stress, consider doing something relaxing to calm the mind, like playing music.

- Since everyone is different, understand yourself and know what tends to make you angry. Once you understand your own weak spots, don't expose them to things likely to upset you.

- There's no need to hear and see everything that happens. You can avoid many annoying things simply by not taking them in. (This is especially valuable advice in the Internet age!)

- Don't entertain false suspicions or exaggerate trivial matters.

- Forgive others, and even all of humanity, because you are not perfect either: the faults we find in others also exist within ourselves.

- Remember that if someone starts to make you angry, you can just wait a little: death will make us all equal eventually. So, rather than being angry, it's better to focus your mind on more important things.

JUSTICE WITHOUT ANGER

In our time, in which it's fashionable for people to vent their every outrage on social media platforms, some people might find it shocking that Seneca believed extreme anger was *never* justified, because nothing good ever comes from it.

Aristotle thought that a moderate amount of anger was desirable, if controlled, because of the way anger encourages soldiers to fight, and the way it can energize human action. But Seneca skillfully demolished this view by pointing out that real anger, or rage, is a vice that can never be moderated. Moreover, anger undermines our rationality, and thus our ability to function as authentic human beings. But Seneca's ultimate takedown of the idea that anger could enhance the performance of soldiers came in the form of a question: If anger can help soldiers to fight more effectively, he asked, why don't we also get them drunk, so they will swing their weapons around more fiercely? Case closed, at least in my opinion.

Seneca fully realized that our world is full of terrible injustices and inhumane events that take place daily. But in one respect, we are somewhat less fortunate today than Seneca was because of the time in which we live. Today, the global news media have made it a lucrative industry to bring every possible outrage into our homes and minds each time we turn on a screen or open a newspaper.

Since bad behavior is plentiful and inevitable, Seneca took

the reasonable view that a wise person should never get angry at any of the events we are assaulted with or hear about on a daily basis. Seneca thought the world to be good overall, due to human kindness and generosity, and human reason. But, as he noted, so many bad things happen that, if every bad behavior made us angry, we would need to be angry each moment of every day. That, of course, would be unlivable.

For Seneca, the alternative approach was to be reasonable and practical. Realistically, he said, we must expect the world to be full of people with terrible character traits. But the way to improve the world is not through the harmful energy of anger, but through the use of reason. For a Stoic, the proper way to look at the world would be like a doctor, expecting to meet a host of diseased patients every day. As Seneca writes,

> A wise person is mentally calm and balanced when facing error, and not an enemy of wrongdoers, but one who helps others to heal. Each day, he leaves his home with this thought in mind: "Today I will meet many addicted to wine, many overcome by lust, many who lack gratitude, many enslaved by greed, and many bewitched by the false promises of ambition." But all these conditions he will treat with kindness, as a doctor treats his own patients.[30]

The other way to look at the world is from the rational and level-headed perspective of a judge presiding over a court of law, who is sometimes forced to punish those who have done wrong. Seneca stresses that a judge should never punish a wrongdoer out of anger, but out of hope that the punishment will encourage the offender to become a better person in the future. A judge who punishes someone out of anger would be as dangerous, and just as undesirable, as an armed soldier swaggering while drunk.

Even though we live two thousand years after Seneca, he provides us with a good, realistic model for social change, because he shows how we can improve the world by relying upon reason alone. Extreme anger will not increase justice or make the world a better place; it will only make the world more miserable, and more out of control. Anger, in the Stoic view, can only increase human suffering.

CHAPTER 5

Wherever You Go, There You Are:
You Can't Escape Yourself

Those who rush across the sea change their weather,
but not their minds.

—Horace, *Letters* 1.11.27

ONE DAY LUCILIUS WAS FEELING A BIT DEPRESSED and wanted to cheer himself up by taking a trip, as many people do today. He thought a change of scenery might help to improve his mood. Unfortunately, the project was a failure: Lucilius's depression was not cured. But as Seneca commented, "You must change the mind, not the location," because "your faults will travel with you wherever you go."[1]

Well, so much for that idea!

I once experienced something similar. Long ago, I had a chance to spend a week in an Italian Renaissance villa—the Villa Saraceno, designed by the famous architect Andrea Palladio (1508–1580)—with ten or twelve friends. But I had recently experienced the breakup of a promising relationship and was still feeling the sting of grief. Despite that, since it was a once-in-a-lifetime chance to stay in a Palladian villa (and cost almost nothing), I decided to go on the trip, which was unforgettable. But when I was alone in my room, I sometimes broke down into tears, because of the grief and disappointment that had followed me there.

When Seneca was writing his letters to Lucilius, he changed locations frequently, traveling here or there to one of his country retreats. In one funny letter, he even found himself staying above a noisy gym and bathhouse in Rome. In amusing detail, he described the sounds of people grunting during their workouts, which drifted up from below to his apartment. I mention this to stress that Seneca was no stranger to travel, nor did he disapprove of it. Seneca felt that everyone needs periods of relaxation to release the mind. He also felt that getting out of Rome with its smoky, polluted air was a good idea, if not a medical necessity.[2]

If Seneca thought travel was fine, though, why did he write so much about how our inner troubles follow us wherever we go—a theme that comes up repeatedly in his writings?

Since Seneca was a Stoic, his attention was focused on how to realistically improve our inner character. Because of that, he opposed the idea that someone could improve his or her mental state, at least in a lasting way, by simply going on a trip. Whatever problems we suffer from internally, they do follow us: "The fault is not in one's circumstances but in the mind itself. . . . His malady follows him."[3] What is to be gained by "getting away from it all," he asks, since our worries will follow us everywhere we go? But to drive the point home, he notes bluntly: "If you want to escape your troubles, you don't need to be somewhere else: you need to be someone else."[4]

Seneca had a specific kind of personality in mind when writing about how people can misuse travel. These are the kinds of people who will use any possible diversion to avoid facing their inner lives—and to avoid whatever it is they need "to work on," as we say today. It's common psychological knowledge that some people stay busy or distracted all the time to fend off feelings of emptiness, loneliness, or depression. Since we live in a consumer society, emphasis is placed on owning external things, participating in external activities, and achieving external accomplishments. By contrast, taking a deep look inside ourselves and then feeling a sense of emptiness, rather than discovering a well-developed and happy personality, could be quite uncomfortable. The Stoic view is not that external things are unimportant, but that true happiness and peace of mind originates from within. So those who fail to develop their inner character are unlikely to be truly happy.

In the same way that "distracted" or "preoccupied" people rush around and misuse the gift of time (chapter 2), the preoccupied also misuse the gift of travel to avoid developing their inner selves. As Seneca notes somewhat pointedly, "If you're always choosing remote spots to chase after leisure, you'll find sources of distraction everywhere."[5]

In the end, he wonders, if each person is trying to flee himself, what is the point of fleeing if there is no escape?

HAVING A REAL DESTINATION

The mind cannot become stable unless it stops wandering.

—Seneca, *Letters* 69.1

For Seneca, having a real destination is of supreme importance. When you have a real destination, you also have focus, consistency, and a goal you're moving closer to. The opposite of having a destination involves a lack of focus, inconsistency, and mere wandering. When you have a real destination, you actually know what you're living for. But that's not true for someone who's wandering or just reacting to whatever happens next.

We can see how having a real destination perfectly ties in with the idea of Stoicism being "a path" (explored in chapter 1), because a path exists to take you somewhere. The way that Seneca repeatedly contrasts the idea of having a real destination with the idea of just wandering cannot be due to chance. Instead, it's a brilliant and intentional metaphor to explain his overall understanding of Stoicism and the importance of focus and consistency in making progress.

Just how important this was for Seneca is confirmed by the fact that it comes up at the very beginning of his second letter to Lucilius. In other words, Seneca brings up the topic of focus and "not wandering" at the earliest possible opportunity:

LETTER 2
From Seneca to Lucilius, greetings
Based on your letter and what I'm hearing, I'm becoming very hopeful about you. You are not rushing around or letting frequent changes of place disturb you. That kind of restlessness is the sign of an unhealthy mind. In my view, the first proof of a stable mind is its ability to stay in one place and enjoy its own company.[6]

Seneca then suddenly changes the subject to talk about selecting and reading the right books, to discuss how "not wandering" is vital in reading also: "If you wish to take in something that will settle reliably in your mind," he says, "you must dwell with a few chosen thinkers and be nourished by their works. Someone who is everywhere is nowhere. Those who travel constantly end up with many acquaintances, but no real friends."[7]

In this way, Seneca shows how both traveling and reading can be harmed by wandering, by not having a real destination. Of course, having access to a research library of thousands of books might be useful. But in terms of becoming a wise human being, deeply absorbing the thoughts of a few solid and proven authors is essential. As Seneca advises, "Study not in order to know more, but to know better."[8]

In both reading and travel, you need some focus and a destination. You don't want to wander to and fro. As he says, people who travel constantly have many acquaintances but no real friends, which is not an exaggeration. For example, I've known and entertained digital nomads, people who constantly travel the world, working from their laptops. And while it works well for some (especially couples), the inability to form lasting friendships while always on the move—and the loneliness that it breeds—is a problem for many.

"Those who follow a path," Seneca writes, "have a destination, but wandering is limitless."[9] While travel is fine, the desire to travel constantly is a sign of "disquiet" or "an unsteady spirit."[10] "As you progress," Seneca tells Lucilius, "take pains above all to be consistent with yourself," because "a change of purpose shows that the mind is drifting at sea, appearing here and there, as if blown around by the wind."[11] (See figure 3.)

For example, if I'm working on a project with mental focus, I can go on the Internet, look up a piece of information on the web, and get back to work immediately. But if I don't have that kind of focus, I can easily surf the web, then Facebook, and then YouTube, wandering around for hours. Doing that now and then

A Student of Stoicism	A Typical non-Stoic
Is traveling with a destination	Is wandering without a path
Is focused and consistent	Lacks focus and consistency
Is settled and calm. Lives in the present moment. Anticipates the future without anxiety.	Feels unsettled. Tries to flee the self. Worries about the future.
Has a guiding purpose	Is blown in different directions by the winds of chance
Realizes that unhappiness is caused by our opinions about things	Thinks that other people or external things make us unhappy
Knows how to avoid or how to deconstruct extreme negative emotions	Experiences extreme negative emotions on a regular basis and doesn't know why
Overcomes adversity by transforming it into something positive or admirable. Keeps moving forward.	Suffers from adversity and discouragement. Feels thwarted by setbacks.
Is grateful to the universe	Complains frequently
Is traveling on the way to freedom and tranquility by learning how to make sound mental judgments	Is enslaved by false opinions, which result in negative emotions and suffering

Fig 3: Seneca's descriptions of how a Stoic differs from a typical non-Stoic, including metaphors related to travel.

is certainly harmless, but doing it daily, as a form of procrastination, might indicate that something is wrong. When people procrastinate, it's often a sign that they find their work to be unfulfilling. In that case, it might make sense to think about finding some more exciting work, if possible.

While Seneca advocates focus and having a destination, he certainly wasn't some kind of joyless "all work and no play" kind of person. Having leisure and free time was something he valued greatly. He even wrote a work *On Leisure*, which you can still read today.[12] Seneca's interests included viticulture, or growing grapes, so he must have been a winemaker. While he gave up drinking wine later in life, he advocated drinking for some people, even up to the edge of intoxication, because of the freeing effect wine can have on the mind.

For Seneca, having leisure time was one of the finest things in life. But leisure is only fulfilling if the mind is stable and well-developed enough to really enjoy it. That's why philosophy, for Seneca, was an essential companion for living a good and happy life. A wise person, for example, will be able to travel and get something profound out of the trip because his or her mind is prepared for the experience, while others just "embark on one journey after another and exchange spectacle after spectacle."[13] In terms of deep enjoyment, what you actually get out of life depends on what you bring to it.

While a wise person or Stoic in training should have a calm and steady mind, many people are restless, discontent, unsettled, and easily irritated. Writing about Seneca's thought, philosopher and historian Mark Holowchak offers a significant insight into why restless people feel that travel will improve their emotional state. It has to do with *expectancy*, "the hope that tomorrow will be better than today." Expectancy, he explains, is usually created through the combination of distress and desire. Distress is the feeling that some ill is present now, and desire comes from "the feeling that some good is lurking on the horizon to replace the ill."[14] In short, if we could just get "there," things would be better.

While Seneca believed that some locations are unhealthy (think beach town, during spring break), he said, "We should live with this belief: 'I was not born for one small corner. This entire world is my homeland.'"[15] Like the other Roman Stoics,

Seneca thought that someone could be happy almost anywhere, even if subjected to exile. As he noted, "The place where one lives doesn't contribute much to tranquility. It's the mind that makes everything agreeable to itself. I've seen gloomy people in a cheerful, pleasant villa, and people working happily in complete isolation."[16]

It's always possible that travel might help some people remove their dissatisfactions with life, based on the belief that things will be better somewhere else. But that belief is more likely to be a case of what some psychologists call the "grass is greener syndrome," based on the saying "the grass is greener on the other side of the fence." While not an official psychological diagnosis, it's certainly a real thing, and it accounts for many failed relationships. Because when relationships end, someone often believes, "My life would be better with someone else." So instead of watering or tending the lawn one already has, a lawn elsewhere seems to be more desirable, or greener, even though that's usually a fantasy.

Sometimes, the grass *might* be greener elsewhere, and another lawn might be a real destination. But people who frequently suffer from expectancy are always likely to be dissatisfied and restless, because wherever they go, there they are. Since you can't escape yourself, the solution to psychological unhappiness usually lies within.

HAVING A GUIDING PURPOSE

For Seneca, having a destination is identical to having a guiding purpose, which is the real point of studying Stoic philosophy in the first place.

Seneca advocates a "steady and calm way of life that follows a single path." But, as he says, many people jump from one purpose to another, frequently changing their plans. It's like the winds of chance blow them here or there. "There are only a few," he says, "who plan their lives and affairs by a guiding purpose." The rest are just swept along, some violently, like objects floating down a fast-moving river. The alternative, he writes, is that "we should decide what we really want, and stand by that decision."[17]

People make mistakes, he says, because they consider the parts of life, but not life as a whole. Similarly, as an archer has a target, we should have an overall goal of life. As he notes in a memorable line, "When someone doesn't know what port he's sailing for, no wind is favorable." In other words, without a destination, people's lives are ruled by chance.[18]

Fortunately, he claims, a compass *does* exist to guide us safely. And that guide is not a religion, a revealed scripture, or anything external, but our own power of clear thinking: "Whenever you want to know what to seek or avoid, look to your Highest Good, the aim of your entire life," because whatever we do should be in harmony with that.[19]

While the idea that "a person should live according to their Highest Good" might sound a bit strange to our modern ears, it made perfect sense to the Roman Stoics. They also knew exactly *what* that Highest Good was for them: it was always striving to live in a way that is honorable and rational, with excellence of character, by aligning your life with the four cardinal virtues of wisdom, courage, moderation, and justice.

CHAPTER 6

How to Tame Adversity

THE CITY THAT DISAPPEARED
IN A FLASH

In the summer of the year 64, Seneca received some terrible news from a friend. The Roman colony of Lugdunum—the modern-day city of Lyon, France—had suddenly burned to the ground in a freak fire. Adding to the shock, the city was destroyed in just a few minutes. Seneca called the fire at Lyon "so unexpected and unheard of, because it was without precedent."[1] As he pointed out, it is rare for fires to consume everything so fiercely that nothing is left behind.

Seneca devotes an entire missive, Letter 91, to the destruction of Lyon by fire. In terms of the powerful feelings it evokes, it's one of his most compelling works. He lyrically describes the frailty of everything created by humans and by nature, and how things can turn into their opposites almost instantly. Peace turns into war, a calm day into a terrible storm. Prosperity collapses into poverty, health into illness. The accomplishments of an entire lifetime can be lost in a single day. An hour is enough time to destroy an empire. "The reality," he writes, "is that things develop slowly, but the way to ruin comes quickly."[2]

The fire of Lyon moved so quickly, and was so unexpected, the city didn't stand a chance. But misfortune isn't uncommon. It's destined to strike us all.

While all of the Roman Stoics wrote about how to handle adversity, Seneca was the master of this subject. He addressed it widely across hundreds of pages. This question, *How should we respond when bad things happen to good people?*, never goes out of style, because the need to confront adversity is part of human nature. Even the richest and most privileged among us cannot avoid pain and suffering, the occasional mishap, and the feeling that things have taken a wrong turn. In fact, Seneca's wise teachings on adversity contribute significantly to the popularity of his writings today. During the worldwide lockdown for the Covid-19 pandemic, during which I wrote part of this book, many book sales were in steep decline due to the impact of halting the world economy. But during the first peak of the pandemic, sales of Seneca's *Letters from a Stoic* soared 747 percent higher than usual.[3] During this highly stressful period, Seneca's teachings about how to live calmly, despite adversity, attracted many new readers.

VIRTUE AND EQUANIMITY: HOW STOICS FIND GOODNESS DESPITE ADVERSITY

Don't desire hardships, but the virtue that allows you to endure hardships.

—Seneca, *Letters* 15.5

We live in an unpredictable world—a world in which we will all experience adversity, hardship, and suffering. How, then, were the Stoics able to live calm and happy lives?

Based on common sense, the Stoics knew that adversity and hardships are just part of life, so they developed ways to anticipate and respond to these inevitable experiences. But most importantly, it was their underlying way of looking at the world that took away the emotional sting most people feel when misfortunes cross their paths. In other words, the Stoics learned how to see the world in a slightly different way than the average person, making hardships feel less painful.

Ultimately, the Stoics believed that a person with a well-developed character would be able to endure adversity with a glad or happy mind. As we saw in chapter 4, this doesn't mean that a Stoic won't experience normal human feelings. But how, the Stoics asked, can we look at the world to prevent those feelings from turning into something extremely negative or debilitating?

We can find the answer in two key Stoic ideas mentioned briefly in the introduction to this book. The first Stoic belief is that virtue, or inner excellence, is the only true good. The second belief is that some things are "up to us" and other things aren't, so we should focus on the things that are actually within our control.

It's now time to take a more in-depth look at these ideas and how they can work together to ease human suffering.

The word *virtue*, unfortunately, sounds stuffy and Victorian. But what virtue or *aretē* meant to the ancient Greeks was simply "goodness" or "excellence." Even an inanimate object can possess excellence. For example, the *aretē* or excellence of a good knife is that it's sharp and cuts well. The virtue of a good horse might be that it's strong and fast. Once we reach the level of human beings, the thing that sets us apart from other animals is that we're *rational*. So for the Stoics, to possess virtue as a human being, we must act in a rational, reasonable, or honorable way. This means we should develop a good and stable character, characterized by equanimity, in which extreme negative emotions don't cause us to lose our mental balance.

Aside from being rational, there are many other virtues. Going back at least to Plato, the Greeks identified four primary or "cardinal" virtues: *wisdom, courage, moderation*, and *justice*, which the Stoics also saw as essential.

The second key idea is that some things are "up to us" or within our power, while others are not. Modern Stoics call this *the dichotomy of control*, and it's central to all of Roman Stoicism.[4] When you think about it carefully, however, there is very little under our total control. Even our bodies and thoughts are not under our control at all times.

To give another example, while we can control our intentions, we can't control the outcomes of things. If you start a business, you might be able to get everything just right in terms of the marketing, which you could, in theory, have total control over. But the company might fail for millions of other reasons, including the possibility that there just isn't enough demand for what the business is offering.

Today, the Stoic philosopher most famous for writing about the dichotomy of control is Epictetus, who was a teenager when Seneca died. But Seneca and earlier Stoics accepted this idea too; they just described it in different ways. Seneca spoke of *virtue* and *Fortune*.* For Seneca, virtue (and our inner character) is up to us, but Fortune or chance is not. (See figure 4.) While

---

* For Seneca, Fortune was akin to being a cosmic power, so I often capitalize it in this book, along with other Stoic terms that refer to cosmic powers such as Nature, Fate, and Logos (reason or rationality).

we should always try to make good use of the things outside of our control (to help create a better world), we should focus first on having a good character, because without virtue or a good character, we won't be able to create anything good in the world either. As Seneca wrote, "Virtue itself is the only good, since nothing is good without it."[5]

The Dichotomy of Control		
Seneca	Virtue / Inner Character	Fortune or Chance
Epictetus	"Up to us"	"Not up to us"

Fig. 4: How Seneca and Epictetus described the dichotomy of control. While virtue and inner character are "up to us" and under our control, things in the domain of Fortune or chance are not fully up to us.

In Stoic philosophy, these two ideas—that virtue is the only true good and that some things are outside of our control—are like two powerful chemical substances. When they are combined and mixed together, an intense reaction occurs, and an entirely new way of viewing the world comes into being.

ONE MAIN DIFFERENCE BETWEEN an average person and a Stoic is that an average person sees external things—things such as having money, a lovely home, and a beautiful family—as being *goods*, while for a Stoic they are only seen as being *advantages*. At first, this might seem like a small difference, or even a verbal quibble. But for a Stoic, this is a crucial distinction, because virtue is the only true good. (That said, if possible, a Stoic will want to have external advantages, just like everyone else.)

For Seneca, "All the things under the power of chance are servants," including money, the body, reputation, and most other things.[6] As he explains, anyone who believes external things to be good puts himself under the power of Fortune, chance, and things outside his control. But the person who understands goodness to be a virtue can find lasting happiness within, regardless of external circumstances.[7]

For a Stoic, anything that's a real good, like virtue, can never be taken away from us, while anything that can be taken away is not a real good—it's just an advantage, or a gift of Fortune. "It's a mistake," Seneca wrote, "to believe that anything good or bad is given to us by Fortune." Rather, Fortune just gives us the raw material for creating good or bad, based on the good or bad qualities within us.[8] Similarly, when speaking to his students, the Stoic teacher Epictetus stressed this point forcefully: "Don't search outside yourselves for what is good; seek it within, or you will never find it."[9]

WHILE BELIEVING THAT MONEY, good health, friends and family, and many other things are advantages we should actively seek out, the Stoics believed that advantages are valuable, but refused to call them "goods." But why did they make this distinction? Part of the answer goes back to Aristotle, who claimed that to lead a truly good or happy life, you also needed "external goods" like health, a certain amount of money, and even good looks. (Aristotle, by the way, was the sharp-dressing son of a wealthy father, who was the court physician to the king of Macedonia.)

To the Stoics, though, Aristotle's belief was absurd, because many people, with age, will lose many or all of these external goods. For example, let's imagine that you develop an excellent moral character over your entire life, but that at a certain age you lose your wealth, your health, your family, and suddenly find yourself facing death. Would that suddenly mean, at this point, that your life is no longer good, or that you've lost your moral character? Of course not. And what about "good looks"? Socrates, who was considered to have been one of the most virtuous people who ever lived, was legendary for looking ugly. People said that Socrates, with his famous pug nose, resembled a satyr.

By insisting that virtue is the only true good, the Stoics affirmed a radical egalitarianism. While it's better for someone to have obvious advantages, even if you're poor, sick, ugly, or dying, it's still entirely possible for you to be a good and virtuous person. And regardless of your circumstances in life, it's still possible to find some way to study philosophy. As Seneca wrote, anyone can develop excellence of mind, if they so desire: "Philosophy doesn't exclude or select anyone. Its light shines for all."[10]

REGARDLESS OF WHETHER OR not you are personally drawn to Stoic ways of thinking, I hope you can now see how these two ideas, when combined, are so powerful. If someone truly adopted the Stoic ideas that "virtue is the only true good" and "many things are outside of our control," this would produce a significant shift in the way most people view and experience the world. And that shift would make any external misfortunes feel much less terrible. Regardless of that, we can summarize Seneca's idea about the relationship between misfortune and virtue in a simple formula: it's not what we bear, but *how* we bear it that matters. While any adversity could strike us, it's how we respond that is a measure of our true character.

PREPARING FOR ADVERSITY

> If you don't want someone to panic during a crisis, train
> him or her beforehand.
>
> —Seneca, *Letters* 18.6

One Stoic approach to reduce the sting of adverse events is called *praemeditatio malorum*, "the premeditation of future adversity." This involves briefly rehearsing potential negative events in your mind before they occur. Should the event then actually take place in the future, you'll be mentally prepared for it, and the emotional shock will be significantly reduced. While this technique doesn't work for everyone and could cause anxiety instead (in which case you shouldn't use it), it has worked exceptionally well for me and for many others. In fact, everyone already has experimented with this who has experienced a fire drill as a schoolchild. Rehearsing a potential disaster in advance increases your ability to cope and think clearly should the imagined disaster ever take place.

Speaking of fire drills, Seneca offers this exact advice to Lucilius, after describing the terrible destruction of Lyon by fire:

> When one doesn't anticipate a disaster, it weighs more
> heavily on us. Shock strengthens the impact, and every
> mortal feels more profound grief when left in astonish-
> ment. Therefore, nothing should be unexpected by us.
> We should send our minds ahead in advance, and we

should consider not just what typically happens but what *could* happen."[11]

Or even more strongly, as he writes elsewhere, "Let us think of anything that could happen as something that will happen."[12]

The basic idea behind the premeditation of adversity is to briefly rehearse any possible misfortune in your imagination—like you're practicing or exercising your Stoic muscles. As Seneca notes, "That which has been long expected is more gentle when it arrives."[13] Also, we should expect adversity to occasionally cross our paths because "hardships arrive through a law of nature."[14] The premeditation of adversity goes back to the earliest Greek Stoics and was used by all of the significant Roman Stoics.[15] Seneca refers to it often across his many writings. One of the most famous places it crops up is at the beginning of the *Meditations* of Marcus Aurelius. Writing a note in his personal journal, Marcus reminds himself: "Say to yourself each morning: Today I will meet with people who are meddling, ungrateful, overbearing, deceitful, envious, and unsocial. They suffer from these flaws through ignorance of good and bad."[16]

True enough: Seneca and the other Stoics realized that the world is full of annoying people. And since they will cross your path, you might as well anticipate it. That will help you to avoid having a negative, emotional reaction when it actually takes place. So the next time you go for a drive in your car, remind yourself that you might encounter a crazy motorist, fueled with road rage. Should that happen, you won't feel surprised in the least, but like a well-trained Stoic, you'll be able to say, "I knew it" or "I expected it."[17]

My best use of *praemeditatio malorum* involved my little son, Benjamin. Shortly after he was born, I bought a townhouse in Sarajevo. While it has a beautiful view, the hard wooden stairs leading up to the third floor, where the bedrooms are located, are extremely steep and dangerous. As we'd say in the United States, "They aren't up to code." The stairs are so hazardous that if Benjamin had fallen down them, he literally could have been killed.

To prevent my son from hurting or even killing himself, I approached the project in stages. First, I took every reasonable precaution I possibly could to prevent this from happening. After I purchased the house, I had a railing installed on the stairway to make the stairs safer for everyone. (It was unbelievable that there was no railing installed, to begin with!) Second, I had a wooden gate made with a lock on it and installed at the top of the stairs. We would lock the gate at night so that no one could tumble down the stairway by accident. Finally, I placed friction tape on the narrow, slippery stairs, to create some traction and make them less dangerous.

That was everything I could physically do, but the stairway remained unsafe. So the next step involved training. Every morning, when Benjamin walked down the stairs with his mom to go to school, I would always say, "Benjamin, be sure to hang on to the railing!" He would say, "Okay!" and proceed accordingly. In fact, I still remind him today.

The last thing I did was to practice *praemeditatio malorum*. Since this was a serious concern, I would imagine Benjamin falling down the stairs and hurting himself. That way, if it actually happened, at least I'd be fully prepared for it. (In other words, I wouldn't panic the way my wife did when our son fell off a slide at kindergarten and hit his head.) I also imagined how *I* would respond to him falling down the stairs, based on the severity of his injuries.

While this sounds like a slightly unpleasant exercise, I'm glad I did it, because, sure enough, one day he did fall down the stairs, when he was six. Fortunately, he was toward the bottom of the stairs when he fell. And while he scraped his back on the hard, sharp edges of the stairs, he was fine. It was just a scare with no severe injuries. The Stoic training I had used allowed me to respond to the misfortune calmly—with concern, but without panic. There was no sense of shock or surprise when it happened, because I had anticipated it.

The Stoic exercise of contemplating future misfortune strongly resembles a technique of modern psychotherapy known as *exposure therapy*, which helps people confront and overcome their fears. In exposure therapy, the patient is exposed bit by bit to the source of the anxiety or phobia, but in tiny doses. Over time, the exposure increases until the fear completely vanishes or is significantly diminished. While exposure therapy can take many different forms, one technique involves exposing yourself to the source of the fear entirely through the imagination. That kind of exposure therapy, which is used today by psychologists, corresponds exactly to the ancient Stoic practice.

As William B. Irvine points out in his recent book, *The Stoic Challenge*, another unexpected benefit of practicing the premeditation of adversity is that it helps someone overcome *hedonic adaptation*. Hedonic adaptation happens when you buy a shiny new object that delights you, but over time you adapt to it and the pleasure of owning it wears off. You might even take it for granted. Seneca, being the keen psychologist he was, described this common experience several times in his writings: "Don't you see," he asked, "that everything loses its force once it becomes familiar?"[18]

Having lived in my house for over five years now, I'm not nearly as excited about the place today as when I first bought it. But if I practice the premeditation of adversity and imagine it being destroyed by a fire or by an earthquake, it makes me once again feel grateful for something I might otherwise take for granted. Similarly, the Stoics recommend that we regularly remind ourselves that our closest family members and friends will one day die, perhaps even tomorrow. Not only is this a fact of nature, but reflecting on it will also help us reduce the emotional shock when they do leave us. But in a positive sense, it encourages us not to take them for granted in the present moment, and to be grateful each day for the time we still have together.

TESTED BY THE UNIVERSE: ADVERSITY AS TRAINING

While Seneca believed that nothing terrible could happen to the inner character of a wise person (see chapter 10), it's a law of nature that everyone will experience adversities. In the Stoic view, however, these adversities are sent to us by "God" or "the universe" as "training exercises," to test us and help us develop our character. (While Seneca uses the term *God* like other Stoics, it's essential to know that the Stoic idea doesn't correspond to the Christian concept of God. The Stoic notion refers to a kind of intelligence present in nature, which they would call *God*, *Nature*, *Fate*, *Zeus*, *the universe*, and many other terms interchangeably. In this book, I use the term "the universe," when possible, to avoid any confusion with the Judeo-Christian idea of God.)

Seneca wrote that while "fire tests gold, adversity tests brave men."[19] Significantly, he wrote an entire work, *On Providence*, about how the universe sends us "tests" so we can develop better characters. As Seneca quoted his old friend Demetrius as saying, "No one seems more unhappy to me than someone who has never faced adversity." The reason why, Seneca explains, is because "such a person has never been able to test himself."[20]

In fact, Seneca emphasizes that a person can never be sure of his strength of character until it is tested: "To have nothing that inspires you, to have nothing that challenges you to take action, to have nothing to test the strength of your mind against—that is not the peace offered by tranquility. It is merely floating becalmed, on top of a dead sea."[21] As he writes elsewhere, the universe is like a father who gives his children a bit of tough love. Only by being stirred up by labors, pains, and losses can we become genuinely robust as human beings. Conversely, "Unimpaired good fortune cannot withstand a single blow."[22]

For Seneca, one of the worst things that could happen to anyone would be to lead a life of extreme pleasure and ease, without having one's character tested. After Seneca, Epictetus used almost identical language. "It is difficulties that reveal a person's character," he wrote. So whenever someone faces adversity, it's like a gymnastic trainer has "matched you against a powerful, young opponent." When someone asked Epictetus *why* this takes place, he replied, "So that you might become an Olympic champion; and that's something that can never be achieved without some sweat."[23]

TRANSFORMING ADVERSITY

> No matter what Fortune sends his way, the wise person
> will transform it into something admirable.
>
> —Seneca, *Letters* 85.40

One of the most inspiring things about Roman Stoicism is how the Stoics believed something good can always come out of an adverse situation. As Seneca wrote, "Disaster is virtue's opportunity."[24] Even the worst misfortune allows us to respond in a virtuous way.

As Seneca explained, regardless of what happens, we must find the good in it, and transform the situation to good. In this way, "It's not what you face, but how you face it that matters."[25]

In the real world, our lives are full of failure. Sometimes, whether in business or love, our best-laid plans just don't work out. Within the first ten years, most small businesses go under. Marriages fail. People lose their jobs, often through no fault of their own. The important thing for a Stoic is to understand that it's just a fact of nature that our plans or objectives will sometimes fail. And when those failures occur, it's our responsibility to learn from them, respond to them with virtue, or turn failure into some other kind of opportunity.

For example, for many years, I ran a small book publishing company that was barely profitable most years. But the skills I learned from running that company allowed me to start an editorial and book design company, which has allowed me to work for some of the most highly regarded publishers in the world. It also allowed me to research and write this book.

Seneca said that a wise Stoic resembles a skilled animal trainer, like a lion tamer. In its natural state, a lion might be fierce, dangerous, and terrifying. But under the influence of a good trainer, a ferocious lion can become a gentle companion, even allowing the trainer to kiss the lion, hug it, and slide his arm between the lion's deadly jaws. For Seneca, the way a Stoic tames adversity exactly resembles the work of the animal handler: "Similarly, the wise person is a skilled expert at taming misfortune. Pain, poverty, disgrace, imprisonment, and exile are feared by everyone. But when they encounter the wise person, they are tamed."[26]

No one is in control of the circumstances we are given in life, but the Stoic takes whatever situation is at hand and makes use of it, transforming it into something valuable. "Whatever might happen," wrote Epictetus, "it's within my power to derive some benefit from it."[27]

In this way, the Stoic aims to make good use of whatever life, or the present moment, happens to offer. As Marcus Aurelius explains, if something negative happens to us, we can "use the setback to employ another virtue."[28] Or as Seneca writes, whatever is bad, the Stoic "turns into good."[29]

Ryan Holiday took this Stoic idea from the writings of Marcus Aurelius and transformed it into the memorable title of his book, *The Obstacle Is the Way* (2014). Marcus Aurelius inspired that title, almost twenty centuries later, with this reminder to himself, which he wrote in his Stoic notebook:

> Our actions may be impeded ... but there can be no impeding our intentions or our dispositions. Because we can accommodate and adapt. The mind adapts and converts to its own purposes the obstacle to our acting.
>
> The impediment to action advances action.
>
> What stands in the way becomes the way.[30]

As we can see from these passages, Seneca, Epictetus, and Marcus Aurelius—the major Roman Stoics—were in full agreement about the value of transforming adversity into something better. More importantly, as they show, no matter what might happen to us, we can always respond in a way that brings goodness into the world.

CHAPTER 7

Why You Should Never Complain

Nothing needs to annoy you if you don't add your
annoyance to it.

— Seneca, *Letters* 123.1

THERE'S NOTHING WORSE THAN HAVING TO SPEND
time around someone who complains constantly. But don't
worry, that's just an observation. It's not a complaint.

As you might imagine, Seneca and the other Stoics were vigorously opposed to complaining, moanings and groanings of all
types. This is not unexpected. But the reason why they rejected
complaining will be surprising to many readers. We'll explore
their thinking about why you should never complain at the end
of this chapter. In the meantime, let's take a look at how people
view complaining today.

My first hope, though, is that you've never had to spend much
time around someone who complains all the time. Chronic complainers remind me of Pig-Pen, the cartoon character from the
comic strip "Peanuts." As Pig-Pen walked around, he was always

surrounded by a large cloud of dust and dirt, wherever he went. A chronic complainer, though, isn't surrounded by a cloud of dust. Instead, he or she is surrounded by a cloud of negative psychic energy, which follows the complainer everywhere. Within that cloud floats a lot of irritation and dissatisfaction, always ready to express itself, along with the desire that someone will respond to the complainer's emotional discontent.

"A BAD DAY AT THE OFFICE"

For many people today, an office environment is a fertile breeding ground for irritation and complaints. Seneca even mentioned this in his writings. He noted that people piled high with business tasks are likely to become irritated. As he said, "When a person is rushing here or there and constantly attending to many matters, a day will never pass so smoothly that some irritation won't arise from someone or something and prepare the mind for annoyance."[1]

The amazing thing, though, is just how much time people waste complaining at work. According to a study by Marshall Goldsmith, quoted by the *Harvard Business Review*, most employees spend ten hours or more per month complaining about their bosses or management, or listening to others complain. Even more striking, almost one-third of all employees spend twenty or more hours per month complaining or listening to complaints![2] Yes, that statistic even surprised me!

Of course, all that energy spent complaining at work is a massive waste of time and productivity, because complaints usually don't lead to any change. In fact, "the more we complain, the more likely the frustration, over time, will increase."[3] But as Peter Bregman, the author of the article, points out, those complaints could lead to change if framed as constructive criticisms instead, and if they were seriously discussed. But many people find the idea of having a real conversation, which could change things, to be a bit threatening. By contrast, it's much easier to complain.

But what *is* complaining, anyway?

If my son performed badly at school today by biting a girl's foot—yes, that happened when he was in first grade!—I could say, "Benjamin acted poorly today," and it would not be a complaint. But if I said, "Benjamin acted poorly today. What a rotten little kid!," that *would* be a complaint. (Of course, I didn't say that!) The first statement is just an observation. The second statement is negative emotional "venting," which usually appears in complaints. In the end, complaining involves expressing emotional dissatisfaction.

For most people, complaining comes so easily that they're often unaware of it: for many, it's a kind of ingrained bad habit. So the only way to break the bad habit is to take a mental step back, notice when complaining happens, and try to stop the behavior.

Noticing this to be the case, and noticing how toxic complainers can be, some years ago Will Brown, a Kansas City pastor, came up with a Twenty-One Days Without Complaining Challenge. As the title implies, the goal of the challenge is to go three full weeks without complaining once. The clever trick is that the challenge involves wearing a little purple bracelet, which Pastor Brown will gladly sell to you. Once you start his A Complaint Free World® challenge, you start counting the number of days you can go without complaining. But as soon as you do complain, you need to move the bracelet to your other wrist and start over, resetting the count back to Day One. As he notes somewhat shockingly on his website: *"The average person takes four to eight months to complete the twenty-one-day challenge* [emphasis added]. But stick with it! Just remember, you can't complain your way to health, happiness, and success."[4]

Given the fact that there are so many complainers in the world, over ten million people have now taken the challenge, which must have resulted in a tidy number of purple bracelet sales, too.

What, however, would the Stoics have thought about this approach? My best guess is that they would have approved, especially with their emphasis on practical, cognitive exercises. For example, Epictetus taught his students how to break bad habits, step by step, over a thirty-day period. Once someone reached the end of the month-long period without repeating the bad habit, he suggested offering thanks to the gods.[5]

Also, while most people complain, some kind of hands-on exercise like this would be beneficial for someone who is a chronic complainer, and perhaps even necessary. One psychologist, Guy Winch, tells an amusing story about complainers. "Optimists," he says, "see a glass half full." "Pessimists," he goes on, "see a glass half empty." But this is what chronic complainers see:

> A glass that is slightly chipped holding water that isn't cold enough, probably because it's tap water even though I asked for bottled, and wait, there's a smudge on the rim, too, which means the glass wasn't cleaned properly and now I'll probably end up with some kind of virus. Why do these things always happen to me?[6]

What, then, would a classical Stoic see?

A Stoic would see a glass of water and view it with gratitude, as a gift from the universe, and be grateful for its life-giving properties. Because in the end, when you complain, you are no longer living in harmony with nature. Instead, according to the Stoics, your lack of gratitude is a condemnation of the harmony and beautiful order of the cosmos, which brought you into being in the first place.

This leads us to a much deeper understanding of why you should never complain, which doesn't rule out the many obvious psychological reasons against complaining. Instead, it points toward a more profound vision of human nature and our own relationship to the greater world.

"FOLLOW NATURE" AND
DON'T COMPLAIN

Zeno, the founder of Stoicism, said that the goal of his philosophy was to "follow nature" or "live in agreement of nature." If we could live in agreement with nature, it would result in "a smooth flow of life," which implies a kind of happiness or tranquility of mind.[7]

This idea to "follow nature" was taken up by the later Roman Stoics, too, like Seneca, Epictetus, and Marcus Aurelius. But, as you might expect, while "follow nature" is a saying that might fit on a bumper sticker, what it means is something far more profound than just an attractive slogan.

For the Stoics, to follow nature, we need to understand nature—both human nature and the cosmos as a whole. And, as they pointed out, we can't fully understand ourselves without understanding the greater universe first.

For the Stoics, the world is permeated by *logos*, which can be translated as "rationality," "intelligence," and by many other terms. What makes human beings unique, they stressed, is that we are creatures capable of rational thought, which makes us different from other animals. This allows us to do science, create societies based on law, launch astronauts into space, write love letters, and many other fine things. But the reason we can understand nature scientifically is because there is some connection between the rationality present in nature's laws, the world's structure, and the rational structure of our own minds. In the end, the Stoic belief in *logos* simply means that there is a rational structure to nature and our own minds.

Because we are rational creatures, we are born with the task of trying to understand the world—Nature as a whole—along with our own human natures, and the relationships that exist between the greater world and our inner selves. And since rationality is the defining characteristic of human nature for the Stoics, we are born to develop our rational capabilities; this will allow us to live peacefully and thoughtfully, develop good inner characters, and contribute to society.

There's nothing unscientific about the fundamental Stoic belief in Logos, and there's nothing irrational about the Stoic belief in Fate either. While "Fate" might sound spooky or superstitious at first, it merely refers to the chains of cause and effect that exist in nature, which modern scientists also believe in. In fact, most of classical physics in Newton's time was based on the idea of "Fate": cause, effect, and deterministic relationships. The Stoic belief in Fate simply means that we must acknowledge and honor the laws of nature, which are unavoidable.

While Logos and Fate are uncontroversial, the final Stoic idea that some modern readers (and modern Stoics) have difficulty with is *Providence*, because they see it as being a religious idea, which is a misinterpretation. Importantly, the Stoic concept of Providence had nothing to do with the Christian idea of providence, and the Stoics didn't believe in a kind of Christian God that exists outside of nature. For the Stoics, "God" *was* Nature.

The Greek word for "providence" is *pronoia*, which means "foreknowledge," and I personally think that the Stoic idea of providence came from the study of living organisms. For example, as we can still see today, living organisms are repositories of biological intelligence and possess the ability to heal themselves, which implies a kind of knowledge. For instance, if I cut my hand, my hand "knows" how to heal itself. If you cut the head off a flatworm, the flatworm knows how to grow a new head. There is also an incredible amount of biological intelligence embodied in the development of a human embryo into a full-grown person. Today, we understand this intelligence to be a by-product of biological evolution, which makes it no less astonishing or worthy of admiration.

From the perspective of the earliest Greek Stoics, however, we modern people would be mistaken to treat Logos, Fate, and Providence as different concepts. For the earliest Stoics, these terms were just different, interchangeable terms for the same thing. According to ancient sources, "Nature," "Logos," "Fate," and "Providence" were seen as being identical.[8]

While modern Stoics sometimes reject these terms, which they mistakenly see as being antiscientific, if they do so they're often overlooking something vital. One significant dimension is the kind of *attitude* that these ancient concepts led to—a rational yet inspired way of seeing and valuing the world—which has stimulated the development of science for centuries. For the Stoics and some other Greek philosophers, *we live in an incredibly beautiful tapestry of a cosmos, governed by universal laws and harmonies, which we ourselves have emerged from, and to which we ourselves are inextricably bound.* Moreover, through rationality, we're able to understand the universe from which we've emerged.

Importantly, this ancient philosophical attitude is not in conflict with modern science—science itself is an outgrowth of it.

Albert Einstein, in his famous essay on "Religion and Science," referred to this as "the cosmic religious feeling," which he found to be "the strongest and noblest motive for scientific research," and the Stoics would have agreed with him.[9] Regardless of the terminology the Stoics used, their overall way of looking at the cosmos and our place in it remains significant today. Einstein himself rejected belief in a personal God (as did the Stoics), and he was not religious in a traditional sense. Despite that, he noted that everyone who has made genuine advances in science "is moved by profound reverence for the rationality made manifest in existence"—a very Stoic observation indeed.[10]

Ultimately, we can see that the Stoics valued nature highly. They believed that nature does nothing in vain, that a kind of rationality is expressed in the laws of nature, and, because of that rationality, nature is wholly good. In other words, if we could see and understand how the universe operates as a whole, from a cosmic vantage point, we would see it as a perfect and beautiful model of excellence.

AT THIS POINT, we can fully grasp what the Stoics meant by "Follow nature." In order to live a happy human life, we must align our minds and wills with nature. In that way, we will strive to be perfectly rational and virtuous, just as nature was, in their view. We will accept Fate, and honor all of nature's laws without complaint. And once we do so, life will flow smoothly, because we'll be living in harmony with reality, in the deepest possible way, and living as rational human beings.

Even though we are mortal and fragile beings, and although we live in a world where pain and suffering are destined to strike our individual lives, there is also something perfect about the work-ings of nature, taken as a whole. Therefore, when we complain, we are expressing disappointment with nature's perfect order.

This is why the Stoics were so opposed to complaining. Since everything in nature follows a rational pattern, even if we can't see its totality at once, complaining about some trivial event is an insult to the goodness of the universe itself.

As if offering an explanation of Zeno's command to "follow nature," Epictetus wrote: "Don't wish things to happen as you desire, but wish them to happen as they do. Then your life will flow smoothly."[11] That is an essential part of his Stoic formula for happiness, freedom, and peace of mind. Put another way, we need to accept Fate and whatever the laws of nature are destined to bring. If not, we will never experience peace of mind.

Going back to the earliest days of the school, the Stoics used a story to illustrate the nature of Fate. This story involves a dog tied to a cart with a leash. As the cart rolls down the road, the dog can happily run alongside the cart, smiling and panting as they move forward together. Alternatively, if the dog fails to keep up with the cart, it will get dragged down the road instead, which would be a painful experience.[12] This is a metaphor about following nature and accepting Fate. It is possible to resist Fate, but not successfully: you'll get dragged along to the same desti-nation, even if you struggle against it. In the words of Cleanthes (c. 330–c. 230 BC), the second head of the Stoic school in Athens, "Fate guides the willing, but drags the unwilling."[13]

That said, the Stoics were not "fatalists" who believed that we couldn't change the world. Because we are part of the web of Fate, our own actions and decisions, through cause and effect, will influence the future and the Fate of others. The impor-tant thing to remember, though, is that fate and the workings of nature will place us in certain situations beyond our control. But we need to accept or respond to these things gracefully rather than complain because they are mandated by nature, which is beyond reproach.

Seneca explained that everyone who is born enters into a contract with life, and part of that contract involves accepting that certain things will happen. And when it comes to these inconveniences, there's no point in complaining about them or being upset. One obvious instance of this is death, because everyone who is born is fated to die. Rather than moan or groan about your impending death, you should accept it peacefully, and see that it's part of life itself.

In one of his funniest remarks, Epictetus said that if someone has a runny nose, it's just silly to complain about it. Because the universe has given us two hands, it's better to wipe your nose instead.

In his *Letters*, Seneca portrays his friend Lucilius as being something of a complainer. And in several letters, Seneca, like the good Stoic therapist he was, helps Lucilius see the futility of complaining. For example, at the beginning of Letter 96, Seneca writes back to Lucilius, and explains why his complaining is wrong:

> You are still upset about something—you still complain. Don't you see that the only bad thing in these situations is your own annoyance and complaining? If you ask me, nothing can be upsetting for anyone unless he thinks something perfectly natural should be upsetting. I will no longer tolerate *myself* on the day I cannot tolerate something else.[14]

Seneca then describes the annoying events everyone must face as merely being "the taxes of being alive":

I will accept whatever happens to me without growing sad or showing an unhappy face. I will pay all my taxes without complaint. All the things at which we groan, and from which we recoil, are just the taxes of life—things, my dear Lucilius, you should never hope or seek to avoid. A long life includes all these things, just as a long journey includes dust, mud, and rain.[15]

For Seneca, it makes no sense that people complain about trivial things that should be expected, rather than living in agreement with nature and accepting the inevitable bumps on the road of life:

To become upset about these things is as laughable as complaining about getting splashed in public or stepping in some mud. Our experience of life is like being in a bathhouse, in a crowd, or on a journey. Some things will be thrown at you and others will strike you by accident. . . . It is amid mishaps like this that you must make this rugged journey.[16]

As he notes, "We shouldn't be surprised by any of the things we are born to encounter. Nor should we complain, because they are faced by everyone."[17]

AMOR FATI:
LOVE YOUR FATE

The nineteenth-century philosopher Friedrich Nietzsche used the phrase *amor fati*, "love your fate," but the idea goes back to the Stoics. Seneca said that the Stoic should "experience whatever happens as though you wanted it to happen to you," because the universe approved of these events. "Crying, complaining, and moaning," he wrote, "are rebellion" against the good order of the universe that brought us into being, and the laws of nature that actively maintain the world.[18] This is just like the advice of Epictetus, quoted earlier: "Want things to happen to you as they do, and not as you desire them to."

But the most beautiful expression of *amor fati*, at least in my mind, comes from these loving lines of Marcus Aurelius, which almost resemble a prayer:

> Every thing that is harmonious with you, oh Universe, suits me also. Nothing is too early or too late for me that is timely for you. Everything that your seasons bring is fruit for me, oh Nature. All things are from you, in you, and all things return to you.[19]

That is certainly a case of following nature and celebrating its wisdom and goodness, coming from a man who experienced a vast amount of personal suffering. (Of his thirteen children, only five survived until adulthood.) We can sense in these words the deep sense of gratitude Marcus Aurelius felt for everything he had received from the beautiful and generous universe, of which he, too, was a part.

For a Stoic, everything we have from the universe is a gift, something on loan to us, which we will one day need to return. But our underlying mindset should be one of gratitude. Because even if we stumble on life's journey or get splashed by a bit of mud, that's no reason to complain about the beautiful world that brought us into being.

CHAPTER 8

The Battle Against Fortune: How to Survive Poverty and Extreme Wealth

The poor person is not someone who has too little, but someone who always craves more.

—Seneca, *Letters* 2.6

RIDING FORTUNE'S ROLLER COASTER

Everyone has some interest in money. And why not? We all have bills to pay. But how much money is too little? How much is excessive? Everyone will have his or her own views about this, but Seneca's are especially interesting. He was one of the wealthiest people during his time, yet he was keenly aware of the psychological and moral dangers involved in the pursuit of financial success. He also experienced losing half his wealth, practically overnight. On Fortune's roller coaster, what goes up often comes down.

Fortuna was a Roman goddess, and, as noted, sometimes I uppercase the term *Fortune* since, for Seneca, it verged on being a cosmic power, like Fate. The Stoic problem with Fortune, whether good or bad, is that it's not up to us or fully within our control. As Seneca pointed out, what Fortune gives you is not truly your own. It can be taken away. By contrast, that which is truly good—a well-developed character—comes from within and is ours to keep.

Seneca writes extensively about Fortune, leaving no doubt that it was his biggest enemy. "The high places," he said, "are the ones struck by lightning."[1] He explains that people who suddenly become wealthy often lose their psychological balance. They "imagine that their good luck will never end and that their gains will not just continue but increase. Having forgotten this trampoline on which human affairs bounce up and down, they feel certain that chance will remain steady for them alone."[2]

As we know, the world is full of stories about lottery winners who have lost all of their winnings. When someone obtains great wealth quickly, that doesn't mean he or she has the skill, or mental equilibrium, to manage it. Back in the dot-com bubble days of the late 1990s, I knew an amateur stock trader who turned fifty thousand dollars into over a million in a very short period, and then lost it all. She was afraid of selling her stocks and then having to pay taxes on the profits. By that refusal to sell, she lost everything when the bubble collapsed. Similarly, there are many public stories of celebrities who have lost vast sums through high living, extravagance, and lack of moderation. As one of many possible examples, when he died Michael Jackson was between four hundred and five hundred million dollars in debt.[3]

In the Middle Ages, the Wheel of Fortune was a famous allegory of wealth's unpredictability (see figure 5). In these illustrations, Fortune or Chance, often wearing a blindfold, rotates a wheel resembling a small Ferris wheel. The wheel lifts those stricken by poverty up from the bottom to the extreme wealth of kings, but it simultaneously drags the wealthy, at the top, back down to the level of beggars. As Seneca wrote, "Every rank in life is subject to change, and whatever befalls someone else could befall you too."[4] Also, since things swing back and forth, no one should be overly confident when things go well, or give up when things go poorly.[5]

Fig 5: The Wheel of Fortune. Lady Fortune's wheel lifts those stricken with poverty up to the wealth of kings and drags the wealthy down into poverty.

Seneca himself was no stranger to the wild swings of Fortune. As I mentioned in the introduction to this book, he skyrocketed to wealth and fame as a Roman senator early in his career, only to be exiled to the island of Corsica for eight years by the Emperor Claudius. This involved Seneca losing half of his wealth and being separated from his wife, right after losing their only child. Then, after finally returning to Rome, Seneca achieved even greater fortune as adviser to the Emperor Nero.

Shortly after being exiled to Corsica and losing so much, Seneca wrote this message to his mother, Helvia, reflecting on his experience:

> I have never trusted Fortune, even when she seemed to offer peace. All those blessings that she generously bestowed on me—money, position, and influence—I stored in a place from which she could reclaim them without disturbing me. I have maintained a great distance between those things and myself; and so she has taken them away, but not torn them away, from me. No one has been crushed by Fortune unless he was first deceived by her gifts.[6]

BEFORE MONEY RULED THE WORLD, EVERYTHING WAS FREE

In Letter 90, Seneca tells a story about how people lived simply and more freely in earlier times, before complex civilization emerged. Seneca's story revolves around the idea of *natural wealth*: nature freely provides what its creatures require. For example, everything that an animal requires to survive in its natural habitat is readily available and requires little effort to obtain.

The same holds true, Seneca claims, for the earliest people. "Nature imposed no painful demands on us," he writes. "Nothing needed for life was difficult to obtain. Everything was prepared for us at our birth." He continues:

> It is *we* who made things difficult for ourselves through contempt for what was easy. Housing, shelter, clothing, and food—things that have now become a huge business—were ready at hand, free, and easily available. Everything then was based on actual need. It is we who made all of these things expensive and objects of envy. It is we who made everything difficult to obtain through many and great technical skills.[7]

The idea that "nature's needs are few" runs throughout all of Seneca's works. It's *we* who make things much more difficult than they need to be. While the lives of the earliest people would have been rustic, they lived safely and freely beneath their thatched roofs. But those who live under marble and gold roofs live in a state of servitude. Commenting on the wealthy Romans of his time, Seneca notes, "The natural measure that limited our desires to actual needs, within our means, has now vanished. These days, if someone wants only what is enough, they are seen as being uncultured and poverty-stricken."[8]

In the end, it was human greed that introduced poverty. By desiring more than was needed, we lost everything. In the earliest times, according to Seneca's story, people cared for one another equally. But then people who were more powerful and greedy "came to lay their hands upon the weaker." They would "hide away things for their own use" and "started to shut out others from the necessities of life."[9] Then, as things developed even further, people became blinded by the idea of wealth and seduced by the desire to display their wealth to others in extravagant ways. This is what we would now call the idea of "fame and fortune," and as Seneca writes, "All such prosperity just wants to be noticed."[10]

Rather than favoring the fame-and-fortune approach, which causes human suffering, Seneca advocated a path of voluntary simplicity. As he wrote to Lucilius, "You should measure all things by your natural needs, which can be satisfied for free or at very little cost. . . . Nature desires nothing beyond some food."[11]

THE DANGERS OF EXTREME WEALTH

> Anyone who has surrendered to the power of Fortune
> has set himself up for great and inescapable mental
> turmoil.
>
> —Seneca, *Letters* 74.6

For Seneca, the dangers of extreme wealth are many. Epicurus, the founder of a rival school to the Stoics, wrote that "for many people, the acquisition of riches has not been the end of their troubles, but merely a change in their troubles."[12] While Seneca disagreed with many teachings of Epicurus, this was not one of them.

As the business writer Timothy Ferriss and others have noted, when people become suddenly wealthy, it amplifies their existing character traits. Some mentally stable people, like Warren Buffett—worth about $83 billion as of this writing— are not fazed by great wealth at all. He still lives in a house that he bought for $31,500 in 1958. He also frequently eats cheap fast food—think McDonald's—and drives an inexpensive car. These facts suggest that his lifestyle is quite staid and that he's not attracted to extravagant living. But for other people, when they become wealthy, it increases their sense of self-importance and amplifies their negative character traits, which Seneca cataloged in detail. As he notes, extreme wealth makes many people unstable, but it affects people differently: "Prosperity is a restless condition; it torments itself. It unsettles the brain, in more ways than one, because it affects people differently. Some people it provokes toward power, others toward self-indulgence. Some it puffs up; others it softens, and totally incapacitates them."[13]

While Seneca's Latin can be translated as "puffs up" or "inflates," we today would refer to this condition as *psychological inflation*. Elsewhere he writes, great wealth "inflates the mind, breeds arrogance, attracts envy, and disturbs reason" to such a degree that people love to have a reputation for affluence, even though that reputation is likely to harm us.[14]

One of the greatest dangers of extreme wealth is that it encourages some people to become addicted to luxury, excess, and living beyond their means. In other words, the virtue of moderation gets thrown out the window. In the worst situation, what were once luxuries become necessities. Offering a case study of out-of-control excess, Seneca tells the story of the Roman lover of luxury, Apicius, who would spend any amount needed to procure the world's finest food. After he spent one hundred million Roman sesterces (an astronomically huge amount of money) on his addiction to fine dining, he discovered that he had "only" ten million left. Afraid that he might die in "poverty" and without his extravagant meals, Apicius killed himself instead.[15]

Another problem associated with extreme wealth is the challenge of maintaining it. Wealthy people, like the rest of us, often live beyond their means. But Fortune is fickle. Once you acquire an expensive piece of property, or two, or three, you need to maintain it all. This requires a large, continuing flow of income. "Preserving great wealth is an anxious task," Seneca wrote, and "great prosperity is great slavery."[16] To maintain great wealth requires new wealth, and the greater one's fortune rises, the more likely it is to collapse, which is a source of worry and misery for anyone who lives beyond his or her means.

As the modern Stoic philosopher William B. Irvine points out, fame and fortune go together because they are both signs of social status. Even if we can't achieve fame and fortune on a massive scale, almost everyone seeks social status: "If universal fame eludes them, they seek regional fame, local renown, popularity within their social circle, or distinction among colleagues. Likewise, if they can't amass a fortune in absolute terms, they seek relative affluence: they want to be materially better off than their co-workers, neighbors, and friends."[17]

Some things never change, and as Seneca pointed out two thousand years ago, the pursuit of social status leads to envy, greed, and ambition. "Regardless of how much you own," he notes, "if someone else has more, you will feel your wealth to be insufficient by the same amount in which you fall short of another. Your madness for success be so great that, if anyone is ahead of you, it will seem that no one is behind you."[18] Wealth can inspire greed because the more money you have, the more you can make.

Finally, another source of misery generated by wealth is the pain of loss. Seneca suggests that "we should keep in mind how much less the pain is from not having wealth than losing it. Then we will realize that, since poverty has less to lose, it is less likely to torment us."[19]

OVERCOMING FINANCIAL WORRY: "PRACTICING POVERTY" AND VOLUNTARY SIMPLICITY

> If you wish to have free time for your mind, you should either be poor or resemble the poor. Study cannot be helpful without a concern for simple living, and simple living is voluntary poverty.
>
> —Seneca, *Letters* 17.5

If you've ever been worried about money, you're not alone. According to a recent survey conducted by H&R Block, 59 percent of all Americans "constantly worry about money to some degree."[20] As Seneca emphasized, even the most wealthy people worry about money, which still holds true. According to Jeremy Kisner, a certified financial planner, "A recent survey revealed that 48% of millionaires, and 20% of ultra-high net worth households ($5–$25 million), were still worried about running out of money in retirement." If you read his short article, "Why Rich People Worry about Money," you'll see that little has changed from Seneca's time, including the reasons for worry.[21]

As I suggested in chapter 3, it's entirely valid to have financial *concerns*, but *worry* is probably not the best term to use. By simply eliminating the term "worry" from my vocabulary and replacing it with "concern," I've become more emotionally resilient, because worry is a negative emotion. By contrast, a concern is something to be addressed with reason. While this might seem like a very small change, the results have been noticeable.

That aside, judging by Seneca's letters, his friend Lucilius chronically worried about financial matters, even though he must have been wealthy. Lucilius was always fretting, wondering about how he could retire and lead a more leisurely lifestyle. And as you might imagine, Seneca had plenty of advice to offer him. Like the multimillionaires who worry about running out of money today, Seneca pointed out that Lucilius's worries were primarily psychological.

Many people today have fully valid financial concerns when it comes to retirement. Still, it's hard to believe that this also applied to Seneca's wealthy friend Lucilius, who seemed to be an expert at making excuses. To address this issue, Seneca spent several letters trying to deconstruct his friend's beliefs about how much money he really needed, along with his view that "poverty" was something terrible. While Seneca used the term "voluntary poverty" to describe a good lifestyle, we today would translate this as *voluntary simplicity*. For Seneca, the person who has enough is truly rich, and the fastest way to become rich is to give up on the endless pursuit of wealth.

Seneca urged Lucilius not to postpone living now, and suggested that he should scale back his well-paying but unfulfilling lifestyle:

> You have sunk into a kind of life that will never bring an end to your miseries and servitude. . . . If you retire from your public position, everything you have will be less, but life will be more fulfilling. As things stand, you have many piles of things heaped up all around, but they don't satisfy you. So which do you prefer: abundance in the midst of scarcity or scarcity in the midst of abundance? Prosperity is not just greedy—it is exposed to the greed of strangers. As long as nothing is enough for you, you will not be enough for others.[22]

As he stresses throughout the letters, only a wise person is satisfied by what he has, and common things, like simple foods, can deliver great pleasure. If you instantly want to become rich, Seneca suggests, stop thinking about adding to your money, but instead subtract from your desires.

Seneca then gives Lucilius a project of "practicing poverty" to see how little he can get by on. In what is now a famous passage, popularized by Tim Ferriss, he writes: "Set aside a certain number of days, during which you will be satisfied with the least amount of food, of the cheapest kind, and with rough and shabby clothing. Then say to yourself: "Is *this* what I was fearing?"[23]

This, of course, is a kind of "exposure therapy" and training for future adversity. Seneca tells Lucilius,

> Endure this for three or four days, sometimes more, so that it's not a game but really a test. Believe me, then, Lucilius: You will feel astonished to be well-fed for just a few cents; and you will realize that your peace of mind does not depend on Fortune. For even when angry, Fortune provides enough for our needs.[24]

Lucilius, he says, should "start to do business with poverty," as a way to find contentment by easing his financial concerns.

According to Tim Ferriss, his friend Kevin Kelly, the author and cofounder of *Wired* magazine, performs an identical practice to the one described by Seneca. He occasionally camps out in his living room for a few days in a sleeping bag and eats only instant oatmeal and instant coffee. This reminds him that he can survive any situation. Kelly traveled the world with a backpack in his twenties, with next to nothing in cash, and seems to have taught himself the practice of voluntary simplicity without any help from Seneca.

One way that I've experimented with Seneca's technique is by creating inexpensive but delicious hot breakfasts at home, starting with two hardboiled eggs, heated pinto beans, and salsa. The gourmet version includes some avocado slices with lemon juice and a bit of tunafish. Sometimes I'll include a few sun-dried tomatoes. Periodically, I calculate the per-breakfast cost for each variation. At today's prices, the least expensive break-fast comes out to $1.50, using canned beans. One of my favor-ite healthy and hot lunches costs $2.50: a reheated turkey burger with a bit of kalamata olive paste on top, served with hot beans and salsa on the side. While I often spend more on food by going out, it's psychologically reassuring to know that I could eat quite well, if needed, for $6 a day or less than $200 a month. Of course, if I went the rice-and-beans route, it would be even less.

For anyone who has financial concerns, it's often a helpful exercise to calculate the least amount of money you could live on, and then experiment with following that lifestyle, at least in part.

A life of voluntary simplicity, as advocated by the Stoics, also allows you greater personal freedom to pursue your own interests. Because a simple lifestyle reduces your expenses, it could reduce the time you need to work, resulting in more free time.[25] As Seneca wrote, "Only a small amount will satisfy nature's needs. She is content with just a little. It's not our hunger that costs us dearly, but our ambition."[26] He also noted, writing to his mother, that "A person who lives within the bounds set by nature will never feel poor; but someone who exceeds those bounds will be chased by poverty even amidst the greatest wealth."[27] For Sen-eca, "The worst kind of poverty is those who feel poor in the midst of their riches."[28]

USING FORTUNE'S GIFTS

> Virtue does not come from wealth, but virtue makes
> wealth and everything else good for humans.
> —Socrates, Plato's *Apology* 30A–B

While Seneca saw how distracting and damaging extreme wealth could be to people with an unsteady character, the Stoics saw wealth, overall, to be an advantage: it's something you should desire, they said, along with good health, if possible, even if wealth and health won't improve your character.

Because Seneca was an advocate of simple living, yet extremely wealthy himself, he was accused of hypocrisy during his lifetime.[29] At the end of his little book *On the Happy Life*, Seneca takes aim at his critics, arguing against them. But his entire thinking about this can be summed up in one simple thought: It's fine to use the gifts of fortune, as long as you're not enslaved to them.

As Seneca told Lucilius, no one can truly be happy until they've risen above wealth. Consequently, those who possess wealth must convince themselves that they would be happy without it. They should view wealth as something that could disappear at any moment.[30] In other words, if you possess wealth or any gift of fortune, you shouldn't become attached to it.

Seneca's most compelling argument for the value of wealth is that a wealthy person can use his financial resources to practice virtue. In other words, people with wealth can use it wisely to benefit others and society.

When I lived in the United States, my next-door neighbor Fred was just such a person. Fred and his daughters own an engineering company that was doing $220 million in sales at the time. While he was wealthy, he was also down-to-earth, easy to talk with, and never once showed the least bit of arrogance or extravagance. In fact, despite being successful in business, Fred's main interest in life was helping other people and trying to improve society. His family's foundation had given millions to the local community. But one program he created, and was understandably proud of, trained thirty people with the skills they needed to get off welfare. When they completed the training, he gave them all permanent jobs—a feat the government had been unable to accomplish.

One day I was over at his house, which had a beautiful view of the countryside but an unassuming, rustic-style interior. As we sat there sipping coffee, he confided to me, "I love working on these projects to make things better. The most interesting problem, which I think about often, is how to eliminate poverty."

Once, when I experienced a personal tragedy, Fred walked over to my house to see how I was doing. When we talked, he said, "When something like that happens, I think you can only put it in God's hands." While Fred was a Christian, those words have a very Stoic ring to them. For as the Stoics said repeatedly, "Some things are not up to us."

In any case, Fred is a perfect example of what Seneca had in mind when saying that if you possess wealth, you have a fabulous opportunity to practice virtue.

When Seneca addressed his critics, who accused him of hypocrisy for being wealthy, he delivered a perfect, stinging response, which makes me feel a sense of delight whenever I read it. "If my wealth flows away," he wrote, "it will only take itself. But if you lose *your* wealth, you will be in shock, and you'll feel as though you've lost your very self. For me, wealth has a place, but for you, it holds the highest value. In the end, I own my wealth, but your wealth owns you."[31]

CHAPTER 9

Vicious Crowds and the Ties That Bind

Do you ask what you should avoid most of all? A crowd.
—Seneca, *Letters* 7.1

TIME FOR A BIT OF THROAT-SLITTING

When Seneca told Lucilius that he should avoid crowds, Seneca had just returned from the gladiatorial games. There he watched and listened to the crowds cheer for other human beings to be killed, right before their eyes, as a form of entertainment.

So when Seneca said we should "avoid crowds," he wasn't just referring to large groups of people in general. He was speaking about mobs or vicious crowds, which can have a terrible effect on our inner character, especially if we get swept away by the crowd's emotions. As he wrote to Lucilius,

> Contact with a crowd is harmful to us: there is no person who doesn't recommend some vice to us, transmit it to us, or smear it on us while we remain unaware. Without

fail, the greater the mob we mingle with, the greater the danger.

But nothing is so harmful to good character than to take a seat at the public games, for then the vice creeps in more easily during the course of our pleasure. Do you understand what I'm saying? I come home more greedy, more conceited, more self-indulgent—and worse than that—I return home more cruel and inhuman, just because I have been around other humans.[1]

Seneca explains that he was expecting some "fun, wit, and relaxation" at the games, but it turned into slaughter when someone drove condemned criminals into the arena. In Seneca's graphic account, "The previous combats were exhibitions of mercy. But now the pretense was over, and it is pure murder. The men have no protective armor. Their whole bodies are exposed, and no one strikes a blow in vain. Every fight ends in death, carried out by sword and flame."[2]

At one point, the mob was getting a bit rowdy, screaming, "Kill him! Whip him! Burn him!" and so on. "And when the games stop for an intermission, someone announces: 'Time for a bit of throat-slitting, now, to keep the action going!'"[3]

Seneca brings this up to make a significant point: Our characters are deeply influenced by the people who surround us in daily life. People are also strongly affected by those around them when they are part of a crowd at political rallies, sporting events, religious events, or gatherings that turn into riots. But the ways in which others affect us, whether in our day-to-day lives or in a crowd, are largely the same: "A single example of self-indulgence or greed does much harm. A close friend who is overly pampered weakens and softens us. A rich neighbor inflames our greed. A mean-spirited companion rubs off his spite, even on a sincere and spotless fellow."[4]

Seneca uses the story of his trip to the games to bring up the idea that the quality of the people we surround ourselves with is essential in terms of improving our character. We'll explore Seneca's thoughts on this shortly, but let's first take a look at how emotions and behaviors "go viral" in large groups, a notable feature of our own Internet age. Surprisingly, this idea that human behavior can be "viral" or "contagious" was clearly described by Seneca, two thousand years ago.

WHEN THINGS GET CONTAGIOUS

Using a metaphor from medicine, Seneca explains that we can become "infected" with the bad qualities of others. In a plague, he noted, we can catch a disease by merely being "breathed on," so we must choose our friends with great care, based on the health of their character. "Make an effort to take on the least infected," he wrote, because "it's the beginning of disease to expose healthy things to sickness."[5]

Significantly, this isn't something Seneca only mentions once. As he writes in another work, "We pick up habits from those around us, and just as some diseases are spread through physical contact, the mind also transmits its ills to those nearby." For example, a greedy person can transmit his infected character to his neighbors. Fortunately, though, "It's the same thing with virtues, but in reverse." So while people with flawed characters can transmit their bad habits to us, people with good characters, who befriend us, can make us better human beings.[6]

What Seneca was writing about would now be described as a form of *unconscious influence*. And in order for us to be unconsciously influenced, it doesn't matter if it's a large group, a small group, or just another person. The process is similar in all cases.

For example, when I was growing up, I never liked being around people who smoked cigarettes. In fact, when I was a youngster, I decided to never go down the road of becoming a smoker. But in my late teens I was surrounded by coworkers and friends who smoked frequently. When we'd go out to lunch, they'd light up while drinking coffee, before and after a meal. Sure enough, it wasn't long before I took up smoking too. After a while, things got worse. Eventually, the smoking habit turned into a pack-a-day addiction. At age twenty-four, though, I quit. Smoking and its effects became too terrible to endure. I even developed a persistent pain in my left lung. Nicotine, as scientists point out, is as addictive as heroin. Quitting was extremely difficult, but after being free from cigarettes for a month, I started to feel normal again.

Similarly, around the same age, my best friend was very smart but also incredibly sarcastic. Sarcastic comments rolled off his tongue in the same way that water pours from a fountain. Unfortunately, through unconscious imitation, I picked up this behavior from him, which ended up being an unpleasant character trait. Some years later, I made an effort to eliminate it.

While Seneca spoke about the dangers of crowds and how habits are contagious, today we talk about things "going viral" on social media, which has become our modern-day locus of crowd behavior. If Seneca was right about the dangers of crowds and how they can adversely affect our mental well-being, perhaps we should be more careful about going online. Hypnotic images, raw emotions, and rage often seem to cascade through online networks and take on a life of their own. With the full-blown development of the Internet, the print era's more serious journalism largely went into eclipse. Unfortunately, the online reporting that has replaced it is often designed to cause outrage, get clicks, and go viral. This cannot possibly be good for us as individuals or as a society.

Back in the 1800s, the social psychologists Gabriel Tarde (1843–1904) and Gustave Le Bon (1841–1931) initiated the study of crowd psychology, which has since become a significant field. Tarde and Le Bon introduced the idea of *herd mentality*, also known as *mob mentality*, which Seneca had written about two thousand years earlier. Scientific studies have shown how people are naturally prone to imitate the behavior of others, both in the real, physical world and online.[7]

But scientific studies aside, any careful observer can see how individual behavior can often become governed by herd psychology on social media. One example of this is how groups respond to news stories with outrage even before the facts are fully known. In some ways, "Twitter mobs," when gripped by an emotional contagion, are no less dangerous than physical mobs. When outrage spreads online, the resulting desire for mob or vigilante justice overthrows the need for due process, which real justice always requires. There are now countless examples of death threats posted publicly online (or privately by email) and people trying to "cancel" the careers of people they feel offended by. Since anyone can get caught up in an emotional contagion, this behavior is not limited to either side of the political spectrum.

In his classic book on herd psychology, *The Crowd* (1895), Gustave Le Bon noted,

> The most careful observations seem to prove that an individual immerged for some length of time in a crowd in action soon finds himself—either in consequence of the magnetic influence given out by the crowd, or from some

other cause of which we are ignorant—in a special state, which much resembles the state of fascination in which the hypnotized individual finds himself in the hands of the hypnotizer.[8]

When the group mind emerges and takes over, he wrote, "An individual in a crowd is a grain of sand amid other grains of sand, which the wind stirs up at will."[9]

As Gabriel Tarde also noted, the fact that people unconsciously imitate one another accounts, at least in part, for herd behavior and the emergence of the group mind. And as a more recent thinker, Tony D. Sampson, points out, it's because of the hypnotic power of imitation that emotions and feelings spread virally across digital networks to infect others.[10]

TAKING A LOOK AT INVISIBLE INFLUENCES

Seneca's interest in how other people influence us is related to *socialization*, a term that became popular in the 1940s. Socialization is the process through which people become assimilated to society's values or to the norms of a smaller subgroup.

Much socialization is intentional and deliberate, like when parents teach their children to be polite, play nice, and follow rules—all important life skills. However, other forms of socialization are more invisible and unconscious: for example, the way people absorb beliefs and behaviors through media, advertising, and peer groups. Because of this, people who study socialization refer to *deliberate socialization* and *unconscious socialization*.

If we want to become well-developed human beings, social-ization is essential. But *how* we are socialized can be for good or ill. For example, parents might socialize a child to be honest and fair, but another family might socialize a child to hold racist views. In Seneca's world, the bloodthirsty crowd he saw at the games, chanting for death and destruction, had been socialized to revel in violence. Put in modern psychological language, as the crowd chanted for death it had become a group mind in the grip of an emotional contagion. Seneca was one of the first to notice how emotions can be contagious, now a scientific field of study. For example, researchers have found that yawning is not only contagious among humans. It's even contagious *across species*: dogs and chimpanzees can catch yawns from human beings.[11] This kind of contagious imitative behavior must be very deep-seated indeed.

While all of the Stoics believed that false beliefs or opin-ions cause human suffering, some of them also realized that we absorb those beliefs through training.[12] For example, many par-ents teach their children that money is an unconditional good. But Seneca, who had the most profound psychological insight of all the Stoics, realized that something deeper was happen-ing. We can see this from his repeated use of metaphors about invisible influences, which he applied to human psychology—"invisible infections," "plagues," and "contagious habits," which, when transmitted "without our awareness," can affect our char-acter. Today, we can now see these descriptions as metaphors for "invisible" or unconscious socialization.[13]

Psychology has taught us that some emotions, ideas, beliefs, and behaviors can have a "magnetic quality" and be transmit-ted without conscious awareness. As we've also learned from hypnosis, *imitation* and *suggestibility* are among the most potent psychological phenomena. Even though imitation and suggestibility work in largely unconscious ways, they are primary factors in making mental states contagious. Psychologists also note that social customs and behaviors are largely adopted through unintentional or unconscious imitation.[14]

While Seneca was perhaps the first thinker to describe this, his insights are even more relevant today. Through mass media and social media platforms, the influence of crowd psychology and emotional contagion has extended far beyond anything Seneca could have imagined. To make things worse, entire industries like advertising and online media actively attempt to manipulate people's feelings, beliefs, and behaviors on a mass level. Unfortunately, this is not a half-hearted effort: it's approached with scientific rigor and based on "measurable results." Each time we click on a viral link or outrage-inducing headline, someone somewhere—or some machine—is keeping track of that link's popularity score.

How Seneca would respond to this brave new world strikes me as clear. He would tell us, "Don't be antisocial, but do take a step back" from anything that resembles crowd psychology or groupthink. Certainly, we should take a huge step back from anything that resembles psychological manipulation. When he said, "Avoid crowds," Seneca didn't imply we should avoid people in general. He did mean, though, that we should be on guard about the influences to which we're exposed. If Seneca could have used our modern terminology, he would have said, "Don't let your thoughts, or your mental autonomy, be swayed by the hypnotic power of the group mind." From a Stoic perspective, the only antidote to unconscious social conditioning is to safeguard our autonomy as rational human beings. And to do that, we must engage in critical thinking.

In this way, Seneca was correct: crowds *can* be dangerous.

THE SEARCH FOR GOOD COMPANY

> We should choose a healthy environment not only for
> our body but for our character too.
>
> —Seneca, *Letters* 51.4

If crowds tend toward infectious, unhealthy behavior, what's the alternative? After describing the violent, jeering behavior he saw in the amphitheater, Seneca advised Lucilius, "Spend time with those who will make you better, and welcome those you can improve. The process is mutual; and people learn while teaching."[15]

If people with unhealthy characters surround us, the first and most crucial step is to escape from their presence. "A large part of sanity," Seneca explains, "consists of letting go of those who encourage insanity and getting far away from a companionship that is mutually harmful."[16] The second step is to surround ourselves with people who have good characters, even if it's a tiny group or a single person. That's because virtuous people can influence us just as strongly as vicious people, but in reverse: "Just as poor health improves in a good location and a healthy climate, it is equally beneficial for a mind, lacking in strength, to associate with a better crowd."[17] In the same way bad qualities can be virally transmitted, good qualities can be contagious too. Seneca would have agreed, at least in principle, with the famous saying of business writer Jim Rohn, "You're the average of the five people you spend the most time with"—so we should choose those people with care.

This again highlights why friendships and meaningful relationships are crucial in Seneca's philosophy. Spending time with people who possess good characters will help us make progress.

"Good people are mutually helpful because they exercise each other's virtues." Even a Stoic sage "needs his virtues activated: for just as he exercises himself, so too is he exercised by another wise person." In the same way that wrestlers and musicians practice and train, wise people need others to practice with and learn from.[18] If we want to be wise and have good characters, we need to have those qualities "activated" in us by another person. And in order to activate another person's good character, we must activate our own.

ONE HUMANITY: BELONGING TOGETHER VS. TOXIC TRIBALISM

> Remove fellowship and you will tear apart the unity of the human race on which our life depends.
>
> —Seneca, *On Benefits* 4.18.4

With their belief that humanity is one due to the spark of reason or *logos* we all share in common, the Stoics made a monumental contribution to the development of human rights. Stoic ideas contributed to ending slavery and ensuring the equality of women in the Western world and on a global basis.

While Aristotle had many fine philosophical ideas and helped to lay the foundations for scientific research, some of his ideas were flawed and damaging. Specifically, Aristotle believed that only men fully possessed reason. In comparison to men, women possessed a lesser degree of reason, while "natural slaves" and "barbarians" (or non-Greeks) lacked reason altogether.[19]

The Stoics, by contrast, believed that all people possess reason in exactly the same way. In other words, *everyone* who is a human being—including men, women, slaves, and people from every country—all possess reason, and the human soul is "always and everywhere the same."[20] The early Christians adopted this idea from the Stoics. As the Christian writer Lactantius wrote, "Wisdom is given to humankind, it is given to all without discrimination . . . *The Stoics understood this to such an extent that they said that even slaves and women ought to do philosophy* [emphasis added]."[21] To put it differently, in the same way that all human beings are born with muscles, all humans are born with reason, too. How we will then develop these gifts is up to us.

While not a Stoic philosopher, the Roman statesman and writer Cicero (106–43 BC) studied Stoicism carefully and was very deeply sympathetic to many Stoic ideas. As a political philosopher, Cicero adopted and developed the Stoic idea of *natural law*, which would have a long and significant history.[22] Natural law is based on the Stoic idea that the laws of nature are rational and that our human rationality, also, originates from nature. Based on these premises, Cicero thought our human laws should be self-evident to reason: ultimately, they should be based on the kind of rationality we see reflected in nature, in the cosmos, and in our own moral sense. As a political philosopher, he defined *law* as "right reason in harmony with nature." If we could see things clearly, Cicero thought, we would want the laws to be identical in Rome, Athens, and every other city because they should be founded on universal reason.[23]

In other words, natural law is universal: it is not invented by humans. Rather, it is discovered. It ultimately comes from Nature, Reason, or "God"—three terms that were synonymous for the Stoics. According to natural law, all people have inherent rights, or natural rights, which are intrinsic to human nature.

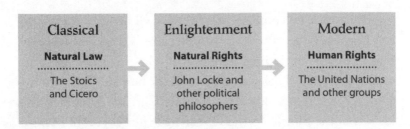

Fig 6: The long development of human rights,
from the Stoics to the United Nations.

While our modern idea of "universal human rights" did not exist
in the ancient world, the seeds of these ideas did exist in the
Stoic idea of natural law, championed by Cicero.[24] The Stoics
had already set forth the concept of human equality. Then, over
the centuries, natural law gave birth to the idea of natural rights,
which in turn gave rise to the modern notion of human rights
(see figure 6).[25] In essence, natural rights *are* human rights.

The Stoic ideas of natural law, as expressed by Cicero,
informed Enlightenment thinkers like John Locke (1632–1704)
and deeply inspired the Founders of the United States.[26] For
example, Thomas Jefferson (1743–1826), who wrote the first draft
of the Declaration of Independence, was, like other Founders,
thoroughly familiar with the ideas of Seneca, the Stoics, and
Cicero.[27] Jefferson's own concept of natural law was Stoic.[28] And
when Jefferson wrote the words, "All men are created equal," it
mirrored the Stoic idea of human equality.[29]

Cicero had explained that a primary function of government
was to protect the life, liberty, and property of its citizens. Centuries later, John Locke identified "life, liberty, and property" as
among the most fundamental natural rights of people. When
Thomas Jefferson wrote the Declaration, he transformed the

natural rights described by Locke into "Life, Liberty, and the pursuit of Happiness." As Jefferson put it,

> We hold these truths to be self-evident, that all men are created equal, that they are endowed by their Creator with certain unalienable Rights, that among these are Life, Liberty and the pursuit of Happiness.

For Jefferson, the rights he listed were "self-evident" to reason, and aspects of "Nature's Law." These rights are both natural rights *and* human rights. And as historian Joseph J. Ellis has noted, Jefferson's lines in the Declaration are "the most quoted statement of human rights in recorded history."[30]

This, then, is the historical trajectory linking Stoic ideas with the development of modern human rights: from the Stoics and Cicero on natural law; through John Locke and the other Enlightenment philosophers; to Thomas Jefferson who drew on them all in his proclamations on human rights.

Jefferson was obviously an important but transitional figure in ending slavery. On the one hand, many believe that he did not fully live up to his high ideals (he was, after all, a slaveholder, and thus at odds with his own moral principles). On the other hand, his commitment to end slavery was profound: he consistently advocated for the elimination of slavery, proposed practical schemes for emancipation, and even enacted a law, while serving as president of the United States, that banned the international slave trade. As Martin Luther King Jr. famously said, "The arc of the moral universe is long, but it bends toward justice." While slavery did not end in Jefferson's lifetime, the lengthy historical arc of eliminating slavery originated from, and was inspired by, Stoic ideas of natural law and human equality. Jefferson made those ideas central in the public mind and vigorously advanced the cause of abolition.

———

IF THE STOICS WERE correct, and the entire human family is one, why is there so much division and polarization in the world today? The short answer is that these divisions have something to do with our biological history as tribal animals. Belonging to a group or a tribe is a natural human need. By definition, people who don't feel a sense of belonging experience loneliness and alienation. Things become problematic, though, when tribalism becomes toxic.

For roughly the last two hundred thousand years, we *Homo sapiens* have lived as tribal creatures. Because of that evolutionary history, tribalism is almost impossible to eliminate. But as the physicist and philosopher Marcelo Gleiser observes, "A tribe without enemies is, almost by definition, not a tribe. As a consequence, tribal dispute and warfare is part of what defines humanity." As he goes on to note,

> *The biggest enemy we have to fight against now is our tribal past.* What served us for so well for thousands of years is now an obsolete concept. It's no more about the survival of this tribe or that one, but about *Homo sapiens* as a species. . . . For the first time in our collective history, we must think of ourselves as a single tribe in a single planet. . . . We are a single tribe, the tribe of humans. And, as such, not a tribe at all.[31]

The Stoics were the first to spell out this idea fully: we're all members of a *cosmopolis*, they said, a worldwide, interconnected community of human beings. In other words, we are citizens of the entire world. Seneca, like other Stoics, taught that human beings should desire to benefit all of humanity, the cosmopolis as a whole. Without the mutual support of others, society would collapse. "We are all parts of a great body," he wrote. "Our companionship is like a stone arch, which would collapse if the stones did not mutually support one another."[32]

A sense of belonging is essential, but toxic tribalism tears people apart and goes against the prosocial vision of the Stoics. In Seneca's words, "You must live for another if you would live for yourself."[33] At its worst, toxic tribalism can lead to the demonization of others, violence, and even genocide. Because of their belief in human unity, if they were alive today, the Roman Stoics would be vigorously opposed to modern *identity politics* in all its forms, because identity politics divides people into different subgroups, based on traits like gender, race, or sexual orientation. It then encourages those groups to compete against one another for special status or power, as if group identity were more important than our fundamental status as human beings. By taking a "divide and conquer" approach, and by fragmenting the human family into competing groups, identity politics represents the ultimate form of toxic tribalism in our time. Its approach increases social division and risks tearing society apart. As Seneca warned, "Remove fellowship and you will tear apart the unity of the human race on which our life depends."[34] For Stoics, humanity is one: we are all brothers and sisters. Rather than dividing society into warring tribes, we should recognize our common humanity and support one another.

144 | BREAKFAST WITH SENECA

THE TIES THAT BIND:
FEELING AT HOME WITH EVERYONE ELSE

> All human beings are born for a life of fellowship, and
> society can only remain healthy through the mutual
> protection and love of its parts.
>
> —Seneca, *On Anger* 2.31.7

Seneca's idea that we belong to a global community of human
beings, united through reason and friendship with others, strikes
us as modern. Because we now live in a planetary civilization,
connected by worldwide trade and communication networks,
global fellowship is part of our daily experience.

But how is it that human society, and even global society,
comes into being in the first place? If the instincts of tribalism
alone governed things, the world would be much more dangerous and polarized than it actually is.

The Stoics had a beautiful explanation for this. It's known
as *okeiōsis*, and seems to go back to Zeno, the founder of the
school.[35] The term comes from the Greek word *oikos*, which
means "house" or "family." *Okeiōsis* refers to the sense of kinship
or being at home that we feel toward other people—the human
affinity we feel for others—and it's the ultimate source of all
Stoic ethics. *Okeiōsis* allows us to see other human beings as near
and dear to us, even if we're not directly related to them. Marcus Aurelius frequently wrote about our kinship with all human
beings and how that kinship forms the basis of society. As he put
it, "All rational creatures are born for the sake of one another."[36]

The most thorough explanation of how natural human affection gives rise to society appears in Cicero's writings, and the
basic idea is simple. "The Stoics," he says, "think that nature

itself causes parents to have affection for their children," and this parental affection is "the source from which developed the common fellowship of the human race in communities." This parental affection for one's offspring is rational and part of natural law. It's even found in other species. When we see the great effort that even nonhuman animals spend on caring for their young, Cicero says, "we seem to be hearing the voice of nature itself."[37] For the Stoics, he explains,

> It is also clear that we've been impelled by nature herself to love those to whom we have given birth. From this impulse arises a common attraction that unites human beings as such; based on our common humanity, we feel kinship with others.[38]

While animals, like bees, work in harmony with one another, "With human beings, these bonds of fellowship are far more intimate. Thus, by nature, we have been fitted to form unions, societies, and states."[39] Further, as we grow older and our reason develops, *okeiōsis* extends our feelings of kinship to others. Through the use of reason and understanding, the kind of natural affection we feel toward our family members becomes applied to society as a whole.

The Stoics had another way of illustrating *okeiōsis,* the ties that bind us together with other human beings. This was explained by the Stoic philosopher Hierocles, who lived around the time of Marcus Aurelius. In one of his writings, Hierocles described the circles of humanity of which we're part (see figure 7), and why "we are eager by nature to win over and make a friend of everyone."[40]

The innermost circle is where we stand as individuals. It represents our individual self. The next circle is that of our imme-

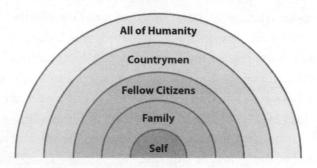

Fig 7: Simplified version of the circles of humanity
from the Stoic philosopher Hierocles.

diate family, parents, siblings, spouses, and children. The third
circle contains more distant family members: aunts and uncles,
grandparents, and cousins. The next circle contains citizens in
our local communities and then fellow countrymen. Finally, the
largest, outermost circle contains humanity as a whole. Many
modern Stoics, including myself, would draw a larger circle yet,
representing nature or the living biosphere, of which we're all a
part. But this idea is not modern. It's part of the ancient Stoic
tradition. As philosophy scholar John Sellars notes,

> The process of widening one's circle of concern should
> not stop once it encompasses all human society. . . . Even-
> tually, one's *okeiōsis* should extend to include the entire
> cosmos, generating a concern for the preservation of all
> human beings and the natural world. . . . When we reach
> this widest possible circle of concern we shall become
> cosmopolitans—citizens of the cosmos.[41]

The wise person, Hierocles suggests, will try to pull in the
outer circles in toward the center, or compress them, so that we
will feel kinship with all of humanity and not just those who are

closest to us. While he admits that a "difference in blood" will remove some affection for those who are farther away, the Stoic goal is to feel affection for humanity as a whole, and not just a sense of kinship for those with whom we're closest.

In this way, as we progress down the path toward becoming wiser and more complete human beings, we won't ignore the needs of those who are nearer and closest to us. Instead, we'll recognize all of humanity and nature as part of the wider, living community of which we're all a part. We'll then see those greater circles, from which we've all emerged, as indispensable for our well-being and flourishing.

CHAPTER 10

How to Be Authentic and Contribute to Society

THE EPICUREAN GARDEN VS.
THE STOIC COSMOPOLIS

Stoicism became the most widespread and successful philosophy of the Roman Empire because it promised a sense of inner tranquility in a stressful world that seemed, as in our own time, dangerously out of control. But Stoicism wasn't the only philosophy that promised inner tranquility to its followers. The Epicureans, named after their founder Epicurus (341–270 BC), made the same claim. And like earlier Greek philosophers, both the Stoics and Epicureans were in search of *eudaimonia* or lasting happiness.

There are some areas in which Epicurean and Stoic thinking overlap. But it's impossible to reconcile other ideas from the two schools because they're just too far apart. In about the first thirty letters Seneca wrote to Lucilius, he includes a saying from Epicurus at the end of the letter. These sayings or epigrams are in perfect harmony with Stoic teachings and cover topics like the importance of simple living and how to achieve wealth through frugality. Even though Seneca considered the Epicureans to be "the opposing camp," he was extremely open-minded when acknowledging the value of genuine wisdom, whatever its source. As he liked to point out to his friend Lucilius, good ideas are the "common property" of humanity, regardless of who expressed them.

Like the modern meaning of the word "stoic," popular stereotypes and the development of language have been unfair to the Epicureans too. Today *epicurean* refers to someone who seeks out pleasure, like a gourmet through fine food. While it's true that the Epicureans did make "pleasure" the foundation and goal of their philosophy, they were far from being hedonists. In fact, "pleasure" for them only meant living a life that was free from pain. And when it came to gourmet dining, nothing could be further from the truth. Epicurus himself mainly ate bread and water, and if he ever had a little cheese to go along with it, he considered it to be a feast.[1]

While the Stoics and Epicureans both sought mental tranquility in life, their views about the universe were entirely different. The Stoics saw the universe as resembling an intelligent organism, of which all living things, including us, are a part. The patterns we see in nature, they maintained, are a reflection of nature's intelligence, in the same way that your hand is a manifestation of biological intelligence. By contrast, the Epicureans believed that the universe was made up of atoms—or tiny particles of matter—that collided randomly and stuck together by chance. Let's stress those two words, just for a moment: *randomly* and *chance*. While atomism is an interesting idea, it doesn't explain the kind of order and patterns we see in nature or biological life, which is very far from random.[2]

We discover another vast difference between the two schools in their ideas about how people should contribute to society.

When Epicurus founded his philosophical school in Athens, he bought a piece of land outside the city, which was called "the Garden." Epicurus's students would hang out at the Garden, which resembled a hippy commune. That's because the Epicureans lived a life in common, but as social dropouts. While the goal was to achieve peace of mind, in practice that meant disengaging from anything that might upset the soul, including the frustrations arising from marriage, having children, and getting involved in politics. As if to sum up his belief in social disengagement, Epicurus famously advised, "Live unnoticed."[3]

For the Stoics, the Epicureans' dropout culture raised serious ethical questions but also inspired opportunities for humor. Epictetus, for example, had a very sharp wit, which is still funny today. Joking to his students one day, he asked them, "Can you imagine a city of Epicureans? 'I won't marry' says one. Another says, 'Nor will I, because one shouldn't marry!' 'No children either! Nor should we perform any civic duties!'"[4]

By contrast, the Stoics strongly emphasized the importance of civic engagement because they understood that we're born to be social animals. For the Stoics, we belong to two different cities or two different commonwealths. The first commonwealth is the city or community where we were born (or where we now happen to live). The second commonwealth is the *cosmopolis*, the "world-city" or "community of the cosmos," which encompasses the entire world and all of humanity. Because of this brotherhood of humanity of which we're a part, the Stoics taught, it's our duty to improve society—not by dropping out and joining a commune, but by actively serving our local communities and society as a whole. That's why so many Stoics, like Seneca and Marcus Aurelius, were statesmen or public servants throughout the Roman Empire. Stoicism called upon them to improve the human condition to the best of their abilities.

For the Stoics, living an authentic life means contributing to society in some way that will benefit others. But since people are different, that service to others will take various forms. We're not, after all, stamped out from a single cookie cutter. Because of that, the first step in living with authenticity is to understand yourself and your unique nature.

KNOW YOURSELF

Each person acquires his character for himself, but accident controls his duties.

—Seneca, *Letters* 47.15

Inscribed on the wall of the temple of Apollo at Delphi in ancient Greece was the famous saying, "Know yourself." While this relates to every aspect of life, it very strongly applies to the question "How can I live authentically and contribute to society?" Because each person is different, we're all best suited for many different tasks and occupations. And then there's the added factor of chance or Fortune that's thrown into the mix. As Seneca explained, while we're all responsible for the quality of our inner characters, what each person does for a living is not entirely under our control.

Even though we don't have full control over our professional careers or what we're able to achieve in life, we should certainly strive for the best—or strive for the best work that's suited for us. Because of this, Seneca writes, "we must first examine ourselves," and then consider what we'd like to undertake. As he explains, we must understand ourselves carefully because people often think they can accomplish more than they're able to.[5] Of course, the opposite is often true. Sometimes people accomplish less than they could, simply because they doubt their abilities.

When discussing these things, Seneca seems to be following the thoughts of an earlier Roman Stoic philosopher, Panaetius (c. 185–c. 110 BC). In his writings, Panaetius described the "four roles" (or four *personae*) that contribute to a person's place in society, including our work and career choices.[6] Rather than calling these "roles," though, let's call them *factors*.

The first factor that influences us is our universal nature as human beings, which, for a Stoic, means the fact that we're rational beings, which allows us to understand the world and act in good ways. The second factor that influences us are all the qualities that nature assigns to us as individuals, which vary widely. As Seneca noted, the qualities given to us by birth will tend to stick with us throughout life.[7] People vary enormously in their physical differences. For example, some people are athletic by nature, and others aren't. But there are even greater differences in people's psychological dispositions, personality traits, and the wide range of talents we all possess.[8] As Seneca notes,

> Some people are too shy for politics, which requires a bold appearance. Others are too arrogant for the royal court. Some cannot keep their anger in check, and any feeling of irritation leads them to say reckless things. Others cannot control their humor and refrain from dangerous jokes. For all such people, retirement is more useful than public employment: an arrogant and impatient nature should avoid provocations to outspokenness that will only bring harm.[9]

In addition to understanding our individual traits and capacities, a third factor that affects us is chance, which is beyond our control: for example, the facts of our upbringing, whether our parents were wealthy or poor, whether we had good or bad teachers, and many other things of that kind. The fourth and final factor is our own will or personal agency: our intention and decision-making. What we decide to apply ourselves to, and the energy with which we pursue our intentions, will all make a significant impact on our careers and how we contribute to society.

In the Stoic view, we must understand our traits so that we don't struggle against nature and try to pursue something beyond our capabilities. It's just not possible to live authentically, with self-awareness, if you don't understand who you are. Finally, it's impossible to live authentically or happily if you try to copy someone else while ignoring your own nature.[10]

As we can see, the Roman Stoics emphasized our universal nature as human beings, or what is common to everyone. But they also recognized the importance of our traits as individuals, which are also given to us by nature. To live happy and fulfilling lives in society, we need to pay attention to both. In this way, the Stoics extended the idea of "following nature" to include our personal traits.

SELF-CONSISTENCY

Above all, strive to be consistent with yourself.
—Seneca, *Letters* 35.4

For Seneca, living with authenticity implies being one person with a stable personality. Without that solid sense of self, a person changes his or her intentions like the shifting winds. "I don't mean," Seneca explains, "that a wise person should always walk in the exactly same way, but that he should follow a single path."[11] This idea relates strongly to Seneca's metaphor that, when traveling, it's important to have a real destination rather than just wandering about randomly.

Consistency, and having some kind of "destination," is a byproduct of having a real philosophy of life. A person with a solid character will be one person instead of many, have an aim in life, and a corresponding sense of intention. But many people aren't sure what they really want until the moment they desire it. As Seneca puts it, many people are not guided by their intentions, just "driven by impulse."[12] Elsewhere, he illustrates this idea with a funny account of what we today might call neurotic behavior:

> There isn't anyone who doesn't change his plans and desires every day. One minute he wants a wife, the next moment only a girlfriend. One minute he wants to rule like a king, then he acts more obliging than the lowest servant. One minute he acts so grandly that he attracts envy, then he acts more humble than the most self-effacing. At one moment he scatters money grandly, and the next moment he steals it.
>
> This is the clearest sign of a mind that lacks awareness: it constantly changes its identity. In my view, there is nothing more shameful than a mind that is inconsistent with itself. Consider it a great accomplishment to act as one person. But only the wise play a single role. The rest of us wear many masks. One minute we will seem frugal and serious, the next moment wasteful and silly. We keep changing our characters, taking on a new role that is its opposite. You should, then, demand this of yourself: play a single character until the curtain falls.[13]

One mark of a good character is that "it is content with itself and thus endures over time. But a bad character is unreliable: it often changes, not for the sake of the better, but just for the sake of being different."[14] Because of this, Seneca urges Lucilius to "adopt, once and for all, a single norm to live by, and make your entire life conform to this standard."[15]

Another way to live with authenticity and consistency is to present yourself to the world as you really are. Seneca writes about how people wear masks in public and engage in acting: once in public and before an audience, we present ourselves in a different way than we'd normally behave at home. This often involves a bit of pretense and display. The problem is that once someone constructs a false persona, adjusted for public display, it creates anxiety due to the likelihood of one's image being discovered as false. That could result in a shock for some, like photos of well-known Hollywood actresses shown without their makeup on. As Seneca notes, "life cannot be happy or free from anxiety for those who constantly live behind a mask," and "it is better to be scorned for one's natural state than to be tormented by constant pretense."[16]

Finally, to live with authenticity, our actual deeds should match our words and our beliefs. As our modern sayings go, "Walk the talk" and "Practice what you preach." Seneca was especially critical of professional philosophers in this regard because they often talk a good game but don't live their lives accordingly. "Philosophy is not a trick to catch the public eye," Seneca wrote, "nor is it devised for show. It's not about words but actions."[17] In short, "Let us say what we feel and feel what we say. Let our words be in harmony with our actual lives. A person fulfills his promise when the person we see and the person we hear are one and the same."[18]

INTELLECTUAL FREEDOM

> We should not, like sheep, simply follow the herd that
> has gone before us.
>
> —Seneca, *On the Happy Life* 1.3

One of the ways that Seneca himself lived with authenticity was through his deep embrace of intellectual freedom. This quality made him one of the best thinkers of his time. It also makes him feel entirely modern. While many people today embrace intellectual freedom in a slightly defiant or arrogant way, Seneca's approach was different: he embraced intellectual freedom out of *humility*. In other words, he realized that human knowledge is limited and uncertain. He realized that, over the centuries, new discoveries will allow us to understand the world and the universe much more deeply. Because scientific understanding evolves, we need to be open-minded. Also, through critical thinking, we ourselves can contribute to the expansion of human knowledge. As he notes, we and future ages will add knowledge to what we have inherited from those who lived before us.[19] For example, writing about scientific discovery, Seneca observes:

> There will come a day when careful research over a long period will bring to light discoveries that are now hidden. A single lifetime, even one devoted entirely to astronomy, is not enough for the investigation of such great matters. . . . A time will come when our descendants will be amazed that we did not know such obvious facts.[20]

As he beautifully describes it, earlier thinkers "opened the way" for future discoveries rather than having exhausted the possibilities of human knowledge.[21] For Seneca, this applied as much to Stoicism as it did to astronomy and other sciences. Because Stoicism is a philosophy and not a religion, it's based on arguments, not beliefs. If you find Stoicism's arguments to be credible, by finding ways to test them, perhaps you'll find it to be useful as a philosophy of life. But a real Stoic would never ask you to take anything on faith. Maybe that's one reason why Stoic philosophy appeals to many people today who classify themselves as secular humanists.

Not surprisingly, Seneca, as an independent thinker, was sometimes critical of the earlier Stoics. For example, Seneca pointed out problems in some arguments of Zeno, the school's founder. He also didn't hesitate to criticize the logic of Chrysippus (c. 279–c. 206 BC), one of the most influential early Stoics, as being overly abstract and lacking in force.[22] For Seneca, being a philosopher means that a person is a critical thinker and not just a believer. While he mostly followed and agreed with the earlier Stoics, he wrote, "I also allow myself to make new discoveries, alterations, and to reject things when needed. I agree with them, but I'm not subservient."[23]

While very few people have noticed this, Seneca *did* extend Stoic thought in significant ways. He carried it forward by combining it with his own profound insights into human psychology and human motivations. Earlier Stoics understood that false beliefs lead to psychological suffering. But Seneca was the first Stoic to explain, in much greater depth, how those false beliefs are assimilated through socialization and social conditioning.

In a very memorable passage, Seneca explains that he will walk in the footsteps of his predecessors while remaining open to new discoveries:

I will indeed use the old road, but if I discover one that is shorter and more smooth to travel, I'll open up a new path. Those who made these discoveries before us are not our masters but our guides. Truth lies open to all—it has not been monopolized. And there is still much to discover for those who will come after us.[24]

STOIC PERSISTENCE: "BECOMING INVINCIBLE"

There are a thousand cases of persistence overcoming every obstacle: nothing is difficult when the mind decides to endure.

—Seneca, *On Anger* 2.12.4

Let's imagine that you understand yourself and your capabilities. You've surveyed the project or career you want to pursue, and everything looks good. It seems to be a perfect fit for your talents and abilities. But then when you press ahead, the project fails.

While the Stoics advocated patience and endurance, I've learned there are times when moving on to something else might be the best rational choice. Moving on could be another way to show persistence, another way to turn adversity into something positive, or might be justified by other reasons. Being persistent doesn't mean you have to be a masochist, pounding your head against the same wall, day after day. Similarly, it doesn't mean that it's virtuous or a good idea to keep pursuing something that might not even be in your best long-term interests. Being persistent means that you keep moving forward or "making progress" in general. The specifics will always vary on a case-by-case basis.

Endurance, for the Stoics, was an essential human quality.

Seneca wrote that "even after a poor harvest, one should sow seed again; often, what was lost to poor soil due to continued barrenness has been made good by one year's fertility." Similarly, "After a shipwreck, sailors try the sea again. . . . If we were forced to give up everything that causes trouble, life itself would stop moving forward."[25]

The Stoics believed that nothing external can harm a wise person who possesses virtue, as long as his or her virtue stays intact. Seneca wrote a long work on this, which you can still read. It's now called *On the Constancy of the Wise Person*, but it was initially titled *On How the Wise Person Receives Neither Injury Nor Insult*.[26] Being invincible doesn't mean that a Stoic isn't vulnerable in a physical sense. As Seneca pointed out, even a Stoic sage can be beaten, lose a limb, or experience extreme physical pain. For a Stoic, those would be unfortunate events but not an injury. The only way to really *injure* a Stoic would be to damage his virtue, goodness, or character.

To illustrate persistence, Seneca uses the example of someone at the Olympic games who wears out an opponent through sheer patience. (The Latin word *patientia* means "endurance.") Similarly, in terms of mental endurance, the wise person, through long training, acquires the patience to wear out, or simply ignore, any attack on his character. Epictetus also uses an analogy from athletic competition. He explains that even if you should falter in an athletic match, no one can prevent you from standing up again and resuming the fight. Even if you should fail at that particular match, you can continue to train and enter the contest again. Then, if you should finally win the victory, it would be as though you had never given up.[27] Sometimes, just being able to keep making progress is a huge victory in itself.

Stoics, like everyone else, will experience adversity and misfortune. What make Stoics invincible is that they don't give up.

Stoics will make the best of whatever circumstances are at hand, even amid failure, disaster, or financial difficulties. If knocked to the ground, Stoics will stand up, brush themselves off, keep training, and keep moving forward.

HOW TO CONTRIBUTE TO SOCIETY

The Romans loved a question that originally came from the Greek philosophical schools. They restated it like this: What is better—a life devoted to serving the Roman government or a life of leisure, devoted to philosophy?

Epicurus had said that a wise person should avoid taking political office if at all possible, since that would threaten a person's mental tranquility. By contrast, the early Greek Stoics said that a wise person should hold political office unless it was impossible, because politics gives the philosopher a way to contribute to society.[28]

Of course, for us today the actual situation is far more complex and nuanced than this kind of simple black-and-white dichotomy. During ancient times, one of the surest ways to contribute to society was by following a political career. It could also be a road to wealth. But today, politics is hardly the only way one can engage in public service. In some cases, it might even be one of the *worst* ways to contribute to the world by wasting your time trying to repair a dysfunctional system. There's also a big difference between working as a government clerk somewhere today and being a chief adviser to the Roman emperor in Seneca's time.

Like us today, Seneca rejected the ancient, black-and-white view of how someone could contribute to society. Like us today, he took a far more nuanced view. While Seneca involved himself in politics like a good Stoic, it sometimes feels as though he was continually advising his friends, through his various writings, that they should seek out retirement from their official government positions and study philosophy instead.

Ironically, while the early Greek Stoics said that a philosopher should participate in politics, none of them actually did. But as Seneca points out, the founders of the Stoa did advance laws, but not just for one state. Instead, they guided "all of humanity," serving people not only in their own time, but "the people of all nations, both present and future."[29] As Seneca writes, "Of course, it is required that we benefit others—many if possible, but if not, a few; and if not a few, then those nearest to us; and if not those nearest, then ourselves. For when we make ourselves useful to others, we engage in public service."[30]

Seneca believed that a Stoic sage would not participate in politics just in any commonwealth or under any situation.[31] If a situation was beyond hope, what would be the use? Also, if a sage decided to pursue a life of leisure instead, he or she would then work to benefit society or posterity through other means.[32] In fact, Seneca saw his own life and work in a similar way. He almost certainly regretted the time he had spent working for Nero and wanted to make things right while he was still alive. As Seneca wrote to Lucilius,

> I am working for later generations, writing down some ideas that may benefit them. There are certain healthy counsels, like the prescription of useful medicines, which I'm now putting into writing. . . . I'm pointing others to the right path, which I found late in life, when I grew tired from going astray.[33]

Significantly, Seneca told Lucilius that his current work was now writing for future generations—writing, in fact, *for us*. He believed this forward-looking work was far more important than anything he could have been doing in the Roman Senate or in the corrupt social and political sphere of his time.

Seneca had an incredible level of confidence in his work. He had no doubt that his writings would find readers far in the future. "I will find favor with future generations," he wrote. Seneca even suggested to Lucilius that he would take Lucilius's name along with his for the ride, preserving it for future readers.[34] Astonishingly, Seneca was fully correct in making this incredibly bold prediction. Today, twenty centuries later, Seneca's *Letters to Lucilius* is among the top-selling works of ancient philosophy. As he confided to his friend, "A person who just thinks of his contemporaries is born for only a few. Many thousands of years will come, and many thousands of peoples: look toward them too."[35]

Whether you are working for those closest to you now or working for future generations, both approaches are worthy of admiration. Seneca shows us that there are countless ways we can *all* contribute to society, whether benefiting one or many. Regardless of our individual skills and inclinations, there's a way open for everyone.

CHAPTER 11

Living Fully Regardless of Death

How long I might live is not up to me, but *how* I live is within my control.

—Seneca, *Letters* 93.7

To live a long life, you need Fate; but to live well depends on your character.

—Seneca, *Letters* 93.2

THE ULTIMATE TEST OF CHARACTER

"Wherever I turn, I see signs of my old age," Seneca wrote to Lucilius. Seneca had just arrived at his villa outside of Rome, where he was having a conversation with his property manager about the high cost of maintaining the disintegrating old building. But Seneca then explained, "My estate manager told me it was not *his* fault: he was doing everything possible, but the country home was old. And this villa was built under my supervision! What will my future look like if stonework of my own age is already crumbling?"[1]

At that time, Seneca was in his late sixties, and he was starting to feel the aches and pains of old age. But he also found old age to be pleasurable. However, the older you get, the more challenging things become. Extreme old age, he said, is like a lasting illness you never recover from; and when the body really declines, it's like a ship that starts springing leaks, one after another.

Where I currently live, in Sarajevo, I see extremely old people, who are quite close to death, on an almost daily basis. It seems that some of my neighbors—thin, frail, and bent over, often walking with a cane at a snail's pace over the old stone streets—could drop over and expire at any moment. That said, seeing extremely elderly people out and about is an inspiring and heartfelt experience for me. First of all, it's lovely to see people who have lived for so long, often against challenging odds, and it's impossible to see them without feeling a great sense of tenderness for them. Second, they are a timely reminder of my own mortality. It's also very different from what I remember seeing in the United States.

Unlike many other countries, the United States has accomplished a world-class disappearing act when it comes to keeping older adults (and any other reminders of death) out of sight and out of mind. With its shiny glass and steel buildings, shopping malls, and spread-out suburbs, the American landscape has been sterilized and artificially "cleaned up" in such a way that extremely old people are rarely seen on public display. But here in a historic European city with ancient stone buildings that go back centuries, and well-established neighborhoods with cobblestone streets, extremely old people, hobbling along, are a happy part of daily life. They remind me that life is not without extreme struggle. And when people die, which can happen at any age, the local religious communities post death notices, with photos of the deceased, in local neighborhoods all over town. It's another nice custom that reminds us of being mortal.

A Stoic wants to live well—and living well means dying well, too. A Stoic lives well through having a good character, and death is the final test of it. While every death will be a bit different, the Roman Stoics believed that a good death would be characterized by mental tranquility, a lack of complaining, and gratitude for the life we've been given. In other words, as the final act of living, a good death is characterized by acceptance and gratitude. Also, having a real philosophy of life, and having worked on developing a sound character, allows a person to die without any feelings of regret.[2]

Seneca frequently thought and wrote about death. Some of this must have been due to his poor health. Because he suffered from tuberculosis and asthma from a young age, he must have sensed the certainty and nearness of his own death throughout his entire life. In Letter 54 he describes, in graphic detail, a recent asthma attack that nearly killed him. But much earlier, probably in his twenties, he was so sick, and so near death, that he thought about ending his own life, to finally stop the suffering. He didn't follow through on that, fortunately, out of love for his father. As he writes,

> I often felt the urge to end my life, but the old age of my dear father held me back. For while I thought that I could die bravely, I knew he could not bear the loss bravely. And so I commanded myself to live. Sometimes it's an act of courage just to keep living.[3]

For a Stoic (and for other ancient philosophers, too), *memento mori*—contemplating our inevitable death—was an essential philosophical exercise, and one that comes with unexpected benefits. As an anticipation of future adversity (see chapter 6), memento mori allows us to prepare for death, and helps remove our fears of death. It also encourages us to take our current lives more seriously, because we realize they're limited. As I've discovered in a practical sense, reflecting on my own death—and the inevitable death of those dear to me—has had a totally unexpected and powerful benefit: feeling a more profound sense of gratitude for the time we still have together.

MEMENTO MORI: REMEMBERING DEATH

The Latin phrase *memento mori* literally means "remember that you have to die." Over the centuries, scholars often would keep a symbolic memento mori image in their study, like a skull, as a reminder of their own mortality.

In the world of philosophy, the model of someone dying well, without an ounce of fear, was Socrates. Imprisoned on trumped-up charges for corrupting the youth of Athens, Socrates was detained for thirty days before facing his death sentence of drinking hemlock poison. At the time of his death in 399 BC, Socrates was around seventy years old. If he had wished, he could have very easily escaped prison, with his friends' help, and then set up life elsewhere in Greece. But it would have gone against everything he believed in. Also, escaping would have permanently damaged his reputation. Since one of Socrates's main goals was to improve society, that implied he should follow society's laws, even if he had been treated unjustly.

This allowed Socrates thirty final days to meet with his friends and his students to continue their philosophical discussions. He had challenged the morality of those who called for his death with a very memorable line: "If you kill me," he said, "you will not harm me so much as yourselves."[4] This thought was much appreciated by the later Stoics, since, in their view, nothing can harm the character of a wise person. During his last meeting with his students, right before his death, Socrates discussed and questioned the possibility of an afterlife. He also said, memorably, that "philosophy is a preparation for death," which was probably the real beginning of the memento mori tradition (at least for philosophers). When his final conversation was complete, Socrates drank the hemlock, and he peacefully passed away, surrounded by his students.[5]

According to Seneca, the philosopher Epicurus said, "Rehearse for death," which is a practice Seneca himself greatly encouraged. For Seneca and the other Roman Stoics, death was "the master fear," and once someone learns how to overcome it, little else remains fearful either.

The Stoic philosopher Epictetus told his students that when you kiss your child goodnight, you should remind yourself that your child could die tomorrow. While it is literally true that your child *could* die tomorrow, many modern readers recoil at the idea of even contemplating such a thought. However, that might be a measure of their reluctance to accept the inevitability of death, or a way of repressing the fact that death can arrive unexpectedly, at any moment. As someone who personally uses this practice, I can tell you that it's perfectly harmless, once you get past any initial discomfort. The huge benefit it brings is the greater sense of gratitude you experience with your loved ones. When you perform this practice, you consciously realize that someday, which nobody can predict, will be your last time together—so you experience much greater gratitude for the time you spend together *now*. As Seneca wisely recommended, let us greedily enjoy our friends and our loved ones now, while we still have them.[6]

WHAT IS IT LIKE emotionally to contemplate your own death or the death of a close family member? I've been experimenting with this for some time now and can report only positive results. That's because, when I think of the mortality of a loved one and the fact that all of our time together is by definition limited, it improves the quality of my life. It makes me feel a much deeper sense of appreciation for all the time we are together. If you don't remember that your time is limited and finite, you are much more likely to take things for granted.

I most often remember death when I'm with my son, Benjamin, seven and a half as I write. That's a delightful age because he's very playful and now capable of having fun conversations. We're also starting to talk about philosophical things.

Of course, it's impossible for most children of his age to grasp the gravity or finality of death, because most of them have never had any firsthand experience of losing a loved one. Children live in a kind of psychological Golden Age, in which all their needs seem magically provided for. Since they live in a protected sphere, most haven't yet been exposed to the more challenging aspects of life.

Because of that, I've been trying to teach Benjamin a little bit about death and the fact that daddy, mommy, and he will someday die. This effort is a bit of basic Stoic training for a kid, and I'm curious if it might be possible to increase his appreciation for the limited time we have together, even at such a young age? At the very least, I hope it will greatly reduce the level of shock he experiences when someone close to him does die, because he'll be expecting it.

The other day, we were driving home after feasting on some fast food, and Benjamin spoke to me about God for the first time in his life. With a boyish sense of delight, he explained to me, "God has some amazing powers, like being able to see and hear everything. But his greatest superpower is that he's invisible!"

I chuckled at his use of the word "superpower," which made God sound like a superhero, just like Spider-Man! But laughter aside, he had opened up the doorway to speak about some profound issues, so I brought up the topic of death.

"Benjamin," I asked, "do you know that, someday, mommy, daddy, and you are going to die?"

"Yes," he replied.

"I'm almost sixty," I explained, "so I could live another twenty years."

"I don't think you'll live quite *that* long," he said. "But maybe something like that." (Thank you, Benjamin! We'll just have to see how things go.)

Then I asked, "Did you know that *you* could die at any time?"

He said, "I don't think I'll die anytime soon."

"But," I replied, "you *could*. This is not something in our control. You are young, so you could live for a very long time. But since we're driving in a car, we could be in a car crash five minutes from now, and we could both be killed instantly. So even if you're very, very young, you can die at any time. If you stay healthy, the chances that you'll live a long life go up. But in the end, when we die is not under our control."

Benjamin nodded and seemed to understand. And fortunately, we arrived home safely a few minutes later.

———

THAT WAS A FEW days ago. Yesterday, I picked up Benjamin at school. He filed out of the school building with a few other kids his age, all wearing facemasks. I was wearing one too.

As of this writing, it's early 2021, during the first year of the

Covid-19 global pandemic. A new wave of infections is now sweeping across Europe, and cases here are at an all-time high. The World Health Organization recently announced that the coming death rate from Covid-19 could now be five times higher than what Europe experienced during the first wave. It certainly *could* happen—who knows? What I do know is that Stoicism can help us face death calmly and with emotional equilibrium, so it's an ideal philosophy for these uncertain times.

After I picked up Benjamin from school, we had to run a few errands on foot, wearing our masks. As we crossed a beautiful, busy street in the old part of Sarajevo, Benjamin slipped his little hand into mine for safety. Crossing a street here can be quite dangerous for adults, not to mention for children.

One of the Stoic practices I learned from Seneca is to treat each day as though it might be my last. Because of that, I ask Benjamin each day, "Do you know that I love you?" He always says, "Yes," and I ask him the question for one reason: if it should really be my last day, I'd like him to know that.

Now at age seven Benjamin has become skilled at expressing his affection. As we walk down the street hand in hand, I can literally feel the love streaming between us, hand to hand between two living beings. Having a child has taught me the beauty of *philostorgia*, a word the Stoics used, which means "family love."

Some people have found Epictetus to be a bit morbid or forbidding for teaching his students to remember that their children are mortal. On the contrary, as I hold Benjamin's hand and we walk down the street, I have a totally different experience. The Stoic practice of remembering our mortality makes me even more grateful for this time we have together. It makes my heart open more widely.

OVERCOMING THE MASTER FEAR

First, free yourself from the fear of death . . . then free
yourself from the fear of poverty.

—Seneca, *Letters* 80.5

In Seneca's philosophy death is "the master fear" because it's usually the worst outcome anyone can think of. Let's imagine that
you're a psychologist, and your client is afraid that something
terrible is going to happen to him or her. You might then say,
"Okay, let's imagine that *does* happen. What's the worst thing
that could happen *next*?"

If you keep asking the same question over and over, to figure
out how bad things could actually get, then, ultimately, your
client will respond, "And then I could die." Since death is termi-
nal, by definition, it's hard to imagine anything worse happen-
ing after that!

In this way, we can see how death stands as "the master
fear." Based on this insight, Seneca and the other Roman Stoics
thought that once we can rid ourselves from the fear of death,
everything else becomes so much easier. With the fear of death
out of the way, other fears lose their power, too.

Overcoming the fear of death, then, is essential to becoming
free. As Seneca writes,

Anyone who dies with the same contentment he had at
birth has become wise. But as it is, we tremble as the danger approaches: our minds fail us and our faces grow pale.
Tears fall but accomplish nothing. What is more dis-
graceful than being overwhelmed with worry at the very
threshold of tranquility?[7]

Epictetus and Marcus Aurelius saw things similarly. As Epictetus noted, the source of all evils and cowardice for human beings "is not death, but rather the fear of death."[8] Seneca said that for someone who has overcome the fear of death, it is possible to let go of life contentedly, with composure, while others feel terror. But those who fear death "clutch and cling to life, even as those who are carried down a rushing stream clutch and cling to briars and sharp rocks."[9]

It's for this reason, Seneca maintains, that death is the ultimate test of character. As he explains to Lucilius (but speaking about himself), someone can say and believe anything, and act bravely while they're alive. But at the point of death, it will become clear whether or not their words were true. At the time of his death, Seneca says, it will become clear "what progress I have really made." In this way, death will pass judgment on us and reveal our authentic characters. He writes,

> Discussions, learned seminars, sayings from philosophers, and high-brow conversations—all of these do not reveal the mind's true strength. Even the most cowardly people speak boldly. What you have actually achieved will only be clear when you take your last breath. I welcome this test and do not fear the judgment.[10]

How, then, to overcome the fear of death? Since the Stoics were philosophers, they tried to look at death rationally. They then presented rational arguments to deconstruct whatever fears might be associated with it. Some of these arguments are very briefly listed below. They are explained more fully in the writings of Seneca and the other Roman Stoics:

1. *Death is just a natural part of life.* When we were born, we

entered into an agreement that, one day, we will die. Death is just a natural part of life. Because of that, and because life and nature are good, we should accept death without fear and without complaint. When writing his letters, Seneca visited his old friend and teacher, Demetrius, an Epicurean philosopher who was in the process of dying. As Demetrius explained to Seneca, the only thing people fear about death is its uncertainty. Otherwise, Demetrius said,

> Someone who is unwilling to die never wished to live, for life is given to us with the condition it will end. . . . Death is a necessity, distributed equally and unavoidably to all. Who can complain about being subject to the same condition as everyone else? The most important element of equality is impartiality.[11]

Put another way, death is not a punishment but merely a consequence of being alive. And since it's a law of nature, applied equally to everyone who lives, there is nothing to fear.

2. *Regardless of what happens at death, we will be fine either way.* In the words of Seneca, "Death either consumes us or sets us free. If we are released, better things remain, since our burden has been removed. But if we are consumed, nothing remains: blessings and evils are removed together." In other words, if the soul is destroyed, there will be nothing left to experience suffering. And if the soul does survive, it will be starting a new adventure in a new form.[12] Whatever may actually happen, neither outcome is harmful.

3. *What is terrible about returning to where you came from?* This is known as "the symmetry argument" and was used by many ancient philosophers. If death is simply nonexistence, when you die you are returning to the same state you were in before you

were born. If this interpretation is correct, the condition that existed before our birth will follow us after death: on either side of life, there is great peace, without any suffering.[13]

When Epicurus famously said, "Death is nothing to us," he wasn't trying to sound superior or look down upon death with contempt. He was merely referring to this argument. Death will be nothing to us, in his view, because there will be no "us" left to suffer from it.[14]

The Stoics believed that the soul, or our mental and biological life-force, is material. Because of this, they left open the possibility that the soul might survive in some way after our physical death, or that it might survive for a period of time. Alternately, it might merge with the intelligence and life-force of the entire universe. Seneca and Marcus Aurelius were not sure if this was likely, but they were both open-minded about the possibility. In any case, regardless of what actually happens, none of the Stoics believed that there was anything harmful in death, even in the worst-case scenario that we are simply annihilated.

WHAT MAKES LIFE WORTH LIVING IN THE FIRST PLACE?

The goodness of life does not depend on life's length but upon the use we make of it.

—Seneca, *Letters* 49.10

A Stoic is attempting to make *progress*, and progress is a journey. For Seneca, there is a definite destination point on that journey: becoming virtuous or "a completed" human being. In Stoicism, this involves developing our character and rationality so that we can understand and possess what is truly good in life. In addition to having developed a solid character, when someone reaches that final destination, human freedom, tranquility, and lasting joy result (see chapter 14). At that point, for Seneca, life is truly complete, and one lives in the fullest way possible. Then a person has attained what Seneca calls "the happy life"—a state of deep and lasting well-being. Even though I shy away from drawing parallels between different traditions, it's difficult to read Seneca's ideas about this state without thinking about the words "enlightenment" or "liberation" in Eastern traditions.

Once someone has attained the happy life, his or her life is truly complete, regardless of its length. For Seneca, this means that once we have achieved true happiness, or a blessed state of mind, living longer will not make us any happier. While living longer won't make us more content, those extra days or years will be like icing on the cake of an already happy life. As he writes, a chief quality of living a virtuous or happy life is that "it doesn't need the future and doesn't count its days." That's because "in whatever time it has, it enjoys a timeless good."[15] For Seneca, finding true happiness is to experience something timeless, which cannot be surpassed; it is "the summit," the whole point of being alive.

As Seneca repeatedly stresses over a dozen times in different writings, it's the quality of one's life that matters, not its quantity or its length. In my favorite description of this, he says life is like a play: it's not the length of the play that matters, but the quality of the performance.[16]

For Seneca, obtaining a virtuous character is what matters in life, not life's duration. To achieve the happy life is to live fully, regardless of its length. By contrast, he points out, many elderly people have simply "existed" for a long time but never truly lived.

Some people, unfortunately, end up dying before they have even started to live fully.

Seneca gives an example of this. He's writing to Lucilius about a mutual friend of theirs, a philosopher named Metronax, who died quite young, in the prime of his life. But while Metronax died young, he had developed a very fine character. Someone might complain that Metronax died in his prime. But Seneca responds:

> He carried out the duties of a good citizen, a good friend, and a good son. He didn't fall short in any respect. While his lifetime was incomplete, his life itself was perfect. Another man might seem to live for eighty years but only *be around* for eighty years—unless by "live" you mean that way in which trees are said to live. I beg you, Lucilius: Let's carry on in this way, so our lives are measured like the most precious objects—not by their size, but by their worth. Let's measure our lives by their performance, not by their duration.[17]

In the end, for Seneca, it's the *quality* of a person's life that allows someone to live fully, not its length.

THE BLESSINGS AND DANGERS OF OLD AGE

> Our good is not merely in living, but in living well. Accordingly, a wise person will live as long as he ought, not as long as he can. . . . He always reflects concerning the quality and not the quantity of his life.
>
> —Seneca, *Letters* 70.4

No one knows how long he or she might live; it's entirely beyond our control. That said, given the significant increases that have taken place in medicine and technology, the chance of someone reaching a ripe old age today, even into their nineties, has increased dramatically since Seneca's time. But with extreme old age come difficulties, like the crumbling stones of Seneca's country villa. At a certain point, an increasingly ancient structure will just collapse, bit by bit. This applies to aging bodies, too.

For Seneca, old age can be a blessing, and it can be one of the most enjoyable times of life. As he writes,

> Let us embrace and love old age. It is full of pleasure if you know how to experience it. Fruits are sweetest when ripe, just before they spoil. Boyhood's charm is greatest at its end. For those devoted to wine, it's the very last drink that delights—the one that puts you under, delivering the final push to inebriation. Every pleasure delays its sweetest moments for last. The most pleasurable time of life is on its downhill slope, but before going over the edge. Even the time spent standing on the outermost edge can have its own pleasures, I believe.[18]

Seneca thought that old age was something to treasure and that old age can be one of the happiest times of life. But there reaches a point where, if you live long enough, a person's life resembles "a lingering death." Perhaps because of their own fear of death, some people believe that life should be preserved at any cost, under any conditions, even if that means keeping a loved one alive unconscious, on a machine, with no hope of recovery. As you might have guessed, Seneca would not have gone along with this approach. He wrote, "What kind of life is a lingering death? Can anyone be found who wishes to waste away amid pains, dying limb by limb, and losing his breath drop by drop, rather than breathing out his last once and for all?"[19]

As Seneca repeatedly noted, "What matters is not how long you live, but how nobly you live,"[20] and being left alone in a hospital room, falling apart limb by limb, is not the noblest way to depart this world. Seneca's philosophy, therefore, has significant implications today for thinking about end-of-life issues.

Both the Greek and the Roman Stoics allowed for suicide under very extreme conditions, which were much more likely to exist in the ancient world than they are today. But suicide aside, there's no question that Seneca would strongly advocate for *euthanasia*, or having a "good death," rather than living on for years in an incapacitated state. As he writes, "Few have passed through extreme old age to death without impairment, and many have lain inert, unable to use their bodies. In this case, the cruelest loss in life is the loss of the right to end it."[21]

Seneca didn't think that old age was something one should yearn for, but he didn't think it was something one should reject, either. In the end, since every life is different, it could be a blessing or a hindrance. As he wrote, "It's pleasant to be with yourself as long as possible—if you've made yourself into someone worth spending time with."[22]

Despite that, there was a definite point where Seneca said he would personally draw the line. As he wrote to Lucilius,

I will not abandon old age as long as it preserves my whole self, by which I mean the whole of my better part. But if it begins to shatter my mind and destroy parts of it—if I can no long *live*, but only breathe—then I will jump free from that crumbling and collapsing edifice.[23]

That makes perfect sense because, for a Stoic, merely being able to keep on breathing without having one's mental faculties—being able to think, to know, and to appreciate—wouldn't be living at all.

LIVING EACH DAY AS IF IT'S YOUR LAST

> I am aiming to live each day as if it is a complete lifetime.
>
> —Seneca, *Letters* 61.1

Everyone has heard the saying, "Live one day at a time." Whether or not that saying goes back to Seneca, it certainly goes back to him in spirit.

As Seneca repeatedly points out, people become anxious by worrying about the future. But that's because they haven't yet "found themselves" enough to fully live in, and to deeply enjoy, the present moment.

Seneca suggests that we should live each day as "a complete life," as if it's our last day of being alive. For Seneca, this idea becomes a brilliant inner practice that ties together many different themes in his work: the fullness of the happy life, the importance of living in the present moment, memento mori, and freeing ourselves from all anxiety, including the fear of death.

As Steve Jobs once said in a speech to college students,

> When I was seventeen, I read a quote that went something like: "If you live each day as if it was your last, someday you'll most certainly be right." It made an impression on me, and since then, for the past thirty-three years, I have looked in the mirror every morning and asked myself: "If

today were the last day of my life, would I want to do what I am about to do today? And whenever the answer has been "No" for too many days in a row, I know I need to change something.[24]

Sadly, we'll never know whether a quotation from Seneca ultimately inspired this daily meditation as practiced by Steve Jobs. But regardless of that, it's undoubtedly a good practice. As a daily meditation, it encourages a person to reflect on his or her life as a whole, including the quality of one's life at that very moment.

Seneca fully believed that each day *could* be our last. He thought we should take our impending death into account without any hint of anxiety, but with happy acceptance, even if that death should arrive today. In practice, this means that we should not leave anything important undone when we go to bed at night. "Let us compose our thoughts," he wrote, "as if we've reached the end. Let us postpone nothing. Let's settle our accounts with life every day."[25] This practice encourages one to take nothing for granted, to look back on one's life with gratitude, and it reminds us to live as fully as possible, according to our deepest values.

For Seneca, being able to go to sleep with gratitude, thinking life might truly be over, was a mark of someone who had lived a complete life. But then, if we should wake up in the morning, "let us receive it gladly," and accept another day with gratitude. "The happiest and most cheerful possessor of himself," Seneca wrote, "awaits the next day without anxiety. Anyone who says, 'I have completed living,' rises each morning with a profit, having gained an extra day."[26]

CHAPTER 12

Give Grief Its Due

Tears fall no matter how we try to hold them back, and
shedding them relieves the mind.

—Seneca, *Letters* 99.15

LET THE TEARS FLOW

The early Greek Stoics held an unusually harsh and strange theory: if a Stoic sage or wise person lost a close friend to death, he
would not weep over his friend's death because such emotions
would originate from false opinions. Seneca rejected this view
strongly and thought that tears of grief are wholly appropriate.
He wrote, "I know that some men can be found whose wisdom is
harsh rather than brave who say that a sage will never feel grief,"
which he found to be inhuman.[1] Elsewhere Seneca wrote, "I do
not remove the sage from the general category of mankind, nor
do I deny him a sense of pain as if he were some kind of rock
with no feelings at all."[2]

For Seneca, the tears we experience when we lose a loved one do not come from faulty judgments. They are the result of natural human feelings at the deepest level of our being. In other words, they are instinctual. In one of his letters, Seneca explains how he wept over the death of a close friend. It's quite safe to assume that Seneca also wept over the death of his only child, a baby who died only twenty days before Seneca was banished to the island of Corsica by the Emperor Claudius. He describes the child dying in the arms of its grandmother—Seneca's mother, Helvia—as she showered the baby with kisses. Marcus Aurelius also lost many children to death, and he is known to have wept in public over the death of his friends.

Seneca believed that when we weep, it's just a natural, physiological response, a natural human feeling (see chapter 4). Because grief and weeping are instinctual, they're not based on faulty beliefs or judgments as negative emotions are. Seneca was well aware that even animals mourn the loss of their offspring. Mother birds experience distress if they return to their nest and discover a missing egg. Even on an interspecies level, dogs often mourn the loss of a beloved master when that person passes away, in the same way people mourn the loss of a pet.

Seneca took grief seriously. In fact, he wrote five separate works consoling friends and family members who had lost loved ones.[3] And in these works, he offers us valuable advice about how to grieve well, how to lessen the sting of grief before it appears, and how to transform grief into something better—happy memories of those we have lost.

Seneca's basic approach to grief is that we should give grief its due. In other words, we should allow our natural tears to flow freely, but never force them, and never make our grief appear to be more intense just because we are in the presence of others.

For Seneca, there are different kinds of tears. *Tears of shock* occur when we first learn of the bitter loss of a loved one and when we see his or her lifeless body, perhaps at a funeral. We have no control over these tears. It's as if they are pushed out of us by nature itself, as the pain of grief causes a person to gasp deeply and shakes the entire body. These kinds of tears are involuntary and beyond our control.[4]

Another kind of tears, which we might call *tears of joy*, appear when we sweetly remember someone we've lost. We think of the person's pleasant voice, the happy conversations we once had, and his or her noteworthy actions. Unlike the harsher tears of shock, these fears are not forced on us, beyond our will, but spring from the happy and sweet memories we recall.[5]

Sometimes, even for a Stoic sage, tears sometimes just well up on their own. When this happens, it's not a negative emotion but simply a mark of a person's humanity. Similarly, Seneca points out, it's possible to experience tears when one feels tranquil and at peace.[6]

FINDING A GOLDEN MEAN

Don't let your eyes be dry when you have lost a friend, and don't let them overflow. We may weep, but we must not wail.

—Seneca, *Letters* 63.1

Even grieving has its own kind of moderation.

—Seneca, *Consolation to Marcia* 3.4

For Seneca, because we're human beings who are deeply bonded with those we love, it's only natural that we will feel grief and shed tears at losing a loved one. It's cathartic too. All that grief cannot be held inside; it needs to be released. Crying is a complex phenomenon, and is not fully understood. But on one level, we now know that crying releases oxytocin and endorphins. These chemicals help to relieve pain and, as mood enhancers, make people feel better and calm.[7]

Seneca had no problem with grief and falling tears, as long as they remained genuine or natural. But some people increase their grief beyond what nature requires. And some people push their grief to the point of madness. For example, little is known about Marcia, the first person Seneca ever wrote to, helping her to overcome her grief. But Seneca wrote to her because she was still in a deep state of despair over losing her son, who had died three years earlier. While Seneca believed that Marcia possessed courage and a strong character, he felt that she had kept the initial shock of her grief alive to the point where it had hardened into a severe kind of illness. As he put it, "You hug and hold onto your grief, keeping it alive in place of your son."[8]

Seneca believed that we should seek some kind of moderation in grief and that it's unnatural for extreme grief to be prolonged for lengthy periods. Seneca also objected to how people sometimes make their grief appear to be worse than it is when displaying it in public. As he told Lucilius, let's allow our tears to flow, "but not compel them to do so. Let us weep according to our real emotion, but not in imitating others. Let's not add anything to our real mourning, or make it greater by copying the example of others. The public display of grief demands more than genuine grief requires."[9]

Seneca noted that, when surrounded by others, people often lament more loudly, so others can hear them. But once the onlookers depart, their own grief declines, since it's no longer on show. Since Seneca valued authenticity, he believed that our sorrow should be genuine, or based on what we and nature require. It should never become a form of acting in front of an audience.

Because of this, Seneca sought a kind of moderation in grief. We don't want our grief to be lacking in love or genuine feeling, but we don't want it to become a form of acting—or, even worse, to resemble a form of madness. When we've lost someone close to us, being overwhelmed continuously by grief can become an unhealthy form of self-indulgence. Alternatively, feeling no sorrow would be insensitive and inhumane. Even in grief, we should seek a balance between reason and genuine affection.[10] As Seneca recommends to his friend Polybius, who lost his brother,

> Let reason maintain a mean that doesn't resemble a lack of love or a kind of madness, and let it keep us in a state of mind that is caring but not anguished. Let your tears flow, but also let them stop. Let sighs be drawn from your deepest breast, but also let them find an end. Govern your mind so that you may win approval both from the wise and from your own family.[11]

In the end, it's natural that grief will dissipate given time. But it's even better if we can grow out of grief, rather than just grow weary of it. As Seneca advised Lucilius, "It's better that you abandon grief, rather than have grief abandon you."[12]

REDUCING THE SHOCK OF GRIEF

> Does anyone weep over something he knew to be inevitable? To complain that someone has died is to complain that person was mortal.
>
> —Seneca, *Letters* 99.8

It isn't possible to prevent grief from arising when we lose a loved one. But it is possible to minimize the shock of grief by realizing in advance that everyone we know is mortal and that, one day, our paths will part for good. Seneca went so far as to suggest that when someone gives birth to a child, it's good to think, "I have given birth to a mortal."[13] Rather than being a heartless thought, it's just a truth about human nature.

Knowing that someone is in the process of dying reduces the shock or surprise of losing them dramatically. When I was twenty-seven, my dad, who had led a remarkable life, was hospitalized. It was also clear that his end was near. About a month later, he died, on December 31. As I used to say, "He went out with the old year." If he had lived just six more days, he would have been seventy-five years old. At the time, I experienced a deep sense of grief. But since everyone was expecting his demise, the initial shock was far less intense than it would have been if he had simply died with no warning.

As Seneca notes, "Those who anticipate the coming of suffering remove its force when it arrives."[14] It's difficult, though, to imagine that those who are young, in the prime of life, or even much younger than us, might suddenly die at any moment. That's why it's helpful to remind ourselves from time to time that it could take place. Even Seneca failed to follow his own advice about this with his close friend Annaeus Serenus, who died at a young age. As Seneca confided to Lucilius, "I wept so excessively for my dear friend." That's because Serenus was so much younger, and, as Seneca said, "I had never imagined it possible for his death to precede mine." He concluded, "Let us continually think as much about our own mortality as about all of those we love. . . . Whatever can happen at any time can happen today."[15]

One of my favorite Stoic ideas is that everything we have,

or believe that we possess, is just "on loan" from the universe. *Everything*. And one day, all those things will need to be returned. Seneca brings this up in his message to Marcia, who was still experiencing extreme grief over the death of her son, as though it had just happened yesterday. Seneca tells Marcia that "All the extraordinary things that glitter around us," including children, honors, wealth, and everything that depends on uncertain chance, "do not belong to us but are only on loan."[16] Not one of them is a permanent gift. Seneca explains further,

> We must love them with the awareness that we have no promise we will have them forever, nor any promise we will have them for long. We must remind ourselves often that we should love things as if they are sure to leave us, or that they are leaving already. Take what Fortune gives, but realize that it comes with no guarantee.[17]

Epictetus said, "Never say that 'I have lost something'; only say, 'I have given it back'"—even if that is a loved one.[18] As Seneca wrote to Polybius, when his brother died, "Let us take joy in what is given to us and let us return it when we are asked."[19] Seneca explained elsewhere that someone who views the world correctly will realize that all his property, and even his life, is a temporary gift of Fortune. He'll then live as if everything were on loan, and he'll be prepared to return those gifts without sorrow when the universe finally reclaims them.[20]

Some readers have wrongly assumed that the Stoics were advocating emotional detachment from those around them by thinking in this way. But nothing could be further from the truth. Knowing that nothing is permanent is just accepting a fact of nature. It has nothing to do with a person's ability to love deeply. Realizing that my loved ones are all impermanent encourages me to treasure them more deeply. It makes me even more grateful for the limited time we have together.[21]

TURNING GRIEF INTO GRATITUDE

Keep remembering but cease to grieve.

—Seneca, *Letters* 99.24

Don't complain about what was taken away, but give thanks for what you were given.

—Seneca, *Consolation to Marcia* 12.2

Seneca has the most brilliant strategy for dispelling grief over the long term. When we lose a loved one, we will certainly grieve for a period. But as that grief begins to fade, we can replace those sad feelings with happy and joyful memories.

Seneca's profound insight is that grief, in a way, is selfish and lacking in gratitude for our loved ones. Rather than being ungrateful and sad, let us be grateful for the wonderful experiences we've had together. As he wrote to a friend who lost an infant son, "Many people do not count how many great blessings they've received and how much joy they've experienced. That is just one reason why your kind of grief is bad: not only is it needless, it is ungrateful too."[22]

He continues,

Do you bury a friendship along with the friend? And why would you mourn him as if he didn't benefit you? Believe me: a large part of those we have loved remains with us, even if chance has removed them. The time that has passed is ours to keep, and nothing is safer than that which was.[23]

Seneca is correct that grief, given time, can be replaced by happy memories. For several years after my father died, I'd feel some seasonal sadness around the time of his death, at the end of each year. It's like there was an empty space where he was supposed to be. Many others who have lost family members have experienced this kind of seasonal sadness too. But that was a long time ago. When I look back at my dad or even his death today, I now feel no grief at all—just a sense of happiness, and a sense of gratitude, for the time we spent together. But when a person's mind is filled with grief and sadness, it's hard to make space for the happy memories and gratitude that would more deeply honor a loved one. Being able to replace grief with gratitude is not just possible; it's crucial for living a happy life.

Seneca says this applies even to people who have lost little children. Their memory can still bring us joy, even if their lives were short. As Seneca tells Marcia, "Your son deserves to make you happy each time you think of him, each time you mention his name—and you will honor him more greatly if you greet his memory cheerfully and with joy, as he used to be greeted while still alive."[24] Rather than grieve, Seneca says, remember all the happy times you spent with your son, and "his boyish, loving caresses."[25]

CHAPTER 13

Love and Gratitude

Anxiety is not appropriate for a grateful mind. On the
contrary, all worry should be dispelled through deep
self-confidence and an awareness of true love.

—Seneca, *On Benefits* 6.42.1

STOIC LOVE AND AFFECTION

As we've seen, the stereotype of Stoics being cold and unfeeling
just isn't true. The Stoics, in fact, took love and affection to be
the primary human emotion. They put love, as an emotion, in
a category all by itself. In Seneca's view, the Stoics had more
love for humanity than any other philosophical school. Love and
affection, they maintained, form the very basis of human society. They realized that parents instinctively love their children.
They also thought that this kind of primary affection could be
extended outward to encompass all of humanity. That is why
Seneca wrote, "Society can only remain healthy through the
mutual protection and love of its parts."[1] Because of this, it's no

exaggeration to say that Stoic ethics is ultimately based on love. The fact that people love one another is an aspect of natural law, which provides a natural basis for human community and society.

As the most humane of the Stoic writers, Seneca frequently mentions the importance of love, affection, and gratitude. But in Seneca's writings, we learn the most about the importance of love through how he speaks about others in his life with kindness and affection. As the classical scholar Anna Lydia Motto noted, "Seneca learned much about love, kindness, and generosity from members of his own family." In his writings, "one detects a deep understanding of the true feeling of love in its different aspects—love for one's family, for one's friends, for one's spouse, for one's fellow men, for one's country."[2]

We all can relate to love as an emotion, but the Roman Stoics stressed a specific kind of love, *philostorgia*. This term could be translated as "family love" or "human affection." This is the kind of love the Stoics applied to humanity as a whole, which is also a form of *philanthropy* or love for all mankind. Marcus Aurelius mentions this kind of love repeatedly. As he reminds himself often, we are born to love others and humanity itself. "Love those people with whom destiny has surrounded you," he wrote, "but love them truly."[3]

Marcus also wrote to express his gratitude to his various teachers. But in a comment Marcus made about one teacher, the philosopher Sextus, he seemed to sum up the entire Stoic attitude toward love and the emotions. Marcus tells us Sextus never showed the slightest sign of anger or any other negative emotion. Instead, "he was totally free of passion (*pathos*) and full of human affection."[4] This, indeed, is the Stoic ideal: to be full of love for others and totally free of violent, negative emotions.

Finally, the Stoics felt that a person should love freely and with generosity, without expecting something in return. In the words of philosopher William O. Stephens, "One can love another without making that love conditional upon its always, or ever, being reciprocated. This is the conviction that love is to be given freely in pure joy with no admixture of sorrow."[5]

STOIC GRATITUDE, ANCIENT AND MODERN

Another Stoic emotion that has been almost entirely overlooked is the natural feeling of gratitude. Gratitude was especially important in Roman culture, and Seneca and the other Roman Stoics stressed the importance of gratitude consistently. Cicero said that "gratitude is not only the greatest virtue, it is the mother of all the rest."[6] Seneca, for his part, wrote that "among our many and great vices, ingratitude is the most common."[7] Seneca wrote a lengthy book, *On Benefits*, which has been called "the first (and, for many centuries, the only) great treatise on gratitude in Western thought."[8] In part, this writing is about the art of giving, appreciating, and returning "benefits" or "favors."

In Seneca's time and before, wealthy Roman patrons had "clients" who would greet them in the morning for benefits or favors—financial, social, or political. They would then walk together through the Forum in Rome. The benefits would often be paid back or returned in some way, so there was an entire social code and cycle that involved giving, receiving with thanks, and returning benefits.[9] This was a kind of glue that held society together, especially among the elite citizens of Rome, but it was not the primary focus of Seneca's writings on gratitude. In fact, in the entire philosophy of gratitude, there was no one who was "as revolutionary and radical as Seneca." That is because, as philosopher Ashraf Rushdy explains, Seneca transformed the way the entire topic of gratitude would be considered by later thinkers. As Rushdy emphasizes, Seneca discussed *all* the kinds of gratitude that would occupy the minds of thinkers following him, including sacred gratitude, cosmic gratitude, secular gratitude, personal gratitude, and more.[10]

As we will see, there are three main types of gratitude, which people have felt for thousands of years. Yet strangely, despite the crucial importance of gratitude in Roman Stoicism, the topic of gratitude in Stoicism has been almost totally ignored.[11]

Love and gratitude go together because they both involve *appreciation*. It would be difficult, if not impossible, to love someone without appreciating him or her. Gratitude, too, is a form of appreciation. The Stoic writer Donald Robertson once gave a talk on "Stoicism and Love," in which he suggested, "It is possible to see Stoicism fundamentally as a philosophy of love."[12] Similarly, we might say, "Appreciation and gratitude frame how a Stoic sees the world." Even though we, and everyone around us, are mortal beings, a Stoic can still relate to them with love, appreciation, and gratitude.[13] While there is nothing mysterious about that, there is another dimension of Stoic gratitude that some readers may find puzzling at first. This "different kind of gratitude" has been called "cosmic" or "nonpersonal" gratitude, and by many other names, because it's not directed toward a specific person.[14]

WHEN I STARTED EXPERIMENTING with Stoic philosophical exercises or meditations, I was surprised to discover that they resulted in feelings of gratitude and appreciation, and have noted some of these instances earlier in this book. For example, when I practiced the "premeditation of future adversity" and imagined my house being destroyed by fire or by an earthquake (chapter 6), it made me feel grateful, once again, for a home that I had become bored with through familiarity. Marcus Aurelius even mentioned this kind of gratitude as a goal of Stoic practice. Rather than seeking out something new, he explained how we could experience happiness by appreciating the things we already have. As he reminded himself, "Don't dream of what you don't already possess. Instead, think about the great blessings you *do* have, for which you feel grateful—and remind yourself of how much they'd be missed if they weren't already yours."[15]

My next experience of gratitude came while practicing memento mori: the Stoic meditation of remembering my own death and the fact that my loved ones are mortal too (chapter 11). Walking down the street with my small son during the peak of the Covid-19 pandemic, both wearing facemasks, feeling the warmth of his hand in my own, I remembered that we are both mortal, and at some point we will be separated for good. But that made me feel a profound sense of gratitude—not just for that very moment of being alive with him, but for whatever remaining time we will have together in the future. By reflecting on our mortality, not only do we treasure life more deeply: it can greatly intensify our feeling of being alive in the present moment.

Another example of Stoic gratitude involved replacing the grief I felt from losing my father with gratitude. I hadn't started reading Seneca yet, but in a natural process over time, my grief evaporated and was replaced by happy memories. I came to feel grateful for the good times we spent together (chapter 12). Seneca recommends this practice to help people overcome grief. In retrospect, if I had consciously focused on gratitude for his life, rather than just letting time do its work, the pain would likely have diminished more quickly.

A further Stoic idea about gratitude is that as we are dying we should be grateful for the life and all the experiences the universe has given us. We'll explore this idea at the end of this chapter.

UNDERSTANDING GRATITUDE

> We should make every effort to be as grateful as possible.
>
> —Seneca, *Letters* 81.19

What makes gratitude interesting is that it's both an emotion and a virtue. Yet, in the words of philosopher Robert Solomon, it's "one of the most neglected emotions and one of the most underestimated of the virtues."[16] Significantly, as he notes, gratitude deals with the way we relate to other people, so it "lies at the very heart of ethics." From a Stoic perspective, this is another way that love and gratitude come together as forms of appreciation: they both make a functioning, ethical society possible. In terms of ethical development, we would not see people who lack either love or gratitude as being virtuous. We would see them as possessing a significant defect in their character. Put another way, without love and gratitude, it's simply impossible to live well. Or as Seneca might have described it, without love and appreciation, it's impossible to live "the happy life."

Throughout the history of modern psychology, psychologists have focused on trying to understand human misery and pathology, even though most people are happy most of the time. In a study from the year 2000, in which people were tested at random, 89 percent were experiencing a state of happiness, while a much smaller percentage was experiencing a state of sadness. The most frequently experienced negative emotion was anxiety.[17] Not surprisingly, according to a 2007 study, happy people live about 14 percent longer than unhappy people.[18]

In recent years, the study of "positive psychology," including the study of gratitude, has emerged as a new field of research. Psychologists like P. C. Watkins have discovered that gratitude is not just "an important facet of emotional well-being." Instead, gratitude "actually *causes* increases in happiness."[19] After years of study, Watkins concluded that "Gratitude enhances well-being because psychologically it *amplifies the good* in one's life." That's "because it clearly identifies who and what is good for individuals."[20] Obviously, the Stoics (and the world's religious traditions) were onto something important by emphasizing the importance of gratitude in daily life. Thousands of years later, psychologists are beginning to catch up by studying gratitude and other positive emotions scientifically.

But what is gratitude, really? At its most basic, gratitude has been described as "the positive recognition of benefits received."[21] It's a feeling of thankfulness or appreciation for receiving something of value, a good or a gift. Many people imagine that you must be thankful *to someone* or *to a person* in order to experience gratitude. And while that's true for some kinds of gratitude, it's not true for *all* kinds of gratitude.

In essence, people experience three main types of gratitude, which I've summarized in figure 8.

1. The first type of gratitude I call *personal* or *civic gratitude* because it's directed at another person. It's the kind of gratitude we experience in a social or civic setting when someone does something nice for us or offers us a gift.

Types of Gratitude	Objects
Personal or Civic	Another Person
Theistic	God or gods
Cosmic, Existential, or Nonpersonal	Nature, the Cosmos, or Existence

Fig 8: Three types of gratitude.

2. The second type of gratitude I call *theistic gratitude* because it is directed at God (or the gods, if you are a polytheist). If you are a religious person—especially if you are Jewish, Christian, or Muslim—this kind of theistic gratitude is very similar to personal gratitude, because those religions view God as *a person*. They also see God as the ultimate giver.

3. The third type of gratitude I call *cosmic, existential,* or *nonpersonal gratitude.* It is different from the first two types of gratitude because it's not directed at a person (like a human or God). Instead, it's directed at nature, the cosmos, or existence itself. Or sometimes it's not directed at anything, but a recognition of blessings received. In a sense, this is a spiritual sense of gratitude, and it was a kind of gratitude the Stoics felt. But it's not directed at a creator God who stands outside the universe. In other words, it's distinct from both personal and theistic gratitude.

Sometimes these different kinds of gratitude can intermingle with one another. For example, every morning, my wife brings a cup of black tea with milk to my bedside table, which I then drink while waking up. (If she doesn't bring me a cup of tea, it means she's upset with me, which always sends an important message!) Of course, when she brings me a cup of tea, I'm very grateful to her as a person, and I always thank her. But then, as I sip the tea, I usually feel other kinds of gratitude, too, which is a perfect way to start the day. Sometimes I feel grateful for the tea and caffeine itself, as my consciousness begins to come into focus. Sometimes I feel thankful for the pleasurable feeling of sitting in such a warm, comfortable bed, and having a solid roof over my head, especially since some people are homeless and forced to sleep outside. Sometimes, I feel grateful for having clean air to breathe. Sometimes I feel grateful for being able to write while drinking my tea. And sometimes, I feel grateful for *all* of those things in a very short period. Besides being grateful to my wife, though, these other kinds of gratitude are not directed at a person. How, then, do we explain these other kinds of gratitude?

If you're a religious person, I hope you won't be upset at me for saying this, but I don't direct my gratitude toward a personal God when drinking my tea. But does that mean I'm an atheist? The answer would be "No." That said, it doesn't mean that I'm a theist either. Personally, I hate being pigeonholed into these kinds of categories. But if I were forced to imprison myself in one of these conceptual boxes, I would probably say: "I'm more of a *pantheist*, like the Stoics were, like Spinoza and Einstein were—and even popular luminaries like Carl Sagan."[22]

Pantheists believe that there is no God "outside" the universe. Instead, they believe that the entire universe is God, including the laws and principles that shape it. Of course, atheism, theism, and pantheism are not scientifically testable concepts. But like Carl Sagan, I find pantheism to be a much more useful *metaphor* than the idea of God as a person who exists outside the cosmos, as someone who drew up a plan for the universe.[23] Certainly, none of the ancient Greek philosophers thought of God in that kind of way.[24] That said, regardless of people's religious beliefs (or lack of beliefs), I can happily get along with anyone, especially if they recognize the importance of love and gratitude. Those are character traits and fundamental human values that should bind all people together, regardless of faith or belief.

A DIFFERENT SENSE OF GRATITUDE

Some people—mainly analytical philosophers (who focus on language) or theologians (who believe in a personal God)—have claimed that it *only* makes sense for someone to be grateful to *a person*: that is, to another human being or to God. In other words, they believe that cosmic or nonpersonal gratitude is not possible. In my view, this is a bit of dubious thinking, which discriminates against people who don't think exactly the same way that the deniers do. It implies that you need to have special, limited beliefs to experience gratitude. It also suggests that certain types of gratitude, which people have experienced for thousands of years, are not intellectually credible but "off-limits."

Seneca believed that human beings should be grateful to both "God" and "Nature." But since the Stoics were pantheists, Seneca carefully pointed out that the terms "God" and "Nature" are *interchangeable*.[25] Pantheism is not atheism, but it isn't theism either. While the idea of God doesn't bother me in the least, I know that religion and the idea of God make some people uncomfortable. So if you're reading through an ancient Stoic text and come across the term "God," you're entirely free to replace that term with the word "Nature" in your mind. No Stoic would fault you for doing so.

Gratitude is a response to generosity, especially to a gift that is freely given. The Persian poet Rumi (1207–1273) found the sun to be a perfect symbol of generosity since, in his words, "its only property is to give and bestow." He wrote, "The sun makes the earth green and fresh and produces various fruits on the trees. Its only function is to give and bestow; it doesn't take anything."[26] Seneca, who wrote around 1,200 years before Rumi, would have agreed with this beautiful metaphor. In fact, Seneca, somewhat amazingly, used it himself. For Seneca and the Stoics, Nature, or the universe, is generous. In one passage, Seneca suggested that the ultimate model of freely given generosity was the work of "the gods," by which he seemed to mean the sun and celestial bodies:

> It is our aim to live according to Nature and to follow the example of the gods. . . . See the great efforts they make every day, the generous gifts they bestow; see the wealth of crops with which they fill the lands! . . . They do all these things without any reward, without any advantage for themselves.[27]

Being philosophers, the Stoics did not believe in the traditional gods of the Greeks and Romans. Instead, the Stoics saw the gods as symbolic personifications of nature's elements and life-giving powers—for example, the sea, life-giving rain, and the fertility present in nature.[28] At other times, Stoics used the phrase "the gods" to denote the sun and other celestial bodies. The movements of the sun and the planets trace out ordered, rational, and predictable mathematical patterns over time, which underscored the Stoic belief in a rational universe, subject to natural law.

As pantheists, the Stoics did not believe in a personal God who stood outside of the universe, like the God of theism and Christianity.[29] But they weren't atheists either. Instead, they believed in a deep, unifying force, present in nature and the cosmos, which we could describe as rational, "divine," resplendent, the source of order and beauty in nature, and something worthy of admiration. As Seneca clearly summed up the Stoic view, "What else is Nature, except God and the divine reason that permeates the entire world and all its parts?"[30] We must also remember that, for the Stoics, God was not supernatural, but material—like a breath or life-force permeating the cosmos.

We can be sure that the Stoics, as philosophers interested in logic and science, thought quite differently about ideas like God than most of their neighbors. For example, they didn't take stories and myths about the gods literally. Rather, they gave them symbolic or allegorical interpretations in harmony with reason. At the same time, though, they didn't shun the religious practices of their time. Like love and gratitude, the Stoics saw reverence and piety as important virtues that held society together.

For the Roman Stoics and for many people today, gratitude can be more than just an interpersonal or social emotion. There are many ways that we can experience and be grateful for gifts and blessings that don't come from other people. For example, Seneca stressed all of the incredible gifts we receive from Nature. In one passage, he lists some of them. He mentions "so many virtues . . . so many skills . . . our mind, from which nothing is hidden," which "is swifter than the heavenly bodies." We have been given "so much food, so much wealth, so many blessings heaped on top of each other." Nature has given us so many gifts, he says, it would be absurd *not* to feel gratitude. As he concludes, "Any correct evaluation of nature's generosity will force you to admit that you have been her sweetheart."[31]

The philosopher Friedrich Nietzsche was an avowed atheist who proclaimed "the death of God." Some have seen him as a prophet of nihilism. But toward the end of his career, Nietzsche experienced a "perfect day" and a spontaneous feeling of deep gratitude. On that day, not only were the grapes ripening under the autumn sun, but, as he described it, "a ray of sunshine had fallen on my life." As he wrote, "I looked behind me, I looked before me, and never have I seen so many good things at once." Then Nietzsche asked, *"How could I fail to be grateful to my entire life?"*[32]

Similarly, Richard Dawkins, the most famous and outspoken atheist of our time, was asked if he ever had a religious experience. While Dawkins said, "I would not call it a *religious* experience," he did say that he has felt a profound sense of *gratitude* for his own existence. He explained some of these experiences in a deeply moving tone of voice:

> When I lie on my back and look up at the Milky Way on a clear night and see the vast distances of space and reflect that these are also vast differences of time as well, when I look at the Grand Canyon and see the strata going down, down, down, through periods of time which the human mind can't comprehend: I am overwhelmingly filled with a sense of *almost worship*. It is not worshipping anything personal, any more than Einstein would have worshipped anything personal. It's a feeling of sort of abstract *gratitude* that I am alive to appreciate these wonders. When I look down a microscope, it's the same feeling. I am grateful to be alive to appreciate these wonders.[33]

Obviously, as atheists, neither Nietzsche nor Dawkins was expressing gratitude for their existence to God. Like my experience of waking up and sipping tea in the morning, many feelings of gratitude are not directed toward anyone. I also believe these experiences of cosmic, nonpersonal, or existential gratitude are quite common. They occur to many people and increase their sense of well-being. They can even occur to atheists. But how can we explain them?

As philosopher Robert Solomon pointed out, we should not always think of gratitude in terms of a personal relationship. Instead, "*Gratitude is a philosophical emotion* [emphasis added]. It is, in a phrase, seeing the bigger picture."[34] In this sense, cosmic gratitude originates from experiencing life in the context of a greater whole. Being grateful for your entire life, for the very existence of a loved one, or for the sublime beauty of nature is not a "grateful to whom?" kind of question. Rather, as Solomon explains, it's *being aware* of these things in a greater context that inspires deep appreciation. As he puts it, "Like many moods, gratitude expands beyond the focus on a particular object to take in the world as a whole."[35] This kind of gratitude is much more than just being a response to a social transaction. As such, it certainly deserves our attention.

STOIC APPRECIATION

In some cases, gratitude can be a form of love. If you tell another person, "I am grateful for your existence," it's equivalent to expressing a kind of love. Sometimes, as a way of expressing love, I will simply say, "I appreciate you."

Central to Stoicism, as a philosophical way of life, is a deep sense of appreciation, from which both love and gratitude emerge. We can deeply appreciate the beauty of a sunset even though it's changing every moment and will soon disappear.

Its transience adds to its unique beauty. Similarly, a Stoic can understand that everything in nature is changing, transient, and impermanent, including our own lives, without reducing his or her depth of appreciation.

Stoics don't seek out external things in order to be happy because happiness comes from within. (Happiness also comes from how we decide to perceive the world, based on our inner judgments.) But a Stoic can find a deep sense of appreciation and gratitude in life's simplest gifts: a sunset, holding the hand of a loved one, or even the most basic meal. While our real goods lie within, we can still feel a deep sense of gratitude for every gift the universe offers to us. At the same time, we can come to see, through the eyes of appreciation, that the finest gifts from the universe are often free, or freely given. Because of that, we can take pleasure in simple things, like a cup of tea on a sunny morning. We can also experience profound happiness and satisfaction without seeking out an endless flow of expensive luxuries. As Seneca pointed out, someone who has enough is already rich. When we view the world with a sense of appreciation, even the most simple experiences have value.

For Seneca, someone who has found happiness or well-being will be able to look back on life with gratitude for everything the universe has given, as he or she is facing death. Similarly, Epictetus repeatedly described life, and the world, as resembling a festival. In his view, when we reach the end of life, we should be grateful for the time we were alive, thankful for the chance we had to participate in the festival. He also said a philosopher should be full of gratitude for the opportunity he had to behold the wonders of the universe and investigate nature's underlying order. He told his students, "May I be thinking, writing, and reading such thoughts when death overtakes me!"[36]

Marcus Aurelius left us with an even more graphic image of

the kind of gratitude a Stoic might feel at the end of life. As he reminded himself in his *Meditations*,

> Pass through this short moment of time living in accord with nature, and make your end cheerful, just as a ripe olive might fall, blessing the earth that bore it and grateful to the tree that gave it growth.[37]

For Marcus, the fact that we will one day die is part of nature's providential order, which we should accept without complaint but with gratitude. The Stoics realized that our lives are tiny, and in some ways insignificant, in relation to the immensity of the entire cosmos. But the very fact that we have been given a chance to participate in such a remarkable universe, and in human society, should be seen as both a gift and an honor.

In the end, we experience gratitude for something good or beautiful we receive—either from a person or from nature, which continually delivers such gifts. Like the light given off by the sun, this generosity is unearned by us, but it's freely given to everyone. The sun, while giving everyone the gift of life, greens the meadows of the earth. But it demands nothing in return. Perhaps in this way, as the Stoics suggested, nature, life, and every gift we receive, all reflect a radiance of generosity, given freely by the universe itself.

CHAPTER 14

Freedom, Tranquility, and Lasting Joy

Freedom is the prize we are seeking. That means not
being a slave to anything—to no compulsion and no
chance events. It means reducing Fortune's power to an
equal playing field.

—Seneca, *Letters* 51.9

BECOMING FREE

Stoicism's ultimate and most radical promise is that true happiness is fully within our reach at this very instant. For the Stoics, "happiness is 'up to us' and not due to luck, because the person who develops a sound character will possess deep inner satisfaction and the best, most enduring kind of happiness."[1]

Most important, the Stoics teach us exactly how to obtain this kind of lasting happiness. While it might take some effort, the Stoics claimed that the end result of "a life truly worth living" is within our grasp. In this final chapter, we'll explore exactly how this lasting happiness comes about, according to Seneca.

For the Roman Stoics, the practical goal of philosophy was to develop a sound or excellent inner character. But one outcome of having a good character is to experience tranquility and peace of mind, and to possess a life that is truly worth living. So having a good character and happiness (*eudaimonia*) go together.[2]

For Seneca—and for Epictetus, the Stoic teacher who followed him—the key to developing a good character and happiness is found in the idea of *freedom* and the process of becoming free. As Seneca notes, "Freedom is the prize we are seeking," and as he writes elsewhere, the promise of Stoic philosophy is "lasting freedom."[3] In fact, for Seneca, "freedom," "having a good character," and "happiness" were so closely related as to overlap.

What *freedom* means for Seneca is not being enslaved by false judgments, extreme negative emotions, anger, compulsions, unhappiness, anxiety about the future, a desire for external objects, feelings of emotional injury, and the opinions or actions of others. These are ideas we've already explored in this book. But in another sense, freedom also means belonging to yourself, living a life that is already complete, and being self-sufficient.

Being a former slave, Epictetus was no less interested in freedom than Seneca. Freedom, not surprisingly, was one of the major themes in his teachings. As Epictetus told his students, "Freedom is the greatest good, and no one who is really free can be unhappy. So if we see someone who is unhappy or miserable, we can know, with confidence, that person is not free."[4]

In a Stoic sense, to be free is to remain undisturbed by anything that is "not up to us," anything that belongs to the realm of chance or Fortune. Freedom also means not being subject to false opinions that give rise to worry, anxiety, anger, and other forms of emotional suffering.

In one definition Seneca offers of *freedom*, he states, "It means not fearing humans or gods, not craving things that are low or excessive, and having complete power over yourself. Just being your own person is a priceless good."[5] When Seneca mentions "having complete power over yourself," he's referring, at least in part, to the freedom of being able to make sound judgments, the opposite of being enslaved by false beliefs and negative social conditioning.

For a Stoic, ultimate freedom is achieved by the ability to make sound judgments. Only then will we truly "belong to ourselves." Only then will we possess real freedom and self-sufficiency. Only then will we be able to look down upon Fortune and not allow our mental happiness to depend on chance events beyond our control.

SELF-SUFFICIENCY AND THE HAPPY LIFE: RISING ABOVE FORTUNE AND CHANCE

We must make our escape to freedom. But this can only happen through disregard of Fortune.

—Seneca, *On the Happy Life* 4.4–5

The way someone becomes free, or becomes self-sufficient, is by rising above Fortune. The more we grant importance to external things outside our control, the less free we will become. Blind greed, Seneca notes, impels us to seek out things that will never satisfy us. If those kinds of external things *could* satisfy us, they would have done so already. But as he points out, we don't often consider "how pleasant it is to ask for nothing, how wonderful it is to be satisfied without depending on Fortune."[6] He writes, "I can show you many things that, once acquired, stole our freedom away. We would still belong to ourselves if those things did not belong to us."[7]

The alternative to seeking happiness in external things is to realize that our real goods, our true sources of happiness, are discovered within. People chase after endless pleasures in the outer world, in things that glitter and shine. But those shiny objects are never satisfying over the long term. By contrast, developing a sound character brings lasting happiness while still allowing us to appreciate the value of external things for what they are. This allows a Stoic, or anyone else for that matter, to experience real fulfillment.

Seneca describes the journey to self-sufficiency and fulfillment in many ways, sometimes using colorful metaphors. He describes it as an ascent, like climbing a mountain. Once the summit is reached, and we've risen above Fortune, we're able to "look down upon the things of Fortune from above" because we're no longer mentally or psychologically under Fortune's spell. Instead, we're free. In one dramatic image, Seneca describes this kind of self-sufficiency as involving total protection from Fortune's attacks: "All the arrows of Fortune that attack the human race," he explains, "bounce off a wise person like hail hitting a roof, which then rattles down the roof and melts away without harming the person inside."[8]

For Seneca, "reaching the summit" means finding the source of real happiness. It also involves possessing an inner joy that no one else could ever take away. As he writes, "The person who reaches the heights knows the source of real joy—finding happiness beyond the control of anyone else."[9]

It's important to realize, though, that this sense of self-sufficiency doesn't mean being aloof to others or uncaring. For Seneca, the Stoic wise person is notable for his or her human kindness. Likewise, it doesn't mean that we shouldn't appreciate the things we possess in the world. The wise person *will* appreciate and use all the gifts of Fortune he or she might possess, but will not rely upon those things for happiness. In addition to deeply treasuring the ones we love, we should make full use of the gifts of Fortune we possess at the moment, but realize that all these things are gifts on loan to us from the universe. They are not fully under our control. A self-sufficient person can appreciate everything deeply but doesn't depend upon external events or possessions to experience lasting happiness. A Stoic's happiness comes from within, from having an excellent character.

Once a Stoic begins to live "a life that is already complete," at that moment, he truly belongs to himself, having achieved a state of inner freedom. Rather than waiting for death to "complete" life, a Stoic should complete life *now*. If one lives with peace and calm in the present moment, one need not worry about the future. In this state, we will have truly found ourselves. Living fully "at home," a Stoic can then spend the remainder of his days in happiness, which no one can take away. As Seneca writes to Lucilius, "Consider how fine it is to complete your life now, before you die, and then to live out your remaining days in peace and self-sufficiency, in full possession of the happy life."[10] This idea of living "a life that is already complete" is closely related to Seneca's idea of living each day as if it's your last, or "trying to live each day as if it's a complete life," discussed in chapter 11. The end result of both approaches is a sense of freedom, living fully in the present moment, and lack of anxiety.

Put another way, the happy life is totally present, right here and now, if we would only choose to claim it. But by seeking it elsewhere, or in other things, people lose the freedom of unshakeable confidence and peace they would otherwise possess.[11]

STOIC JOY AND LASTING HAPPINESS

Believe me, real joy is a serious matter!
—Seneca, *Letters* 23.4

Joy is your goal, but you're wandering off course! You
think you'll arrive there among riches and official
accolades. That is to say, you seek joy surrounded by
anxieties! You chase after these things as if they'll bring
happiness and pleasure when, in fact, they are sources
of pain.
—Seneca, *Letters* 59.14

For the Stoics and other Greek philosophers, true happiness,
eudaimonia, differed from our modern idea of happiness significantly. For modern people, happiness is a temporary feeling,
a mood, or a passing emotional state. For the Greeks, though,
eudaimonia was a lasting excellence of character—"an enduring,
continuous, and relatively stable state of mind."[12] That major difference between modern and ancient views helps to explain why
ancient philosophers took happiness so seriously.

For Seneca, "Only an excellent mind develops real tranquility."[13] The result of having an excellent character, which arises
from virtue, is "steadiness of joy." As Seneca writes to Lucilius,
"If a wise person is never lacking in real joy, you have a good
reason to desire wisdom. But this joy only springs from awareness of the virtues. To experience this joy, you'll need courage,
justice, and moderation."[14]

We all have the seeds of these virtues (and other virtues)
within us, but in order for them to fully flower, they need

cultivation. Like a garden, our character requires tending. In this process, we also need to exercise our rationality. We need to weed out our false judgments and opinions, many of which we've been encouraged to embrace, unconsciously, from social conditioning. This includes removing things from the mind that are not truly "our own": things like fear, worry, the false promises of society, the desire for empty pleasures, and the pain and emotional suffering that arise from false beliefs. As Seneca writes, "Our mind is never greater than when it sets aside those things that are not its own: It makes peace for itself by fearing nothing; it creates wealth for itself by desiring nothing."[15]

By removing those things that are not our own, and by developing a steady character based on sound judgments, a remarkable transformation of the personality takes place, which results in lasting joy. Seneca explains:

> Once we have driven away all things that disturb or frighten us, there follows unbroken tranquility and unending freedom. For when pleasures and pains have been banished, a boundless joy comes in to replace all that is trivial, fragile, and harmful—a joy that is unshaken and unwavering. Then follow peace and harmony of the mind, and true greatness coupled with gentleness, since ferocity is always born from weakness.[16]

In my view, this passage is Seneca's most detailed and compelling description of the final goal of Stoic training. It also brings us back to the metaphor of the sun and the clouds, mentioned at the end of chapter 3.

When we become psychologically self-sufficient and experience Stoic joy, our personality becomes steady and radiant. In this way, it metaphorically resembles the sun, always shining, even when clouds float beneath it that might block out its light for a moment.[17]

Seneca tells us that the most advanced Stoic will sometimes experience small disturbances. Like everyone else, a fully developed Stoic sage will share normal human feelings, instinctual responses, and will be startled by unexpected events. But those disturbances will be temporary, just like clouds floating across the face of the sun. Thanks to the Stoic's steadiness of character, he or she will quickly "return home," to a state of inner harmony, joy, and tranquility.

ACKNOWLEDGMENTS

THANKS TO GILES ANDERSON, QUYNH DO, AND ALANE Mason for making this book happen, and to Nancy Green for her excellent editing. Special praise is also due to the team at Norton for their incredible work: Drew Elizabeth Weitman, Rebecca Munro, Elisabeth Kerr, Nicola DeRobertis-Theye, and Jason Heuer.

I am grateful to John Sellars, Donald Robertson, and Massimo Pigliucci for the engaging conversations I had with them while writing this work. Of course, they are not responsible for my own views. I am also thankful to William O. Stephens for the feedback he provided on the introduction and chapter 1, and to Rob Colter for his comments on the entire manuscript. I similarly appreciate the feedback received from Kai Whiting, Judith Stove, and Sandra Muratović.

The Stoic philosophical quotations in this book were newly translated by me, working in collaboration with Elizabeth Mercier, a Latin and Greek professor at Purdue University. Working with Liz to build a bridge between Seneca's thought and the modern world was a memorable undertaking. We both hope that you will enjoy these fresh translations of Seneca and, more importantly, the access they provide to his still living ideas and arguments.

APPENDIX:
STOIC PHILOSOPHICAL EXERCISES

THE STOICS WERE PHILOSOPHERS WHO BASED THEIR ideas and conclusions on rational thinking. That said, like other ancient philosophical schools, they practiced various exercises to reinforce their ideas. They also used meditations for therapeutic purposes, to psychologically reframe situations, and to reduce human suffering. Other meditations focused on remembering the processes of nature and our own relationship to the whole.

What follows is a brief listing of some philosophical exercises you can find in the writings of the Roman Stoics.

Several of these they adopted from earlier philosophers. Many, but not all of them, are discussed earlier in this book. For further reading, see *Stoic Spiritual Exercises* by Elen Buzaré.

Remember the dichotomy of control. Some things are up to us, and some things are not. Place your focus on what is up to you, like developing a good character, and not on the things of chance or Fortune that are beyond your control.

Remember the role of judgment. Things in themselves do not upset us. It's our judgments, or opinions about things, that create suffering.

Contemplation of the sage. Imagine that a wise person like Socrates is watching over your actions. If facing a difficult situation, ask yourself how the wise person would respond to it.

Philosophical journaling. Create your own personal notebook of Stoic meditations and teachings, the way Marcus Aurelius did, as reminders to yourself. Take central Stoic ideas and rephrase them, expressing them in your own words, or explain in your journal how you could apply them.

The daily review. At the end of each day, reflect upon your actions. Ask yourself these questions: What did I do well? What did I do poorly? How could I improve? What did I leave undone?

Transform adversity into something better. When you encounter adversity, transform it into something better. You can always create goodness in any situation if you respond to it with virtue.

Premeditation of adversity. Briefly rehearse in your mind any adversities you might face in the future. Then let those thoughts go. By contemplating adversities in advance, you will rob them of power should they actually arrive.

The Stoic reserve clause. When you start a project, go on a trip, or make a plan, say to yourself, "Fate willing." Keep in mind that, despite your best intentions, something beyond your control might interfere with your plans.

Contemplation of the whole. Realize that you are just a tiny part of the entire universe, but a part of the universe nonetheless. For a moment, expand your mind to encompass the entire cosmos, and experience your connection with the whole.

The view from above. Imagine that you are far above the Earth in space and looking down upon it. Then remember how small, in the grand scheme of things, your personal troubles really are.

Contemplation of change. Meditate on how all things in nature are in constant change, and how everything undergoes continual transformation over short or long periods of time.

Contemplation of impermanence. Realize that everything you have is on loan to you. Remember that it is fine to appreciate the gifts of Fortune while they are on loan to us, but one day we will give them back.

Memento mori. Reflect on your own mortality, on the mortality of those you love, and on death as just the final, natural stage of being alive. Be grateful for the time you have remaining and strive to use it wisely.

Live with gratitude. Each day, realize that everything we have is a gift from the universe. At the end of life, look back on your entire life as a gift, with a sense of gratitude.

Live in the present moment. Don't let your mind race ahead and worry about the future, because that is a source of anxiety. Instead, plan for the future rationally, and remember that the present moment is all we have. Should you start to feel anxious, be mindful of that, and return your attention to the present moment. Remember that when future events arrive, you will face them with the same rationality you have today.

Act for the common good. Remind yourself that you are part of the entire human community and that we are all born to help one another. Remember to act for the good of others.

Weigh your impressions with care. Don't take things at face value and make hasty judgments. Take a step back and carefully weigh the evidence before forming an opinion. If you lack enough firm evidence, suspend making a judgment entirely.

NOTES

PREFACE
1. Seneca, *Letters* 104.26.
2. Seneca, *Letters* 5.4.
3. Massimo Pigliucci, *How to Be a Stoic: Using Ancient Philosophy to Live a Modern Life* (New York: Basic Books, 2017), 230.

INTRODUCTION: A LIFE TRULY WORTH LIVING
1. See John Sellars, *The Art of Living: The Stoics on the Nature and Function of Philosophy* (London: Bristol Classical Press, 2009), chapter 2, "The Socratic Origins of the Art of Living."
2. For a sense of what this stoa, which housed paintings, looked like, see the drawing at https://www.stoicinsights.com/about-stoicism/.
3. Epicurus, cited and translated by Martha Nussbaum in *The Therapy of Desire: Theory and Practice in Hellenistic Ethics* (Princeton: Princeton University Press, 1994), 13.
4. Seneca, *Letters* 8.2. On ancient philosophy being compared to a medical art and "the art of living," see John Sellars, *The Art of Living*, chapters 2 and 3.
5. Seneca, *Letters* 76.16.
6. I am thankful to Massimo Pigliucci for pointing out this more nuanced meaning of the term *eudaimonia* that applies specifically to the Stoics.
7. While Plato and Aristotle set the stage by analyzing civic responsibilities and how to improve the life of the city-state, the Stoics went further by emphasizing the brotherhood of all humanity on a global scale. Seneca wrote that, of all the philosophical schools, the Stoics had

the greatest love for humanity as a whole. In his *Meditations*, Marcus Aurelius, too, constantly reminded himself that his every action should attempt to improve the common good of society.

8. Emily Wilson, *The Greatest Empire: A Life of Seneca* (New York: Oxford University Press, 2014). Another biography of Seneca is James Romm, *Dying Every Day: Seneca at the Court of Nero* (New York: Knopf, 2014). The almost impossible task of writing an accurate biography of Seneca stems from the fact that the Roman historians, by modern standards, are often extremely unreliable. Unfortunately, there are no firsthand accounts of Seneca's life written by people who knew him. The account of Seneca written by Dio Cassius (c. 155–c. 235) in his *Roman Histories*, which appears to be the most unreliable, was written well over a century after Seneca's death. The account of Tacitus (c. 56–c. 120) in his *Annals* appears to be far more solid.

9. Tacitus, *Annals* 15.62.

10. This line from Socrates was a favorite among the Roman Stoics. Epictetus quotes it at the end of his "manual" or "handbook"; see Epictetus, *Handbook* 53.4. Another Roman senator, Thrasea Paetus, who was also a Stoic and put to death by Nero, is reported to have said, "Nero can kill me, but he cannot harm me." See Emily Wilson, *The Greatest Empire*, 154.

11. Seneca, *Letters* 123.6.

12. Seneca, *Letters* 122.14.

13. Seneca, *Letters* 115.9.

14. As Brad Inwood has noted, Seneca was "an original and innovative exponent" of Stoic philosophy, "one whose distinctive contribution seems to be a sensitivity to the value of first-hand experience in ethics and moral psychology." Inwood, *Reading Seneca: Stoic Philosophy at Rome* (Oxford: Clarendon Press, 2005), 3.

CHAPTER 1: THE LOST ART OF FRIENDSHIP

1. Seneca, *Letters* 48.2–3. Seneca also wrote a work *On Friendship*, of which only short fragments survive. On the topic of friendship in Seneca, with plentiful quotations, see Anna Lydia Motto and John R. Clark, "Seneca on Friendship," *Atena e Roma* 38 (1993): 91–96.

2. Seneca, *Letters* 106.12.

3. According to the Stoic Aristo, quoted by Seneca in *Letters* 94.16, unless someone has a medical disease, all "madness" or mental suffering originates from holding false opinions. Seneca agreed with this view. In *On*

the Tranquility of Mind, Seneca is approached by his friend Serenus, as though Seneca is a doctor. Serenus, the patient, explains his mental suffering, and Seneca responds as a philosophical therapist to cure the condition. For a letter that strongly resembles a cognitive therapy session between Lucilius and Seneca, see *Letters* 24. Lucilius is anxious because he has been named the target of a lawsuit; Seneca aims to help Lucilius overcome his anxiety by using a step-by-step therapeutic approach.

4. Seneca, *Letters* 40.1.

5. Seneca, *Letters* 9.12. According to Cicero, the Stoics believed that friendship should be pursued for its intrinsic value, not for what you could get out of a friendship in a utilitarian way (Cicero, *On Ends* 3.70).

6. See John M. Cooper, "Aristotle on the Forms of Friendship," *The Review of Metaphysics* 30, no. 4 (1977): 648.

7. See Nancy Sherman, "Aristotle on Friendship and the Shared Life," *Philosophical and Phenomenological Research* 47, no. 4 (1987): 610.

8. Seneca, *Letters* 6.1.

9. Seneca, *Letters* 6.1.

10. A summary of Plato, *Symposium* 203E–204A.

11. Diogenes Laertius, *Lives of the Eminent Philosophers* 6.54.

12. For the evidence, see John Sellars, *The Art of Living: The Stoics on the Nature and Function of Philosophy* (London: Bristol Classical Press, 2009), 59–64.

13. For more on the extreme dichotomy between the sage and non-sages, see John Sellars, *The Art of Living*, 59–64; Sellars, *Stoicism* (London: Routledge, 2014), 36–41; and Tad Brennan, *The Stoic Life: Emotion, Duties, and Fate* (Oxford: Oxford University Press, 2005), chapter 4. The modern philosopher Lawrence C. Becker also rejected the early Stoic idea that virtue was an all-or-nothing matter, along with the strict dividing line between sages and nonsages, as being "untenable." See Becker, *A Modern Stoicism*, 2nd ed. (Princeton: Princeton University Press, 2017), 132–33 and following.

14. Introduction to Seneca, *Letters on Ethics to Lucilius*, translated by Margaret Graver and A. A. Long (Chicago: University of Chicago Press, 2015), xx.

15. Evidence suggests that Zeno, the founder of Stoicism, also identified Socrates as being a sage. See René Brouwer, *The Stoic Sage: The Early Stoics on Wisdom, Sagehood and Socrates* (Cambridge: Cambridge University Press, 2014), 109, 164.

16. Emily Wilson, *The Greatest Empire: A Life of Seneca* (New York: Oxford University Press, 2014), 146.

17. Seneca, *Letters* 57.3.
18. Seneca, *Letters* 71.36.
19. On what Marcus Aurelius was trying to accomplish in the *Meditations*, see John Sellars, *Marcus Aurelius* (London: Routledge, 2021), 20–36. As William O. Stephens and others have pointed out, a better title for the *Meditations* of Marcus Aurelius might be "Memoranda," since it consists of notes to himself about Stoic principles to remember on a daily basis. Stephens, *Marcus Aurelius* (New York: Continuum, 2012), 2.
20. Seneca, *On Anger* 3.36.3–4.

CHAPTER 2: VALUE YOUR TIME: DON'T POSTPONE LIVING

1. Seneca, *Letters* 1.1.
2. Seneca, *Letters* 1.2.
3. Seneca, *Natural Questions*, preface 1.2.
4. Seneca, *On the Shortness of Life* 2.1 and 1.3.
5. Seneca, *On the Shortness of Life* 2.1–2.2.
6. Seneca, *Letters* 3.5.
7. Seneca, *Letters* 106.1 and 22.8.
8. Seneca, *On Tranquility of Mind*, 12.2–3.
9. Seneca, *On the Shortness of Life* 3.5.
10. Zeno, cited by Diogenes Laertius, *Lives of the Eminent Philosophers* 7.121–22.
11. On the Stoic metaphors of slavery and freedom, see the introduction by A. A. Long to Epictetus, *How to Be Free: An Ancient Guide to the Stoic Life* (Princeton: Princeton University Press, 2018). For the use of these metaphors in Seneca, see Catharine Edwards, "Free Yourself! Slavery, Freedom, and the Self in Seneca's Letters," in *Seneca and the Self*, eds. S. Bartsch and D. Wray (Cambridge: Cambridge University Press, 2009), 139–59.
12. Seneca, *Letters* 22.11.
13. Epictetus, *Discourses* 2.1.22.
14. Epictetus, *Discourses* 4.1.113.
15. Seneca, *On the Shortness of Life* 9.1.
16. Seneca, *On the Shortness of Life* 14.1.
17. Seneca, *On the Shortness of Life* 14.1–2. For more on Seneca's idea of a timeless community of wise people, see the conclusion to Catharine Edwards, "Absent Presence in Seneca's Epistles: Philosophy and Friendship," in *The Cambridge Companion to Seneca*, eds. Shadi Bartsch and Allesandro Schiessaro (New York: Cambridge University Press, 2015), 41–53.

18. Seneca, *On the Shortness of Life* 15.2.

19. Seneca, *Letters* 62.2. In his lost work *On Marriage*, of which only fragments survive, Seneca said that a wise person will never feel lonely because he or she will have so many friends from the past. See Liz Gloyn, *The Ethics of the Family in Seneca* (Cambridge: Cambridge University Press, 2017), 222.

20. Seneca, *On the Shortness of Life* 15.5–16.1.

CHAPTER 3: HOW TO OVERCOME WORRY AND ANXIETY

1. Seneca, *Letters* 5.8.

2. Marcus Aurelius, *Meditations* 4.7.

3. Seneca, *Letters* 101.8.

4. Marcus Aurelius, *Meditations* 12.26. On Marcus Aurelius reading Seneca, see John Sellars, *Marcus Aurelius* (London: Routledge, 2021), 12.

5. Paraphrase of Seneca, *Letters* 89.1.

6. Seneca, *Letters* 13.13.

7. Seneca, *Letters* 78.13.

8. Seneca, *Letters* 44.7.

9. Seneca, *Letters* 13.4.

10. Marcus Aurelius, *Meditations* 7.8.

11. Seneca, *Letters* 13.8–9.

12. Epictetus, *Handbook* 5.

13. Cited in Donald Robertson, "The Stoic Influence on Modern Psychotherapy," in *The Routledge Handbook of the Stoic Tradition*, ed. John Sellars (London: Routledge, 2017), 375. Robertson is a cognitive behavioral therapist who has studied Stoicism in depth. His first work (2010) on the relationships between Stoicism and CBT is entitled *The Philosophy of Cognitive-Behavioural Therapy (CBT): Stoic Philosophy as Rational and Cognitive Psychotherapy*, 2nd ed. (London: Routledge, 2020). His more recent book, *How to Think Like a Roman Emperor: The Stoic Philosophy of Marcus Aurelius* (New York: St. Martin's Press, 2019), explores the parallels between the thinking of Marcus Aurelius and cognitive behavioral therapy, in addition to other topics.

14. Seneca, *Letters* 5.7.

15. Seneca, *Letters* 5.8.

16. Epictetus, *Handbook* 5.

17. Seneca, *Letters* 92.18.

18. Seneca, *Letters* 27.3.

CHAPTER 4: THE PROBLEM WITH ANGER

1. Seneca, *On Anger* 1.1.2.
2. The web pages of the American Psychological Association that address anger management overlap with about 95 percent of Seneca's advice in his book *On Anger*. See "Controlling Anger Before It Controls You" (https://www.apa.org/topics/anger/control) and "Strategies for Controlling Your Anger: Keeping Anger in Check" (https://www.apa.org/topics/strategies-controlling-anger).
3. Seneca, *On Anger* 1.1.3–4.
4. Seneca, *On Anger* 2.36.6.
5. Seneca, *On Anger* 3.1.4.
6. Seneca, *On Anger* 3.1.5.
7. Seneca, *On Anger* 1.2.1.
8. Seneca, *On Anger* 2.36.5–6.
9. Seneca, *On Anger* 1.5.3.
10. Seneca, *On Anger* 1.19.1.
11. Seneca, *Letters* 71.27.
12. Epictetus, *Discourses* 3.2.4.
13. Seneca, *On Mercy* 2.5.3.
14. Seneca, *On Anger* 1.10.2. My interpretation of the four primary kinds of emotions recognized by the Stoics follows that of John Sellars, "Stoicism and Emotions," in *Stoicism Today: Selected Writings*, Volume 2, ed. Patrick Ussher (CreateSpace, 2016), 43–48.
15. Chrysippus, one of the most important and influential of the early Greek Stoics, in his lost work *On Passions* or *On Affections*, had defined the passions as originating from incorrect judgments and as resembling forms of mental illness. He also described a therapy of the passions. Teun Tieleman, *Chrysippus' On Affections: Reconstruction and Interpretation* (Leiden: E. J. Brill, 2003), 132 and chapter 4.
16. Margaret R. Graver, "Action and Emotion," in *The Brill Companion to Seneca: Philosopher and Dramatist*, eds. Gregor Damschen and Andreas Heil (Leiden: E. J. Brill, 2014), 272.
17. For the most important study of Stoic psychology during the entire tradition, see Margaret R. Graver, *Stoicism and Emotion* (Chicago: University of Chicago Press, 2014).
18. Seneca outlines the three-step cognitive theory of emotion in *On Anger* 2.4.1–2. In terms of the "three movements," I follow the interpretation of Robert A. Kaster, introduction to Seneca, *On Anger*, in Seneca, *Anger, Mercy, and Revenge* (University of Chicago Press, 2010), 6–8, and Brad

Inwood, *Reading Seneca: Stoic Philosophy at Rome* (New York: Oxford University Press, 2005), 61–63.

19. Seneca, *On Anger* 2.4.2.
20. Seneca, *On Anger* 2.29.1.
21. Seneca, *On Anger* 2.22.2.
22. Epictetus, *Discourses* 1.20.7.
23. Rollo May, *The Courage to Create* (New York: W. W. Norton, 1975), 100.
24. Seneca, *On Anger* 2.1.4.
25. Seneca, *On Anger* 1.8.1–2.
26. Seneca, *Letters* 116.3.
27. American Psychological Association, "Controlling Anger Before It Controls You," section on "Strategies to Keep Anger at Bay." https://www.apa.org/topics/anger/control.
28. Epictetus, *Handbook* 30.
29. Marcus Aurelius, *Meditations* 12.25.
30. Seneca, *On Anger* 2.10.7.

CHAPTER 5: WHEREVER YOU GO, THERE YOU ARE: YOU CAN'T ESCAPE YOURSELF

1. Seneca, *Letters* 28.1.
2. At the beginning of Letter 104, Seneca describes how he traveled to his villa at Nomentum, eighteen miles outside of Rome, because he was coming down with a fever. But once he got outside smoke-filled Rome and arrived at the villa, he felt just fine.
3. Seneca, *Letters* 17.12.
4. Seneca, *Letters* 104.8.
5. Seneca, *Letters* 104.7.
6. Seneca, *Letters* 2.1.
7. Seneca, *Letters* 2.2.
8. Seneca, *Letters* 89.23.
9. Seneca, *Letters* 16.9.
10. Seneca, *Letters* 69.1.
11. Seneca, *Letters* 35.4.
12. You can find a translation of *On Leisure* in Seneca, *Hardship and Happiness* (Chicago: University of Chicago Press, 2014), 219–32.
13. Seneca, *On Tranquility of Mind* 2.14.
14. M. Andrew Holowchak, *The Stoics* (New York: Continuum, 2008), 185.
15. Seneca, *Letters* 28.4.
16. Seneca, *Letters* 55.8.

17. Seneca, *Letters* 23.7–8.
18. Seneca, *Letters* 71.2–3.
19. Seneca, *Letters* 71.2.

CHAPTER 6: HOW TO TAME ADVERSITY

1. Seneca, *Letters* 91.1.
2. Seneca, *Letters* 91.6.
3. Jack Malvern, "Stuck at Home, Stoic Britons Get Philosophical," *The Times*, April 23, 2020. https://www.thetimes.co.uk/article/stuck-at-home -stoic-britons-get-philosophical-boh7jdnrb.
4. The term *dichotomy of control* was coined by the modern Stoic philosopher William B. Irvine in his book *A Guide to the Good Life: The Ancient Art of Stoic Joy* (Oxford: Oxford University Press, 2009), 86–89. The eminent scholar of ancient philosophy, A. A. Long, believes that this idea, as an ethical premise, ultimately "goes back to Socrates in Plato's *Apology*, where he says that no harm can come to the good man in life or death, which implies that virtue is 'up to us,' and happiness is impervious to fortune" (personal communication).
5. Seneca, *Letters* 76.16.
6. Seneca, *Letters* 66.23.
7. Seneca, *Letters* 74.1. Also see *Letters* 74.5–6.
8. Seneca, *Letters* 98.2.
9. Epictetus, *Discourses* 3.24.112.
10. Seneca, *Letters* 44.2.
11. Seneca, *Letters* 91.3–4.
12. Seneca, *Letters* 24.15.
13. Seneca, *Letters* 78.28.
14. Seneca, *On the Happy Life* 15.5.
15. The early Greek Stoic Chrysippus wrote, "A blow that has not previously been foreseen strikes us harder" (quoted in Cicero, *Tusculan Disputations* 3.52). For a study of the premeditation of adversity in Stoicism and in Seneca, see Mireille Armisen-Marchetti, "Imagination and Meditation in Seneca: The Example of the *Praemeditatio*," in *Oxford Readings in Classical Studies: Seneca*, edited by John G. Fitch (Oxford: Oxford University Press, 2008), 102–13.
16. Marcus Aurelius, *Meditations* 2.1.
17. Seneca, *Letters* 76.35.
18. Seneca, *Natural Questions* 4B .13.11.
19. Seneca, *On Providence* 5.9.

20. Seneca, *On Providence* 3.3.
21. Seneca, *Letters* 67.14.
22. Seneca, *On Providence* 2.6.
23. Epictetus, *Discourses* 1.24.1–2.
24. Seneca, *On Providence* 4.6.
25. Seneca, *On Providence* 2.4.
26. Seneca, *Letters* 85.41.
27. Epictetus, *Handbook* 18.
28. Marcus Aurelius, *Meditations* 6.50.
29. Seneca, *Letters* 45.9.
30. Marcus Aurelius, *Meditations* 5.20 (Gregory Hayes translation).

CHAPTER 7: WHY YOU SHOULD NEVER COMPLAIN

1. Seneca, *On Anger* 3.6.3.
2. Cited by Peter Bregman, "The Next Time You Want to Complain at Work, Do This Instead," *Harvard Business Review* (May 17, 2018). https://hbr.org/2018/05/the-next-time-you-want-to-complain-at-work -do-this-instead.
3. Bregman, "The Next Time You Want to Complain at Work, Do This Instead."
4. Will Bowen, "A Complaint Free World." https://www.willbowen.com /complaintfree/.
5. Epictetus, *Discourses* 2.18.13.
6. Guy Winch, "How to Deal with Chronic Complainers: What They Want and What They Need Are Very Different Things," *Psychology Today* (July 15, 2011). https://www.psychologytoday.com/intl/blog/the -squeaky-wheel/201107/how-deal-chronic-complainers.
7. See Arius Didymus, *Epitome of Stoic Ethics*: "live in agreement with nature" (6b) and "happiness is a smooth flow of life" (6e). Also compare Diogenes Laertius, *Lives of the Eminent Philosophers* 7.87–89.
8. In her book *Determinism and Freedom in Stoic Philosophy* (Oxford: Oxford University Press, 2001), Susanne Bobzien has collected the evidence and ancient sources confirming this. See also the article by Mikolaj Domaradzki, "Theological Etymologizing in the Early Stoa," *Kernos* 25 (2012), 125–48, especially page 134. https://journals.openedition.org /kernos/2109.
9. Albert Einstein, "Religion and Science" (*New York Times Magazine*, November 9, 1930), reprinted in Albert Einstein, *Ideas and Opinions* (New York: Modern Library, 1994), 42.

10. Albert Einstein, "Science and Religion" (Address at Princeton Theological Seminary, May 19, 1939), in Einstein, *Ideas and Opinions*, 52–53.

11. Epictetus, *Handbook* 8.

12. A. A. Long and D. N. Sedley, *The Hellenistic Philosophers*, Volume 1, 62A (Cambridge: Cambridge University Press, 1987), 386. It is reported that the story of the dog and the cart was used by Zeno and Chrysippus.

13. Cleanthes, quoted in Seneca, *Letters* 107.11.

14. Seneca, *Letters* 96.1.

15. Seneca, *Letters* 96.2–3.

16. Seneca, *Letters* 107.2.

17. Seneca, *Letters* 107.6.

18. Seneca, *Natural Questions* 3, preface 12.

19. Marcus Aurelius, *Meditations* 4.23.

CHAPTER 8: THE BATTLE AGAINST FORTUNE: HOW TO SURVIVE POVERTY AND EXTREME WEALTH

1. Seneca, *Letters* 19.9.

2. Seneca, *Letters* 98.8.

3. https://www.newsweek.com/was-michael-jackson-debt-he-died-look-king-pops-finances-1349255.

4. Seneca, *On Tranquility of Mind* 11.10.

5. Seneca, *Natural Questions* book 3, preface 1.7.

6. Seneca, *Consolation to Helvia* 5.4.

7. Seneca, *Letters* 90.18.

8. Seneca, *Letters* 90.19.

9. Seneca, *Letters* 90.40.

10. Seneca, *Letters* 119.11.

11. Seneca, *Letters* 119.12–13.

12. Epicurus, quoted in Seneca, *Letters* 17.11.

13. Seneca, *Letters* 36.1.

14. Seneca, *Letters* 87.31.

15. Seneca tells this tale in *Consolation to Helvia* 10.8–11.

16. Seneca, *Consolation to Polybius* 9.5 and 6.4.

17. William B. Irvine, *On Desire: Why We Want What We Want* (New York: Oxford University Press, 2006), 31.

18. Seneca, *Letters* 104.9.

19. Seneca, *On Tranquility of Mind* 8.2.

20. The survey was conducted in February 2019. https://www.hrblock.com/tax-center/wp-content/uploads/2019/07/Lifestages-survey-results.pdf.

21. Jeremy Kisner, "Why Rich People Worry about Money." https://www .jeremykisner.com/rich-people-worry-money/.
22. Seneca, *Letters* 19.6–7.
23. Seneca, *Letters* 18.5.
24. Seneca, *Letters* 18.7.
25. For an overview of voluntary simplicity with a reading list, see http:// simplicitycollective.com/start-here/what-is-voluntary-simplicity-2.
26. Seneca, *Letters* 60.3.
27. Seneca, *Consolation to Helvia* 11.4.
28. Seneca, *Letters* 74.4.
29. Anna Lydia Motto, one of the leading Seneca scholars of all time, weighed the evidence to see if Seneca was guilty of hypocrisy. Her verdict was "no." See Anna Lydia Motto, "Seneca on Trial: The Case of the Opulent Stoic," *The Classical Journal* 61, no. 6 (1966): 254–58. Also see the discussion by Ward Farnsworth in his book, *The Practicing Stoic: A Philosophical User's Manual* (Boston: David R. Godine, 2018), chapter 13, "Stoicism and its Critics."
30. Seneca, *Letters* 18.13.
31. Seneca, *On the Happy Life* 22.5.

CHAPTER 9: VICIOUS CROWDS AND THE TIES THAT BIND

1. Seneca, *Letters* 7.2–3.
2. Seneca, *Letters* 7.3–4.
3. Seneca, *Letters* 7.5.
4. Seneca, *Letters* 7.7.
5. Seneca, *On Tranquility of Mind* 7.4.
6. Seneca, *On Anger* 3.8.1–2.
7. For a brief summary of several studies, see https://en.wikipedia.org /wiki/Herd_mentality.
8. Gustave Le Bon, *The Crowd: A Study of the Popular Mind*, Book 1, chapter 1. Translation from Project Gutenberg: http://www.gutenberg.org /ebooks/445.
9. Le Bon, *The Crowd*, Book 1, chapter 1.
10. See Tony D. Sampson, *Virality: Contagion Theory in the Age of Networks* (Minneapolis: University of Minnesota Press, 2012).
11. See R. M. Joly-Mascheroni, A. Senju, and A. J. Shepherd, "Dogs Catch Human Yawns," *Biology Letters* 4.5 (2008): 446–48. https://www.ncbi .nlm.nih.gov/pmc/articles/PMC2610100/; and E. A. Madsen, T. Persson, S. Sayehli, S. Lenninger, and G. Sonesson, "Chimpanzees Show

a Developmental Increase in Susceptibility to Contagious Yawning: A Test of the Effect of Ontogeny and Emotional Closeness on Yawn Contagion," *PloS One* 8.10 (2003). https://www.ncbi.nlm.nih.gov/pmc /articles/PMC3797813/.

12. The insight that we learn some false beliefs through socialization goes back at least to the Stoic Chrysippus. However, Chrysippus only seems to have considered deliberate socialization, not the kind of unconscious transmission that Seneca describes clearly. See Teun Tieleman, *Chrysippus' On Affections: Reconstruction and Interpretations* (Leiden: E. J. Brill, 2003), 132 ff., and Graziano Ranocchia, "The Stoic Concept of Proneness to Emotion and Vice," *Archiv für Geschichte der Philosophie* 94, no. 1 (2012): 74–92.

13. At the beginning of Letter 60, Seneca provides an emphatic explanation of how Lucilius picked up his beliefs about the value of wealth as a child from his parents and others responsible for his upbringing.

14. See, for example, J. W. Bridges, "Imitation, Suggestion, and Hypnosis," chapter 18, in J. W. Bridges, *Psychology: Normal and Abnormal, with Special Reference to the Needs of Medical Students and Practitioners* (New York: Appleton, 1930), 311–24. Available from the American Psychological Association: https://psycnet.apa.org/record/2008-08475-018.

15. Seneca, *Letters* 7.8.

16. Seneca, *Letters* 94.69.

17. Seneca, *On Anger* 3.8.2.

18. Seneca, *Letters* 109.1–2.

19. For Aristotle, neither women nor slaves possessed the mental capacity to benefit from the study of politics. Additionally, as he wrote in *Politics* 1260a11, "natural slaves" lack the power of deliberation entirely. Women possess the power of deliberation, "but in a form that lacks authority," which excludes them from participating in politics. By contrast, Plato, who was Aristotle's teacher, believed that women could be guardians of the state.

20. Daniel S. Richter, *Cosmopolis: Imagining Community in Late Classical Athens and the Early Roman Empire* (New York: Oxford University Press, 2011), 68. In chapter 4, Richter highlights the vast differences between the views of Aristotle and the Stoics on human equality.

21. Lactantius, *Divine Institutes* 3.25, cited and translated in Richter, *Cosmopolis*, 67. For more on human equality and slavery in early Stoic philosophy, see Lisa Hill and Prasanna Nidumolu, "The Influence of

Classical Stoicism on John Locke's Theory of Self-Ownership," *History of the Human Sciences* (May 2020): 6–7.

22. On natural law in Stoicism and Cicero, see Maryanne Cline Horowitz, "The Stoic Synthesis of Natural Law in Man: Four Themes," *Journal of the History of Ideas* 35, no. 1 (1974): 3–16; Elizabeth Asmis, "Cicero on Natural Law and the Laws of State," *Classical Antiquity* 27, no. 1 (2008): 1–33; and Fernando H. Llano Alonso, "Cicero and Natural Law," *ARSP: Archiv für Rechts- und Socialphilosophie / Archives for Philosophy of Law and Social Philosophy* 98, no. 2 (2012): 157–68.

23. Cicero, *On the Republic* 3.33.

24. Philosophy scholar Phillip Mitsis concluded that the Stoics gave "expression to the notion of natural human rights." The Stoics, with their idea of the cosmopolis, lived "in a moral climate conducive to the recognition of their fellow citizens' needs and rights—rights that the Stoics think we all share in virtue of the fact that we are human." Mitsis, "The Stoic Origin of Natural Rights, in *Topics in Stoic Philosophy*, ed. Katerina Ierodiakonou (Oxford: Oxford University Press, 1999), 176–77.

25. Our modern idea of human rights—for example, the Universal Declaration of Human Rights, developed by the United Nations in 1948—combines aspects of universal, natural law with civil and international law. Interestingly, this had been an important question for Cicero: how closely can civil law be brought into harmony with natural law?

26. Paul Meany, "Why the Founders' Favorite Philosopher Was Cicero," FEE (May 31, 2018). https://fee.org/articles/why-the-founders-favorite -philosopher-was-cicero/. I am grateful to Meany for his articles on Stoicism, Cicero, natural law, and natural rights, which encouraged me to investigate the Stoic contribution to the development of natural and human rights.

27. In fact, when Thomas Jefferson died, he had a volume of Seneca's writings open on his bedside table, and Jefferson listed Cicero as a major influence on his drafting of the Declaration of Independence. John Locke, who influenced Jefferson's thinking on natural rights, also read the Stoic philosophers and recommended them to his students.

28. M. Andrew Holowchak, "Thomas Jefferson," section 2.2, "Nature and Society," *Stanford Encyclopedia of Philosophy*. https://plato.stanford.edu /entries/jefferson/.

29. As the political historian Charles McIlwan noted, "The idea of the equality of men is the profoundest contribution of the Stoics to political thought, that idea has colored its whole development from their day to

ours, and its greatest influence is in the changed conception of law that in part resulted from it." McIlwan, *The Growth of Political Thought in the West: From the Greeks to the Middle Ages* (New York: Macmillan, 1932), 8.

See also chapter 3, "The Cosmopolis in Human Rights," in Tony Honoré, *Ulpian: Pioneer of Human Rights*, 2nd ed. (Oxford: Oxford University Press, 2002), which documents how Stoicism led to the ideas of human equality, freedom, and the dignity of all in the Roman legal tradition, especially in the work of the jurist Domitius Ulpianus or Ulpian (c. 170–c. 228).

30. Joseph J. Ellis, *American Sphinx: The Character of Thomas Jefferson* (New York: Alfred A. Knopf, 1997), 53.

31. Marcelo Gleiser, "The Trouble with Tribalism," *Orbiter* (July 18, 2019). https://orbitermag.com/the-trouble-with-tribalism/.

32. Seneca, *Letters* 95.52–53.

33. Seneca, *Letters* 48.2.

34. Seneca, *On Benefits* 4.18.4.

35. Ilaria Ramelli, *Hierocles the Stoic: Elements of Ethics, Fragments, and Excerpts* (Atlanta: Society for Biblical Literature, 2009), xxxv.

36. Marcus Aurelius, *Meditations* 4.3. He repeats this "doctrine" and elaborates it throughout the *Meditations*, exploring how "we were born to help one another" (11.18).

37. Cicero, *On Ends* 3.62.

38. Cicero, *On Ends* 3.62–63.

39. Cicero, *On Ends* 3.63.

40. Ramelli, *Hierocles the Stoic*, 89–91.

41. John Sellars, *Stoicism* (London: Routledge, 2014), 131.

CHAPTER 10: HOW TO BE AUTHENTIC AND CONTRIBUTE TO SOCIETY

1. Epicurus wrote to one friend, "I am thrilled with pleasure in the body when I live on bread and water," and in another letter he wrote, "Send me some preserved cheese, so I may have a feast when I like." See Cyril Bailey, *Epicurus: The Extant Remains* (Oxford: Clarendon Press, 1926), 131.

2. The stark difference between the Stoic view of rationality in nature and a random world of colliding atoms and is summed up nicely in a phrase that Marcus Aurelius often used to describe the divide between the Stoics and the Epicureans: "providence or atoms."

3. This saying of Epicurus, *lathe biōsis* or "live unknown," was widely

known in the ancient world. See for example the essay of Plutarch, *Is "Live Unknown" a Wise Precept?* In Plutarch, *Moralia*, Volume 14 (Cambridge, MA: Harvard University Press, 1967), 318–43.

4. Epictetus, *Discourses* 3.7.19.
5. Seneca, *On Tranquility of Mind* 6.2.
6. The Roman writer Cicero presents the ideas of Panaetius in the first two books of his work *On Duties*, an important work on Stoic ethics. The description of the four *personae* appears in Cicero, *On Duties* 1.107–115. In the discussion that follows here, I draw on both the ideas of Panaetius and Seneca, since Seneca expressed the same thoughts in his writings.
7. Seneca, *Letters* 11.6.
8. One of the most accurate psychological tests ever devised measures "the Big Five personality traits." These are identified as openness to experience, conscientiousness, extraversion, agreeableness, and neuroticism (and their opposites). Interestingly, when people are tested for these traits, it's possible to predict where they fall on the political spectrum with a high degree of accuracy. This suggests that many or even most people identify with political orientations based on their personality traits rather than through a process of critical thinking.
9. Seneca, *On Tranquility of Mind* 6.2.
10. Cicero, *On Duties* 1.110–111, reporting on the thought of Panaetius.
11. Seneca, *Letters* 20.2.
12. Seneca, *Letters* 37.5.
13. Seneca, *Letters* 120.21–22.
14. Seneca, *Letters* 47.21.
15. Seneca, *Letters* 20.3.
16. Seneca, *On Tranquility of Mind* 17.1 and 17.2.
17. Seneca, *Letters* 16.3.
18. Seneca, *Letters* 75.4.
19. Seneca, *Letters* 64.7 and 64.9.
20. Seneca, *Natural Questions* 7.25.4.
21. Seneca, *Letters* 79.5.
22. For some criticisms of Zeno's arguments, see Seneca, *Letters* 82.9 and 83.9. Seneca, *On Benefits* 1.4.1, describes Chrysippus's acumen as being so finely pointed that, rather than being compelling, it only delivered "pinpricks."
23. Seneca, *Letters* 80.1.
24. Seneca, *Letters* 33.11.
25. Seneca, *Letters* 81.1–2.

26. James Ker, introduction to *On the Constancy of the Wise Person*, in Seneca, *Hardship and Happiness* (Chicago: University of Chicago Press, 2010), 143.

27. Seneca, *On the Constancy of the Wise Person* 9.4–5 and Epictetus, *Discourses* 3.25.4.

28. See Seneca, *On Leisure* 2.2. As Diogenes Laertius put it, "The Stoics say that a wise person will take part in politics, if nothing hinders him . . . since, by doing so, he will restrain vice and promote virtue" (*Lives of the Eminent Philosophers* 7.121). For an in-depth study of Seneca's views on public service and leisure, see chapter 10, "The Philosopher on Political Participation," in Mariam T. Griffin, *Seneca: A Philosopher in Politics* (New York: Oxford University Press, 1976).

29. Seneca, *On Leisure* 6.4–5.

30. Seneca, *On Leisure* 3.5.

31. Seneca, *On Leisure* 8.1.

32. Seneca, *On Leisure* 6.4.

33. Seneca, *Letters* 8.2–3.

34. Seneca, *Letters* 21.5.

35. Seneca, *Letters* 79.17.

CHAPTER 11: LIVING FULLY REGARDLESS OF DEATH

1. Seneca, *Letters* 12.1.

2. William B. Irvine, one of the first philosophers to have experimented with Stoicism as a modern way of life, has noted that a primary aim of "a philosophy of life" is to make sure that you have a good life and don't "mislive." One sign of having a good life is that, when you reach your final moments of being alive, you won't feel regret that you wasted your life. See Irvine, *A Guide to the Good Life: The Ancient Art of Stoic Joy* (New York: Oxford University Press, 2009), 1–2.

3. Seneca, *Letters* 78.2.

4. Plato, *Apology* 30C–D.

5. On the trial of Socrates and his death, see Plato's dialogues, *The Apology* (where Socrates defends himself while on trial), *The Crito* (where Socrates explains his unwillingness to escape prison), and *The Phaedo* (where Socrates drinks the hemlock, surrounded by his students). These dialogues can all be found in Plato, *The Last Days of Socrates*, translated by Hugh Tredennick and Harold Tarrant (New York: Penguin, 1993).

6. Seneca, *Letters* 63.8.

7. Seneca, *Letters* 22.16.

8. Epictetus, *Discourses* 3.26.38.

9. Seneca, *Letters* 4.5.

10.   Seneca, *Letters* 26.6.

11.   Seneca, *Letters* 30.10–11.

12.   Seneca, *Letters* 24.18. Marcus Aurelius also uses this argument in *Meditations* 8.58. It actually goes back to Socrates, who used the argument at his trial. See Plato, *Apology* 40C–D.

13.   Seneca, *Letters* 54.4–5.

14.   As Epicurus wrote, death is nothing to us, because "when we exist, death has not come, and when death has come, we don't exist" (Diogenes Laertius, *Lives of the Eminent Philosophers* 10.125).

15.   Seneca, *Letters* 92.24–25.

16.   Seneca, *Letters* 77.20.

17.   Seneca, *Letters* 93.4.

18.   Seneca, *Letters* 12.4–5.

19.   Seneca, *Letters* 101.13–14.

20.   Seneca, *Letters* 101.15.

21.   Seneca, *Letters* 58.34.

22.   Seneca, *Letters* 58.32.

23.   Seneca, *Letters* 58.35.

24.   Text of Steve Jobs's Commencement Address at Stanford University, June 12, 2005. https://news.stanford.edu/2005/06/14/jobs-061505/.

25.   Seneca, *Letters* 101.7.

26.   Seneca, *Letters* 12.9.

CHAPTER 12: GIVE GRIEF ITS DUE

1.   Seneca, *Consolation to Polybius* 18.5. On the belief of the Greek Stoics that a sage would not feel grief: Diogenes Laertius, *Lives of the Eminent Philosophers* 7.118.

2.   Seneca, *Letters* 71.27.

3.   Seneca's *Consolation to Marcia* addresses Marcia's extreme state of grief, lasting three years after the death of her son Metilius, and was probably written during the reign of Caligula (AD 37–41). *Consolation to Helvia* was written to Seneca's mother to address her sorrow over Seneca's banishment to the island of Corsica. *Consolation to Polybius* addresses Polybius's grief over his brother's death and was written while Seneca was in exile on Corsica (AD 41–49). Seneca's Letter 63 is a letter of consolation written for Lucilius after the death of Flaccus, a friend of Lucilius's. Seneca's Letter 99 to Lucilius includes the text of a letter Seneca wrote to Maurullus after he lost an infant son. Seneca's *Letters* were written in the period of AD 63–65.

4.   Seneca, *Letters* 99.18–19.

5. Seneca, *Letters* 99.19.
6. Seneca, *Letters* 99.18 and 99.20.
7. Oxytocin is a hormone associated with bonding, love, sex, and stress reduction. Endorphins are opioids associated with pain reduction, stress reduction, and feelings of euphoria. It's no wonder people often feel better and calmer after crying.
8. Seneca, *Consolation to Marcia* 1.5. Seneca's *Consolation to Marcia* was written during the reign of Caligula, which probably makes it his earliest surviving prose work.
9. Seneca, *Letters* 99.16.
10. For these two arguments, see Seneca, *Consolation to Polybius* 18.6 and *Consolation to Helvia* 16.1.
11. Seneca, *Consolation to Polybius* 18.6.
12. Seneca, *Letters* 63.12.
13. Seneca, *Consolation to Polybius* 11.2.
14. Seneca, *Consolation to Marcia* 9.5.
15. Seneca, *Letters* 63.14–15.
16. Seneca, *Consolation to Marcia* 10.1.
17. Seneca, *Consolation to Marcia* 10.3.
18. Epictetus, *Handbook* 11.
19. Seneca, *Consolation to Polybius* 11.3.
20. Seneca, *On Tranquility of Mind* 11.1.
21. For a similar view from someone who has also experimented with looking at life from a Stoic perspective, see Scott LaBarge, "How (and Maybe Why) to Grieve Like an Ancient Philosopher," in *Virtue and Happiness: Essays in Honour of Julia Annas*, edited by Rachana Kamtekar (Oxford: Oxford University Press, 2012), 320–42.
22. Seneca, *Letters* 99.4.
23. Seneca, *Letters* 99.4.
24. Seneca, *Consolation to Marcia* 3.4.
25. Seneca, *Consolation to Marcia* 5.4. Marcia's son Metilius had two daughters, so he was not a child when he died. But as Seneca illustrates, even very young children can be a source of happy memories.

CHAPTER 13: LOVE AND GRATITUDE

1. Seneca, *On Anger* 2.31.7.
2. Anna Lydia Motto, "Seneca on Love," *Cuadernos de Filología Clásica. Estudios Latinos* 27, no. 1 (2007): 80.
3. Marcus Aurelius, *Meditations* 6.39.

4. Marcus Aurelius, *Meditations* 1.9.

5. William O. Stephens, *Stoic Ethics: Epictetus and Happiness as Freedom* (New York: Continuum, 2007), 154.

6. Cicero, *Pro Plancio* 80.

7. Seneca, *On Benefits* 1.1.2.

8. Edward J. Harpham, "Gratitude in the History of Ideas," in *The Psychology of Gratitude*, eds. Robert A. Emmons and Michael E. McCullough (New York: Oxford University Press, 2004), 22.

9. Seneca was often critical of this system. But he was also part of it: his relationship with Nero could be described as a patron–client relationship.

10. Ashraf H. A. Rushdy, *Philosophies of Gratitude* (New York: Oxford University Press, 2020), 46–47.

11. The only scholarly article I've been able to find devoted to gratitude in Stoicism is by my friend Aldo Dinucci, a scholar of Stoicism in Brazil. It's about gratitude in Epictetus and is written in Portuguese. See Antônio Carlos Rodrigues and Aldo Dinucci, "A eucharistia em Epicteto," in *Epistemologias da religião e relações de religiosidade*, eds. Celma Laurinda Freitas Costa, Clóvis Ecco, and José Reinaldo F. Martins Filho (Curitiba: Editora Prismas, 2017), 17–44.

12. Donald Robertson, "Stoicism and Love," presentation from Stoicism Today Conference 2014. Video at https://youtu.be/W4sawA2ohdE.

13. On the Stoic approach to loving others with an awareness of their mortality, see William O. Stephens, "Epictetus on How the Stoic Sage Loves," *Oxford Studies in Ancient Philosophy* 14 (1996): 193–210.

14. Several modern philosophers have explored this topic. These are some of the writings I studied while writing this chapter, listed in order of their publication dates. On the gratitude of Epicurus toward nature but not toward the gods: N. W. De Wit, "The Epicurean Doctrine of Gratitude," *American Journal of Philology* 58, no. 3, (1937): 320–28. On why the experience of "cosmic gratitude" or "transpersonal gratitude" does not call for belief in God: George Naknikian, "On the Cognitive Import of Certain Religious States," in *Religious Experience and Truth: A Symposium*, ed. Sidney Hook (New York: New York University Press, 1961), 156–64. On nonpersonal gratitude, gratitude toward nature, and "free-floating gratitude": E. R. Loder, "Gratitude and the Environment: Toward Individual and Collective Ecological Virtue," *Journal Jurisprudence* (2011): 383–435. On gratitude toward nature: Nathan Wood, "Gratitude and Alterity in Environmental Virtue Ethics," *Environmental*

Values 29, no. 4 (2020): 481–98. A recent exploration of cosmic gratitude: chapter 8, "Cosmic Gratitude," in Ashraf H. A. Rushdy, *Philosophies of Gratitude* (New York: Oxford University Press, 2020), 219–53.

15. Marcus Aurelius, *Meditations* 7.27.

16. Robert C. Solomon, foreword, in *The Psychology of Gratitude*, eds. Robert A. Emmons and Michael E. McCullough (New York: Oxford University Press, 2004), v.

17. Philip C. Watkins, *Gratitude and the Good Life: Toward a Psychology of Appreciation* (Dordrecht: Springer, 2014), 3.

18. Watkins, *Gratitude and the Good Life*, 5.

19. Watkins, *Gratitude and the Good Life*, 7.

20. Watkins, *Gratitude and the Good Life*, 8.

21. Robert A. Emmons, "The Psychology of Gratitude: An Introduction," in *The Psychology of Gratitude*, eds. Robert A. Emmons and Michael E. McCullough (New York: Oxford University Press, 2004), 5.

22. For a list of well-known pantheists, see https://en.wikipedia.org/wiki/List_of_pantheists. Philosopher Michael Levine believes that "there are probably more (grass-root) pantheists than Protestants, or theists in general, and pantheism continues to be the traditional religious alternative to theism for those who reject the classical theistic notion of God." Levine, *Pantheism: A Non-Theistic Concept of Deity* (London: Routledge, 1994), 14.

23. Carl Sagan's son, the science writer Dorion Sagan, wrote, "My father believed in the God of Spinoza and Einstein, God not behind nature, but as nature, equivalent to it." Lynn Margulis and Dorion Sagan, *Dazzle Gradually: Reflections on the Nature of Nature* (White River Junction, VT: Chelsea Green, 2007), 14.

24. See the discussion in David Fideler, *Restoring the Soul of the World: Our Living Bond with Nature's Intelligence* (Rochester, VT: Inner Traditions, 2014), 32.

25. For "Nature" as a term for "God," see Seneca, *On Benefits* 4.7.1–2 and 4.8.3 and *Natural Questions* 2.45.3.

26. These words appear at the beginning of Rumi's discourses. Jalaluddin Rumi, *Signs of the Unseen: The Discourses of Jalaluddin Rumi*, translated by W. M. Thackston, Jr. (Boston: Shambhala, 1994), 1.

27. Seneca, *On Benefits* 4.25.2. Similarly, when Marcus Aurelius referred to the gods as being "visible," he was referring to the celestial bodies (*Meditations* 12.28).

28. For some examples of this, see Mikolaj Domaradzki, "Theological Ety-

mologizing in the Early Stoa," *Kernos* 25 (2012): 125–48. https://journals
.openedition.org/kernos/2109.

29. As philosopher Michael P. Levine stresses, pantheism is not a form of
theism and it's not a form of atheism either. Instead, it's an alternative to
them. While pantheism doesn't posit the existence of a personal God,
it does suggest that there is a unifying force in nature: everything that
exists constitutes a unity, and this all-inclusive unity is in some sense
divine. See Levine, *Pantheism*, 25.

30. Seneca, *On Benefits* 4.7.1.

31. Seneca, *On Benefits* 2.29.5.

32. Friedrich Nietzsche, *Ecce Homo: Nietzsche's Autobiography*, trans.
Anthony M. Ludovici (New York: Macmillan, 1911), 7. Modified.

33. Richard Dawkins, speaking during the Intelligence Squared Debate,
"Atheism Is the New Fundamentalism," November 2019. A video clip of
Dawkins's remark can be seen at https://youtu.be/lheDgyaItOA, 1:44.

34. Robert C. Solomon, foreword, in *The Psychology of Gratitude*, eds. Robert A. Emmons and Michael E. McCullough (New York: Oxford University Press, 2004), ix.

35. Solomon, foreword, in *The Psychology of Gratitude*, x.

36. Epictetus, *Discourses* 3.5.11. The metaphor of life as a festival, which we
should feel grateful for upon leaving, appears several separate times in
the *Discourses* of Epictetus. See also Epictetus, *Discourses* 3.5.10–11 and
4.1.105–106.

37. Marcus Aurelius, *Meditations* 4.48.

CHAPTER 14: FREEDOM, TRANQUILITY, AND LASTING JOY

1. William O. Stephens, *Stoic Ethics: Epictetus and Happiness as Freedom*
(New York: Continuum, 2007), 154.

2. As Epictetus explained, "If virtue holds out this promise—to produce
happiness, freedom from suffering, and serenity—then progress toward
virtue, surely, is also progress toward these states of mind." Epictetus,
Discourses 1.4.3.

3. Seneca, *Letters* 17.7.

4. Summary of a short dialogue in Epictetus, *Discourses* 4.1.52.

5. Seneca, *Letters* 75.18.

6. Seneca, *Letters* 15.9.

7. Seneca, *Letters* 42.8.

8. Seneca, *Letters* 45.9.

9. Seneca, *Letters* 23.2.
10. Seneca, *Letters* 32.5 and 32.3. "A life that is already complete" is a memorable phrase from the translation of Margaret Graver and A. A. Long. My translation of the same passage: "In order to surpass all constraints, in order to be released and truly free, one must live a fully completed life" (*Letters* 32.5).
11. Seneca, *Letters* 44.7.
12. Stephens, *Stoic Ethics*, 141.
13. Seneca, *Letters* 56.6.
14. Seneca, *Letters* 59.16.
15. Seneca, *Letters* 87.3.
16. Seneca, *On the Happy Life* 3.4.
17. Seneca, *Letters* 92.17.

FOR FURTHER READING:
SENECA'S PHILOSOPHICAL WRITINGS

IF YOU WANT TO READ SENECA'S PHILOSOPHICAL writings, it's important to know that there are many collections, selections, and anthologies in the English language, most of which are incomplete. While most of these anthologies tend to be quite good, there are only two *complete* editions of his writings. The editions published by the Loeb Classical Library (Harvard University Press) contain Seneca's Latin texts with facing English translations, but they are decades old and lack a contemporary tone. Alternatively, *The Complete Works of Lucius Annaeus Seneca* published by the University of Chicago Press is much more recent and, without question, the most delightful, readable translation of Seneca's writings available as a complete edition.

Many people who start reading Seneca begin with the mass-market Penguin edition of Seneca's *Letters from a Stoic*, translated by Robin Campbell, which is now in its seventieth printing. (Over the last twelve years alone, it has gone through thirty-seven printings.) There is nothing wrong with that very popular and easy-to-find edition if you want a taste of Seneca's letters.

But you should be aware that *Letters from a Stoic* is a very small selection of his letters, and some of the letters it contains are incomplete. Therefore, if you decide that you are serious about reading Seneca and want the entire collection of his letters, your choice is simple. Get the wonderful *Letters on Ethics to Lucilius*, translated by Margaret Graver and A. A. Long (University of Chicago Press). That is a complete edition and the best translation available. Both the print edition and the e-book edition are excellent productions.

In the bibliography of works cited, I've included all the Seneca translations that I own and have read. From my website StoicInsights.com, you can also download a free copy of *Seneca: A Reader's Guide*, which contains some helpful resources, including some suggestions on the order in which you might want to read Seneca's writings. Listed below are all of Seneca's major philosophical writings, in alphabetical order, and in what volumes you will find these works in the Chicago translations. This is a complete listing of Seneca's philosophical writings, many of which can be found in other sources as well. Happy reading!

SENECA'S PHILOSOPHICAL WRITINGS

THIS ALPHABETICAL LISTING SHOWS WHERE YOU CAN find all of Seneca's philosophical writings in *The Complete Works of Lucius Annaeus Seneca* published by the University of Chicago Press. For the publication data for each volume, see the bibliography of works cited in the next section.

Consolation to Helvia
In Seneca, *Hardship and Happiness*

Consolation to Marcia
In Seneca, *Hardship and Happiness*

Consolation to Polybius
In Seneca, *Hardship and Happiness*

Letters
In Seneca, *Letters on Ethics to Lucilius*

Natural Questions
In Seneca, *Natural Questions*

On Anger
In Seneca, *Anger, Mercy, Revenge*

On Benefits
In Seneca, *On Benefits*

On Clemency
In Seneca, *Anger, Mercy, Revenge*

On the Constancy of the Wise Person
In Seneca, *Hardship and Happiness*

On the Happy Life
In Seneca, *Hardship and Happiness*

On Leisure
In Seneca, *Hardship and Happiness*

On the Shortness of Life
In Seneca, *Hardship and Happiness*

On Providence
In Seneca, *Hardship and Happiness*

On Tranquility of Mind
In Seneca, *Hardship and Happiness*

BIBLIOGRAPHY OF WORKS CITED

BASED ON A PUBLISHER'S WHIM, SENECA'S NAME CAN
appear as "Seneca," "Lucius Annaeus Seneca," or "Seneca the
Younger." In listing Seneca's published works below, the various
forms of his name have not been arranged alphabetically, since
they all refer to the same person. Instead, the titles of the translations are arranged in alphabetical order. For a complete listing
of Seneca's philosophical writings and where to find them in *The
Complete Works of Lucius Annaeus Seneca* (University of Chicago
Press), see the previous section.

Aristotle. *Nicomachean Ethics.* Translated by Terence Irwin. 2nd ed. Indianap-
olis, IN: Hackett, 1999.

Aristotle. *Politics.* Translated by Ernest Barker. Oxford: Oxford University
Press, 1995.

Armisen-Marchetti, Mireille. "Imagination and Meditation in Seneca: The
Example of the *Praemeditatio.*" In *Oxford Readings in Classical Stud-
ies: Seneca*, edited by John G. Fitch, 102–113. Oxford: Oxford University
Press, 2008.

Arius Didymus. *Epitome of Stoic Ethics.* Translated by Arthur J. Pomeroy.
Atlanta: Society of Biblical Literature, 1999.

Asmis, Elizabeth. "Cicero on Natural Law and the Laws of State," *Classical
Antiquity* 27, no. 1 (2008): 1–33.

Bailey, Cyril. See *Epicurus: The Extant Remains.*

Bartsh, Shadi, and Alessandro Schiessaro, eds. *The Cambridge Companion to Seneca*. New York: Cambridge University Press, 2015.

Becker, Lawrence C. *A Modern Stoicism*. 2nd ed. Princeton: Princeton University Press, 2017.

Bobzien, Susanne. *Determinism and Freedom in Stoic Philosophy*. Oxford: Oxford University Press, 2001.

Brennan, Tad. *The Stoic Life: Emotions, Duties, and Fate*. Oxford: Oxford University Press, 2005.

Bridges, J. W. "Imitation, Suggestion, and Hypnosis." Chapter 18 in J. W. Bridges, *Psychology: Normal and Abnormal, with Special Reference to the Needs of Medical Students and Practitioners*, 311–24. New York: Appleton, 1930. Available from the American Psychological Association: https://psycnet.apa.org/record/2008-08475-018.

Brower, René. *The Stoic Sage: The Early Stoics on Wisdom, Sagehood and Socrates*. Cambridge: Cambridge University Press, 2014.

Buzaré, Elen. *Stoic Spiritual Exercises*. Lulu: 2011.

Cicero. *On Duties (De Officiis)*. Translated by Walter Miller. Loeb Classical Library. Cambridge, MA: Harvard University Press, 1913.

———. *On Ends (De Finibus)*. Translated by H. Rackam. Loeb Classical Library. Cambridge, MA: Harvard University Press, 1914.

———. *On the Republic (De Re Publica) and On the Laws (De Legibus)*. Translated by Clinton Walker Keyes. Loeb Classical Library. Cambridge, MA: Harvard University Press, 1928.

———. *The Republic* and *The Laws*. Translated by Niall Rudd. Oxford: Oxford University Press, 1998.

———. *Pro Archia. Post Reditum in Senatu. Post Reditum ad Quirites. De Domo Sua. De Haruspicum Responsis. Pro Plancio*. Translated by N. H. Watts. Loeb Classical Library. Cambridge, MA: Harvard University Press, 1923.

———. *Tusculan Disputations*. Translated by J. E. King. 2nd ed. Loeb Classical Library. Cambridge, MA: Harvard University Press, 1945.

Cooper, John M. "Aristotle on the Forms of Friendship." *The Review of Metaphysics* 30, no. 4 (1977): 619–48.

Damschen, Gregor, and Andreas Heil, eds. *Brill's Companion to Seneca: Philosopher and Dramatist*. Leiden: E. J. Brill, 2014.

Diogenes Laertius. *Lives of the Eminent Philosophers*. Translated by R. D. Hicks. 2 vols. Loeb Classical Library. Cambridge, MA: Harvard University Press, 1925.

———. *Lives of the Eminent Philosophers*. Translated by Pamela Mensch. New York: Oxford University Press, 2018.

De Wit, N. W. "The Epicurean Doctrine of Gratitude," *American Journal of Philology* 58, no. 3 (1937): 320–28.

Domaradzki, Mikolaj. "Theological Etymologizing in the Early Stoa," *Kernos* 25 (2012), 125–48. https://journals.openedition.org/kernos/2109.

Edwards, Catharine. "Free Yourself! Slavery, Freedom, and the Self in Seneca's Letters." In *Seneca and the Self*, edited by Shadi Bartsch and David Wray, 139–59. Cambridge: Cambridge University Press, 2009.

———. "Absent Presence in Seneca's Epistles: Philosophy and Friendship." In *The Cambridge Companion to Seneca*, edited by Shadi Bartsch and Alessandro Schiessaro, 41–53. New York: Cambridge University Press, 2015.

Einstein, Albert. "Religion and Science" (published in the *New York Times Magazine*, November 9, 1930). In Albert Einstein, *Ideas and Opinions*. New York: Modern Library, 1994, 39–43.

———. "Science and Religion" (Address at Princeton Theological Seminary May 19, 1939). In Einstein, *Ideas and Opinions*, 44–52.

Ellis, Joseph J. *American Sphinx: The Character of Thomas Jefferson*. New York: Alfred A. Knopf, 1997.

Emmons, Robert A., and Michael E. McCullough, eds. *The Psychology of Gratitude*. New York: Oxford University Press, 2004.

Epictetus. *Discourses, Fragments, and Encheiridion*. Translated by W. A. Oldfather. 2 vols. Loeb Classical Library. Cambridge, MA: Harvard University Press, 1925–1928.

———. *Discourses, Fragments, Handbook*. Translated by Robin Hard. Oxford: Oxford University Press, 2014.

———. *How to Be Free: An Ancient Guide to the Stoic Life. Encheiridion and Selections from Discourses*. Translated and with an introduction by A. A. Long. Princeton, NJ: Princeton University Press, 2018.

Epicurus: The Extant Remains. Edited and translated by Cyril Bailey. Oxford: Clarendon Press, 1926.

Farnsworth, Ward. *The Practicing Stoic: A Philosophical User's Manual*. Boston: David R. Godine, 2018.

Fideler, David. *Restoring the Soul of the World: Our Living Bond with Nature's Intelligence*. Rochester, VT: Inner Traditions, 2014.

———. *Seneca: A Reader's Guide*. https://www.stoicinsights.com/seneca-readers-guide.

Griffin, Mariam T. *Seneca: A Philosopher in Politics*. New York: Oxford University Press, 1976.

Gleiser, Marcelo. "The Trouble with Tribalism." *Orbiter* (July 18, 2019). https://orbitermag.com/the-trouble-with-tribalism/.

Gloyn, Liz. *The Ethics of the Family in Seneca*. Cambridge: Cambridge University Press, 2017.

Graver, Margaret R. *Stoicism and Emotion*. Chicago: University of Chicago Press, 2007.

———. "Action and Emotion." In *The Brill Companion to Seneca: Philosopher and Dramatist*, edited by Gregor Damschen and Andreas Heil, 257–76. Leiden: E. J. Brill, 2014.

Harpham, Edward J. "Gratitude in the History of Ideas." In *The Psychology of Gratitude*, edited by Robert A. Emmons and Michael E. McCullough, 19–36. New York: Oxford University Press, 2004.

Hierocles. See Ramelli, *Hierocles the Stoic: Elements of Ethics, Fragments, and Excerpts*.

Hill, Lisa, and Prasanna Nidumolu. "The Influence of Classical Stoicism on John Locke's Theory of Self-Ownership," *History of the Human Sciences* (May 2020): 1–22.

Holowchack, M. Andrew. *The Stoics: A Guide for the Perplexed*. New York: Continuum, 2008.

Honoré, Tony. *Ulpian: Pioneer of Human Rights*. 2nd ed. Oxford: Oxford University Press, 2002.

Horowitz, Maryanne Cline. "The Stoic Synthesis of Natural Law in Man: Four Themes," *Journal of the History of Ideas* 35, no. 1 (1974): 3–16.

Inwood, Brad. *Reading Seneca: Stoic Philosophy at Rome*. Oxford: Clarendon Press, 2005.

Inwood, Brad. See Seneca, *Selected Philosophical Letters*.

Irvine, William B. *On Desire: Why We Want What We Want*. New York: Oxford University Press, 2006.

———. *A Guide to the Good Life: The Ancient Art of Stoic Joy*. New York: Oxford University Press, 2009.

———. *The Stoic Challenge: A Philosopher's Guide to Becoming Tougher, Calmer, and More Resilient*. New York: W. W. Norton, 2019.

LaBarge, Scott. "How (and Maybe Why) to Grieve Like an Ancient Philosopher." In *Virtue and Happiness: Essays in Honour of Julia Annas*, edited by Rachana Kamtekar, 320–42. Oxford: Oxford University Press, 2012.

Llano Alonso, Fernando H. "Cicero and Natural Law," *ARSP: Archi für Rechts- und Socialphilosophie / Archives for Philosophy of Law and Social Philosophy* 98, no. 2 (2012): 157–68.

Le Bon, Gustave. *The Crowd: A Study of the Popular Mind*. Public domain translation of the original text, *Psychologie des Foules* (1895). http://www.gutenberg.org/ebooks/445.

Levine, Michael P. *Pantheism: A Non-Theistic Concept of Deity*. London: Routledge, 1994.

Loder, E. R. "Gratitude and the Environment: Toward Individual and Collective Ecological Virtue," *Journal Jurisprudence* (2011): 383–435.

Long, A. A. *Epictetus: A Stoic and Socratic Guide to Life*. Oxford: Oxford University Press, 2002.

Long, A. A. See Epictetus, *How to Be Free*.

Long, A. A., and D. N. Sedley. *The Hellenistic Philosophers*. Volume 1: *Translations of the Principal Sources with Philosophical Commentary*. Volume 2: *Greek and Latin Texts with Notes and Bibliography*. Cambridge: Cambridge University Press, 1987.

Marcus Aurelius. *Marcus Aurelius*. Edited and translated by C. R. Haines. Loeb Classical Library. Cambridge, MA: Harvard University Press, 1916.

———. *Meditations*. Translated by Gregory Hayes. New York: Modern Library, 2002.

———. *Meditations*. Translated by Martin Hammond. London: Penguin, 2006.

———. *Meditations: The Annotated Edition*. Translated, introduced, and edited by Robin Waterfield. New York: Basic Books, 2021.

Margulis, Lynn, and Dorion Sagan. *Dazzle Gradually: Reflections on the Nature of Nature*. White River Junction, VT: Chelsea Green, 2007.

May, Rollo. *The Courage to Create*. New York: W. W. Norton, 1975.

McIlwan, Charles. *The Growth of Political Thought in the West: From the Greeks to the Middle Ages*. New York: Macmillan, 1932.

Meany, Paul. "Why the Founders' Favorite Philosopher Was Cicero." FEE (May 31, 2018). https://fee.org/articles/why-the-founders-favorite -philosopher-was-cicero/.

Mitsis, Phillip. "The Stoic Origin of Natural Rights." In *Topics in Stoic Philosophy*, edited by Katerina Ierodiakonou, 153–77. Oxford: Clarendon Press, 1999.

Motto, Anna Lydia. "Seneca on Trial: The Case of the Opulent Stoic," *The Classical Journal* 61, no. 6 (1966): 254–58.

———. *Seneca Sourcebook: A Guide to the Thought of Lucius Annaeus Seneca*. Amsterdam: Adolf M. Hakkert, 1970. (An index to all of Seneca's philosophical writings.)

———. "Seneca on Love," *Cuadernos de Filología Clásica. Estudios Latinos* 27, no. 1 (2007): 79–86.

———, and John R. Clark, "Seneca on Friendship," *Atena e Roma* 38 (1993): 91–96.

Naknikian, George. "On the Cognitive Import of Certain Religious States." In *Religious Experience and Truth: A Symposium*, edited by Sidney Hook, 156–64. New York: New York University Press, 1961.

Nietzsche, Friedrich. *Ecce Homo: Nietzsche's Autobiography*. Translated by Anthony M. Ludovici. New York: Macmillan, 1911.

Nussbaum, Martha. *The Therapy of Desire: Theory and Practice in Hellenistic Ethics*. Princeton: Princeton University Press, 1994.

Pigliucci, Massimo. *How to Be a Stoic: Using Ancient Philosophy to Live a Modern Life*. New York: Basic Books, 2017.

Plato. *Euthyphro. Apology. Crito. Phaedo. Phaedrus*. Translated by Harold North Fowler. Loeb Classical Library. Cambridge, MA: Harvard University Press, 1914.

———. *The Last Days of Socrates*. Translated by Hugh Tredennick and Harold Tarrant. New York: Penguin, 1993.

———. *Lysis. Symposium. Gorgias*. Translated by W. R. M. Lamb. Loeb Classical Library. Cambridge, MA: Harvard University Press, 1925.

Plutarch. *Is "Live Unknown" a Wise Precept?* In Plutarch, *Moralia*, Volume 14. Translated by Benedict Einarson and Philip H. De Lacy. Loeb Classical Library. Cambridge, MA: Harvard University Press, 1967.

Ramelli, Ilaria. *Hierocles the Stoic: Elements of Ethics, Fragments, and Excerpts*. Atlanta: Society for Biblical Literature, 2009.

Ranocchia, Graziano. "The Stoic Concept of Proneness to Emotion and Vice," *Archiv für Geschichte der Philosophie* 94, no. 1 (2012): 74–92.

Richter, Daniel S. *Cosmopolis: Imagining Community in Late Classical Athens and the Early Roman Empire*. New York: Oxford University Press, 2011.

Robertson, Donald. "The Stoic Influence on Modern Psychotherapy." In *The Routledge Handbook of the Stoic Tradition*, edited by John Sellars, 374–88. London: Routledge, 2017.

———. *How to Think Like a Roman Emperor: The Stoic Philosophy of Marcus Aurelius*. New York: St. Martin's Press, 2019.

———. *The Philosophy of Cognitive-Behavioural Therapy (CBT): Stoic Philosophy as Rational and Cognitive Psychotherapy*. 2nd rev. ed. London: Routledge, 2020.

Rodrigues, Antônio Carlos, and Aldo Dinucci. "A eucharistia em Epicteto." In *Epistemologias da religião e relações de religiosidade*, edited by Celma Laurinda Freitas Costa, Clóvis Ecco, and José Reinaldo F. Martins Filho, 17–44. Curitiba: Editora Prismas, 2017.

Romm, James. *Dying Every Day: Seneca at the Court of Nero*. New York: Knopf, 2014.

Rumi, Jalaluddin. *Signs of the Unseen: The Discourses of Jalaluddin Rumi.* Translated by W. M. Thackston, Jr. Boston: Shambhala, 1994.

Rushdy, Ashraf H. A. *Philosophies of Gratitude.* New York: Oxford University Press, 2020.

Sampson, Tony D. *Virality: Contagion Theory in the Age of Networks.* Minneapolis: University of Minnesota Press, 2012.

Sellars, John. *The Art of Living: The Stoics on the Nature and Function of Philosophy.* London: Bristol Classical Press, 2009.

———. *Stoicism.* London: Routledge, 2014.

———. "Stoicism and Emotions," in *Stoicism Today: Selected Writings,* Volume 2, edited by Patrick Ussher, 43–48. CreateSpace, 2016.

———. *Marcus Aurelius.* London: Routledge, 2021.

———, ed. *The Routledge Handbook of the Stoic Tradition.* London: Routledge, 2017.

Seneca, Lucius Annaeus. *Anger, Mercy, Revenge.* Translated by Robert A. Kaster and Martha C. Nusbaum. Chicago: University of Chicago Press, 2010.

Seneca. *Dialogues and Essays.* Translated by John Davie. Oxford: Oxford University Press, 2007.

Seneca. *Dialogues and Letters.* Translated by C. D. N. Costa. New York: Penguin, 1997.

Seneca the Younger. *Epistles.* Translated by Richard M. Gummere. 3 vols. Loeb Classical Library. Cambridge, MA: Harvard University Press, 1917–1925.

Seneca, Lucius Annaeus. *Hardship and Happiness.* Translations by Elaine Fantham, Harry M. Hine, James Ker, and Gareth D. Williams. Chicago: University of Chicago Press, 2014.

Seneca. *Letters from a Stoic.* Translated by Robin Campbell. New York: Penguin, 1969.

Seneca, Lucius Annaeus. *Letters on Ethics to Lucilius.* Translated by Margaret Graver and A. A. Long. Chicago: University of Chicago Press, 2015.

Seneca the Younger. *Moral Essays.* Translated by John W. Basore. 3 vols. Loeb Classical Library. Cambridge, MA: Harvard University Press, 1928–1935.

Seneca. *Natural Questions.* Translated by Thomas H. Corcoran. 2 vols. Loeb Classical Library. Cambridge, MA: Harvard University Press, 1971.

Seneca, Lucius Annaeus. *Natural Questions.* Translated by Harry M. Hine. Chicago: University of Chicago Press, 2010.

Seneca, Lucius Annaeus. *On Benefits.* Translated by Miriam Griffin and Brad Inwood. Chicago: University of Chicago Press, 2011.

Seneca. *Selected Letters*. Translated by Elaine Fantham. Oxford: Oxford University Press, 2010.

Seneca: Selected Philosophical Letters. Translation and commentary by Brad Inwood. Oxford: Oxford University Press, 2007.

Sherman, Nancy. "Aristotle on Friendship and the Shared Life." *Philosophical and Phenomenological Research* 47, no. 4 (1987): 589–613.

Solomon, Robert C. Foreword. In *The Psychology of Gratitude*, edited by Robert A. Emmons and Michael E. McCullough, v–xi. New York: Oxford University Press, 2004.

Stephens, William O. "Epictetus on How the Stoic Sage Loves," *Oxford Studies in Ancient Philosophy* 14 (1996): 193–210.

———. *Stoic Ethics: Epictetus and Happiness as Freedom*. New York: Continuum, 2007.

———. *Marcus Aurelius: A Guide for the Perplexed*. New York: Continuum, 2012.

Tacitus. *The Annals: The Reigns of Tiberius, Claudius, and Nero*. Translated by J. C. Yardley. Oxford: Oxford University Press, 2008.

Tieleman, Teun. *Chrysippus' On Affections: Reconstruction and Interpretation*. Leiden: E. J. Brill, 2003.

Watkins, Philip C. *Gratitude and the Good Life: Toward a Psychology of Appreciation*. Dordrecht: Springer, 2014.

Wilson, Emily. *The Greatest Empire: A Life of Seneca*. New York: Oxford University Press, 2014.

Wood, Nathan. "Gratitude and Alterity in Environmental Virtue Ethics," *Environmental Values* 29, no. 4 (2020): 481–98.

INDEX

"ABC Theory of Emotion" (Albert Ellis): based on Stoic philosophy, 54

abolition of slavery: and Stoic ideas, 138, 141–42

addiction, 41

advantages. *See* goods vs. advantages in Stoic philosophy

adversity, 88–102; as an opportunity to manifest virtue or goodness, 7; as something we should expect, 7; as a test of character, 7, 95; as training, 99–100; transforming adversity into something good, 100–102; and virtue, 89–95, 100–102

American Psychological Association (APA), 61, 72–73, 226n2

amor fati (love your fate), 113–14

anger (or rage), 60–78; arises from mental judgments, 63–64, 70–71; as avoidable, 64; develops in a three-step process, 67–69; harmful effects of, 62–63; how to cure, 69–74; not a solution to injustice, 76; Stoic theory of, 67–69; symptoms of, 61–62; "a temporary form of insanity," 60; it "topples" mind and reason, 62–63; ways to avoid, 74–76. See also *On Anger* (Seneca)

anxiety, 46–59; and cognitive theory of emotion, 48; concern vs. worry, 53, 123; and feedback loops, 51–52; how it arises, 47–48; how to overcome anxiety, 52–59; and imagination, 47, 49–52; of maintaining wealth, 121–22, 123–34; and mindfulness (*prosochē*), 53; and testing impressions, 53; and worrying about the future, 47–48, 49–50, 53, 56; worrying about worrying (meta-worry or meta-anxiety), 52

Apicius, 121

appreciation: appreciating the gifts of Fortune, 187, 210; relationship to love and gratitude, 195, 203–4; in Stoic philosophy, 168, 194, 195, 196, 203–5. *See also* gratitude; love

Aristo of Chios: on false beliefs and mental suffering, 222n3–223

Aristotle: believed external goods are needed for *eudaimonia*, 93–94; his rejection of human equality, 138; on three levels of friendship, 20–22

atomism, 149

authenticity. *See* living with authenticity

unconscious influence, 131–34. See also
crowd psychology

virtue (excellence of character), 5–6, 87;
and adversity, 85–95, 100–102; as an
all-or-nothing state, 24–25; as being
rational and honorable, 91–92; as
consistently good, 6; and dichotomy
of control, 91–93; meaning of *aretē*
(virtue), 90–91; as the only true
good, 5–6, 94; results in *eudaimonia*
or well-being, 7, 211–12; as the
source of goodness in the world, 6.
See also cardinal virtues (wisdom,
courage, moderation, and justice)
voluntary poverty. *See* voluntary simplicity
voluntary simplicity: Seneca on, 124–26;
in Stoic philosophy, 14

wandering vs. having a destination,
37–38, 81–83, 154
Watkins, P. C.: on gratitude, 196
Wilson, Emily: biography of Seneca, 9;
on the Stoic sage, 27
wealth, 115–28; and addiction to luxury,
121; anxiety of maintaining it, 121–

22, 123–24; dangers of extreme
wealth, 120–22; and envy, 122;
and fame and fortune, 120, 122;
and greed, 122; and living within
one's means, 126; natural wealth,
118–20; nonattachment to, 127;
and pain of loss, 122; provides an
opportunity to practice virtue, 127–
28; and psychological inflation,
121; and Seneca's detachment
from the gifts of Fortune, 118,
127–28; and social status, 122; and
voluntary simplicity, 124–26; how
wealth affects people differently,
120, 121. *See also* Fortune; poverty
work and leisure, 39, 84–85
worry. *See* anxiety

Zeno of Citium: criticized by Seneca,
157; founder of Stoic philosophy,
3; ideas on Stoic sage, 24–25;
influenced by Socrates and the
Cynic philosophers, 24–25; on
living in agreement with nature, 5;
and *okeiōsis*, 144; saw Socrates as a
sage, 22n14; and Stoic paradoxes, 41

ABOUT THE AUTHOR

DAVID FIDELER HAS WORKED AS A COLLEGE PROFES-
sor, editor and publisher, and the director of a humanities center. He studied ancient Greek philosophy and Mediterranean
religions at the University of Pennsylvania and holds a PhD in
philosophy. Fideler is the author of *Restoring the Soul of the World*
and other books. Born in the United States, he currently lives in
Sarajevo with his wife and son.